DEVOTIONAL BIBLE STUDIES

by
F.E. Marsh

KREGEL PUBLICATIONS
Grand Rapids, Michigan 49501

Devotional Bible Studies © Copyright 1980
and published by Kregel Publications,
a division of Kregel, Inc. All rights reserved.

Library of Congress Cataloging in Publication Data

Marsh, Frederick Edward, 1858-1919.
   Devotional Bible Studies - Pearls, Points and
Parables.

   Reprint of the ed. published by Gospel Pub.
House, New York.
   Includes indexes.
   1. Homiletical illustrations. I. Title.
[BV4225.M3   1980]   251'.08   79-2548
ISBN 0-8254-3230-8

Contents

vi / Contents

x / Contents

Introduction

Devotional Bible Studies speak for themselves. The plan of this volume is to give a title as a foundation, then a text as a door of entrance to the subject, then an incident as suggesting the outline of the house of thought, then Scripture references as separate rooms to visit, then a pearl of thought, as unfolding the view to be seen by the out-looker, presenting in capsule form the message of the subject.

The purpose of the book is to help the busy worker for Christ. The Christ is the Wheat of God's Word, which is wrapped up in the package of suggestion and outline, that the grain may be ground in the mill of the individual's meditation, and then the flour of result to be passed on, that cakes of truth may be baked for the benefit of others.

This treasury of devotionals, originally entitled, *Pearls Points and Parables,* developed from Marsh's belief the Word of God is enlivening, enlightening, enduring, emancipating and encouraging. For the Christian Bible student, who aspires with Paul "that I may know Him and the power of His resurrection," this work offers the opportunity through study and devotion to be found in Christ and to become more like Christ.

A double index will be found: one index of titles and one index of texts. The starred texts are the foundation passages of Scripture and the rest of the texts are found in the body of the Bible study.

The Word of God

ENLIVENING IN CONTACT
for it is quick and powerful,   Heb. 4. 12

ENLIGHTENING IN OPERATION
for it maketh wise the simple,   Psa. 19. 7

ENDURING IN SUBSTANCE
for it abideth for ever, -   -   1 Peter 1. 23

EMANCIPATING IN MINISTRY
for the truth makes free,   John 8. 32

ENNOBLING IN EFFECT
for it communicates its nature,   John 17. 17

ENFORCING IN AUTHORITY
for it is the sword of the Spirit, Eph. 6. 17

ENCOURAGING IN PROMISE
for they do not fail,   1 Kings 8. 56

Devotional Bible Studies

A Beautiful Life

"The beauty of the Lord our God be upon us" (*Psalm xc*:17)

"It is said a distinguished artist was once employed to paint the likeness of an empress. She was far from beautiful, and yet he was expected to make a beautiful portrait. He visited all parts of the empire, and took the portraits of all the beautiful women in the different cities, and made a composite picture from them. By an exquisite touch of art he put into the composite picture the expression of the countenance of the empress. It was the countenance of the empress, but there were also the features of the princesses of the land."

As the likeness of the empress was beautified by the beauties of the land, so Christ, in all His beauty, should be seen in us.

> His compassionate love will cause us to be compassionate in heart (2 Cor. v:14);
>
> His patient endurance will enable us to patiently endure (Heb. xii:3);
>
> His meek spirit will make us meek in spirit (Matt. xi:29);
>
> His holy walk will prompt us to walk in holiness (1 Pet. i:15);
>
> His faithfulness in service will inspire us to be faithful too (John xvii:4);
>
> His prayerful dependence will lead us to be prayerful (John xiv:16; xvi:26);
>
> and His beautiful character will constrain us to be lovely (Heb. vii:26).

* * * *

A Holy life needs no commendation; it is its own commendation, and is bound to command attention.

I

DEVOTIONAL BIBLE STUDIES

A Bed Quilt

"He shall give you another Comforter" (*John xiv:*16)

A poor woman, who was not able to get out to a Church service as she was wont, sent her little boy with the instruction that he was to bring home as much of the sermon as he could. When the boy got home he had forgotten all he had heard.

"Well, do you remember the text?" queried the mother.

"Yes," the text was, "God says, He is going to send us another bed quilt."

An additional bed quilt was sorely needed, for the only one the mother had was worn and thin, and it was not sufficient to keep her and the boy warm. The mother could not remember such a text as the boy mentioned, so she asked one who was present at the service what the text was, and she replied, "I will send you another Comforter." The boy knew the bed quilt was a comforter to him when he was cold, so he concluded the Comforter was a bed quilt.

What a number of believers there are who need this bed quilt, namely, the comfort of the Comforter. They are cold because He does not possess them in power.

He is (1) The *Friend* to counsel us by the *Truth* (John xvi:13).
(2) The *Fulness* to supply the deficiencies in our spiritual character (Eph. v:18).
(3) The *Fruit* to make us correspond to His nature (Galatians v:22).
(4) The *Fibre* to knit us in love with all God's saints (1 Cor. xii:12, 13).
(5) The *Fire* to purify, vivify, and cleanse all our being (Acts xi:24).
(6) The *Fervour* to inspire us in love and zeal in God's service (Acts vi:8-10).
(7) And the *Fuel* to feed our spiritual life to its strength and progress (John vi:63).

*   *   *   *

The Holy Spirit witnesses *in* us by an uncondemning heart before the Lord, and He witnesses *to* us by the assuring statements *in* His Word.

A Christian: What Is He?

"A Christian" (1 *Pet. iv:*16)

"It seems to have been pretty generally taken for granted, that the sounds which most strikingly assail the ear at close range must also be those that reach the farthest. This, however, is far from the truth, as indeed, might be easily proved. We listen with charmed ears to the varied sounds of a military band, passing us on the march at a short distance. Our ears are invaded by a tumultuous ocean of sound waves which none the less are perfectly agreeable to our sense of hearing. All is not only harmonious, but well balanced. The reeds easily hold their own against the brass. The cymbals now and again pleasantly strike us with their crash, and ever and anon the shrill little piccolo trills out high above the rest. Yet as the troops move on into the distance, these more piercing but thinner voices may be the first to fade, presently passing out of hearing altogether, and leaving the horns alone in competition, and when all else is lost, probably the vast waves put in motion by the membrane of the drum will be the last to reach the ear."

Wave sounds are not the only things which are taken for granted. One thing which is often taken for granted is, that because a certain individual passes as a Christian, he therefore is one.

A Christian is One who believes on Christ (John iii:36);
One who is abiding in Christ (John xv:4);
One who is walking after Christ (Luke ix:23);
One who is obedient to Christ (John xiv:21);
One who is indwelt by Christ (Gal. ii:20);
One who witnesses unto Christ (Acts i:8);
One who is looking for Him (Phil. iii:20).

*   *   *   *

A Christian is "a man in Christ," therefore he is not a man on earth looking up to heaven, but a man in heaven looking down on earth.

3

DEVOTIONAL BIBLE STUDIES

A Holy Place, Life, and Companionship

In Christ (*Phil. iii:9*); Like Christ (*Phil. ii:5*); "With Christ"(*Col. iii:3*)

I asked a student what three things he most wished for.· He said, "Give me books, health, and quiet, and I care for nothing more." I asked a miser, and he cried, "Money, money, money!" I asked a pauper, and he faintly said, "Bread, bread, bread!" I asked a drunkard, and he called loudly for strong drink. I asked the multitude around me, and they lifted up a confused cry, in which I heard the words, "Wealth, fame, and pleasure!" I asked a poor man, who had long borne the character of an experienced Christian. He replied, that all his wishes might be met in Christ. He spoke seriously; and I asked him to explain. He said, "I greatly desire three things: first, that I may be found in Christ; secondly, that I may be like Christ; thirdly, that I may be with Christ."

Paul illustrates these things in his five desires of Phil., iii:8-12.

> "I may win Christ."
> "Be found in Him."
> "That I may know Him?"
> "I might attain."
> "I may apprehend."

*   *   *   *

Wholeness and holiness are akin in sound and substance. Holiness to the Lord is expressed in wholeheartedness to, and for, Him.

Aiming for the Goal

"I press toward the mark" (*Phil. iii:14*)

In an art gallery, before a great painting, a young artist said to Ruskin: "Ah! if I could put such a dream on canvas!"

4

ALL, AND NO COMPROMISE

"Dream on canvas!" growled the stern old critic. "It will take 10,000 touches of the brush on the canvas to put your dream there."

The dream could only become a reality by dint of hard work. Success is found in the mine of labor, where it has to be dug for. The stones which flash most are those which are ground most. Polishing means patient application, but then the polish is the reward. "Trifles make perfection, but perfection is no trifle."

Persistence will surely meet with blessing (Rom. ii:7).

Pains may mean pain in performance, but they shall result in pleasure (2 Pet. i:10).

Plod may get prods as he walks, but he shall reach his destination (Heb. xi:9, 10).

The travail of birth will result in another life to live, and this may mean an influence for good (Isa. lxvi:8).

The river in its flow may pass undesirable places, but it will minister blessing to some (Ez. xlvii:9-11).

The wind in its rush may overturn, but it will also purify some fear-haunted souls (Acts ii:2-37).

Have a mark, and press towards it, and let nothing hinder in pressing towards it (1 Cor. ix:24).

*   *   *   *

Aim, attention, activity are essentials of success in any grade of life, and more especially in the Christian life. Aim true, attend well, and be active in all, and something will be done.

All, and no Compromise

"Utterly destroy" (1 *Sam. xv:3*)

At one of our seaside resorts, a cab proprietor was fined $50 and costs, for not having licenses for twenty-seven carriages. His excuse was, that they were relics of antiquity, kept to lend out while others underwent repair. Some make a like plea when their sins are discovered; they do not sin as a regular business, though it is true they keep some of the old relics of antiquity. If we keep the devil's carriages, even under such a pretence, we shall find them turn into funeral cars ere long. Do not keep wine in the cellar, and you will not drink it. He who has a pistol may shoot.

The Lord demands a clean sweep of all that is sinful. This may be gathered if the word *"all"* is pondered in the following Scriptures:

> Christ died to redeem us from *"all* iniquity" (Tit. ii:14).
> We are to "cleanse ourselves from *all* filthiness" (2 Cor. vii:1).
> We are to avoid *"all* appearance of evil" (1 Thess. v:22).
> We are to lay aside *"all* malice" and *"all* evil speakings" (1 Pet. ii:1).
> We are to put away *"all* bitterness" (Eph. iv:31), and *"all* * * * anger"* with its accompanying evils (Col. iii: 8).

*   *   *   *

The Best Thing to do is to obey. Obedience to the Lord's command proves our love and loyalty to Him. When we obey His behests, He will not deny us His blessings.

"All Things Become New"

(2 Cor. v:17).

"If any man is in Christ, there is a new creation" (*2 Cor. v: 17*, R. V. margin)

"That man wants a prop on each side of him," said Bishop Taylor Smith, on one occasion, when a curate near London, of some unhappy specimen at a tramps' breakfast. "No, sir," replied the worker, himself a reclaimed tramp; "he wants a new stem right down the middle."

ANGEL IN THE MARBLE

So the Lord works with men. He does not prop us up; He makes us anew; hence the believer is

A "new creature" (2 Cor. v:17);
He sings a "new song" (Ps. xl:3);
He is in the "new covenant" (Heb. viii:13);
Has a "new name" (Rev. ii:17);
Carries out a "new commandment" (John xiii:34);
Walks in a new life (Rom. vi:4);
And is going to the "new Jerusalem" (Rev. xxi:2).

*   *   *   *

The new creation is the production of the Holy Spirit, and whenever that production exists, likeness to Him who produced it is evident, even as the child is like its parent.

Angel in the Marble

"He shall purify the sons of Levi" (*Mal. iii:3*)

"We need a lot of chipping." So said a saint as we were talking together about the Lord's gracious dealings with His people. The saying suggested to my mind the Lord Jesus as the loving Sculptor at work upon the marble of our humanity. There is an angel in the marble, because the pierced hand of the Artist has it in His mind and brings it out by His skill, but there is a "lot of chipping" to be done before the beautiful image of His holy character stands out, displaying the perfection of His work. The hard stone of unbelief, the rough points of self-will, the prominences of worldly ambition, the sharp angles of pride, the ugly faults of temper, the stubborn marks of hereditary trait, and the dark veins of selfishness, are some of the things He removes.

The Lord uses various similes to illustrate His dealings with us.

He uses the sieve of sifting to get rid of the chaff of worldliness and to preserve the corn of consecration (Amos ix:9).

7

He uses the rod of chastisement to remove from us the folly of wilfulness and to train us in the ways of righteousness (Heb. xii:5, 6).

He puts us in the crucible of refining to remove the dross of unbelief, and waits to see the face of His own character in the silver of our life (Mal. iii:3).

He uses the knife of pruning to cut off the fruitless branches of profession, and to strengthen the fruitful branches of love (John xv:2).

He puts us in the fire of trial to burn up the evil remnants of old habits formed in sin, and to test the reality of our faith in Christ (1 Pet. i:7).

He puts us on the wheel of fashioning to save us from the uselessness of an aimless life, and to make us a vessel meet for His use (2 Tim. ii:21);

And He pours the metal of our inner nature into the mould of His truth, that He may keep us from the shapelessness of worldly ambition and make us answer to the humility of His character (Rom. vi:17, margin).

* * * *

The hammer of His word and the chisel of His grace, are used by the hands of Him, whose hands were once transfixed for our benefit on Calvary's cross.

Appearances, the Poinsetta

"Judge not according to the appearances" (*John vii:24*)

The poinsetta is a beautiful flower, in which the leaves close to the bud take on such a rich color, that they are often mistaken for the blossom itself, which is, however, a very insignificant thing. "So men often cultivate their secondary powers to a brilliant hue, while the heart is shamefully neglected and appears miserably small."

The spiritual man does not do this,

He seeks first the kingdom of God (Matt. vi:33),

He has the spiritual on the top and the body under (1 Cor. ix:27),

He looks at the seen unreal with the eyes of the real unseen (2 Cor. iv:18),

He looks not at the present but for a future glory (Heb. xi:10),

ASSURANCE

He has his eyes on the eternal, and can thus truly live in
   the present (Heb. xi:27),
He sets his affection on things above in contrast to those
   who solely mind earthly things (Col. iii:2),
And he walks with God among men, and not as men walk
   with themselves (Gen. v:22).

*   *   *   *

It is not the glamour of outward appearance that tells
with heaven, but the glow of a consecrated heart.

Assurance

"Verily, verily, I say unto you" (*John v:24*)

A poor Scotchwoman, in Glasgow, who had attended
some evangelistic meetings, resolved that she would rest
her soul for her salvation on the words of the Lord Jesus
as found in John v. 24: "Verily, verily, I say unto you,
he that heareth My word, and believeth on Him that sent
Me, hath everlasting life, and shall not come into condemnation; but is passed from death unto life." Major
Whittle, the evangelist, wrote the words on a card, and
gave it to her. She became very happy, so much so, her
little boy was attracted by the joy of his mother, and
asked what had happened. She told him the best way
she could; the consequence was, he too was led to trust
in the Saviour. But the next morning she felt very
different. Despondency and doubt had taken the place of
peace and joy. She betrayed the state of her mind by the
gloom on her face. Harry noticed it at once, and asked
her what was the matter. She replied: "I thought I was
saved, but my feelings are all gone." "But," said the little
fellow, "Mither, has the verse changed?" Quick as a
flash he turned to the Bible and got the little card and
read it, and looking up radiantly, replied: "Why, no
mither; it's just the same." And then he turned to the
Bible, and read it there with great joy, shouting almost
as he cried: *"It's a' here, mither, the verse is just the*

same!" The unalterable word of the living God is the only ground for assurance.

(1) The Word is the *anchor* to keep the barque of our being steady amidst the storms of life (Heb. vi:18).

(2) It is the *harbor-light* which shows us where the port of the Lord's protecting presence is (Phil. ii:16).

(3) It is the *foundation* upon which the believer can rest in safety (1 Pet. i:23).

(4) It is the *soil* in which the grace of faith grows (Acts xx:32).

(5) It is the *cable* that communicates to us the electric current of God's power (Heb. iv:12).

(6) It is the *telephone* by means of which we hear the voice of the Lord speaking to us to our joy and comfort (1 Thess. ii:13).

(7) And it is the *atmosphere* by means of which we see the brightness of the coming glory (John xvii:17).

* * * *

To add the words of our reason to the Word of God's revelation, is not only to demonstrate our folly, but to ask the Lord to add the rod to our back (Prov. xxx:6).

A Telling Argument

"From you sounded out the 'Word of the Lord" (1 *Thess. i*:8)

A woman who had been a drunkard was standing at an open air service, when she observed a person who had formerly been one of her bad companions, suddenly leave the crowd and walk quickly away. Hurrying after her she found her in great distress of soul. "Oh," she said, "I listened to the speakers, but when I saw you standing there so wonderfully changed from what you used to be, I could stand it no longer." She was induced to return to the meeting, and decide for Christ.

The above incident shows the effectiveness of witness-bearing. Christ is more honored by our witnessing than by our talking.

The blind man witnessed to Christ's sight-giving power (John ix:25).

BANKRUPT

The demoniac witnessed to Christ's delivering grace (Mark v:20).
The leper witnessed to Christ's cleansing touch (Mark i:45).
The woman witnessed to Christ's satisfying love (Luke vii:37).
The crooked woman witnessed to Christ's straightening might (Luke xiii:13).
The raised man witnessed to Christ's quickening life (Luke vii:15).
The disciples witnessed to Christ's excellent glory (John i:14; 2 Pet. i:16).
The saints at Thessalonica witnessed to Christ's effective working (1 Thess. i:9, 10).

*   *   *   *

To know the truth as in Jesus we must be true to the truth we know. Walking in the truth, truth walks with us, imparts His secrets, and speaks for itself.

Bankrupt

"I am poor and needy" (*Ps. xl*:17)

"Here's a man wants to speak to you," said a Christian worker to me at the close of a gospel meeting held in a concert hall.

"Well," I said, to a shabbily-dressed man, with a bleared look and a breath strongly pungent with whiskey.

"I want salvation," he said, in a voice shaky with emotion.

"You can have it," I replied, "by accepting Christ as your Saviour, and giving up the drink."

I prayed for him, and as I was praying, he whimpered out in a most pathetic voice, *"Poor me!"* It was the cry, the groan of a soul feeling the lash of sinful habit, and the iron grip of sin. *"Poor me!"* How much bottled-up misery there was in that wail of despair, for wail of despair it was; and yet there was a deep longing to be free from the Satanic grip which held him.

DEVOTIONAL BIBLE STUDIES

Thank God for the gospel which comes to the "poor me" just as he is, and breaks the power of sin, as well as blots out the iniquity.

The woman who was a sinner (Luke vii:37-50),
The demon-possessed man (Mark v:15),
The devil-gripped Mary Magdalene (Luke viii:2),
The despised publican (Luke xviii:13),
Coveteous Zacchæus (Luke xix:2-10),
Self-righteous Saul of Tarsus (Acts ix:18),
And religious Nicodemus (John iii:1-16), are some of the poor me's, that Christ met and blest. He is still the same. None but Jesus can do helpless sinners good; but blessed be His name, there is no "poor me" that He cannot save. His blood is the panacea for every ill of sin, and He Himself the Satisfier of every heartache.

*   *   *   *

Satisfaction does not depend on possessions or position, but on disposition. What is your disposition towards Christ? If it is faith in Him, and love to Him, then you are satisfied with Him, and have all things in Him.

Beauty and Fragrance

"Sweet Flowers" (*Canticles v:13*)

Walking along Magdalen Green, in Dundee, my sense of smell was suddenly greeted by a sweet fragrance. I instinctively turned to whence it came from, and saw a row of mignonette, modestly blooming against a stone wall. Its sweetness betrayed its presence. The same thing is true of a beautiful Christian character—it speaks for itself by its sweetness of temper and attractiveness of grace.

What a beautiful nosegay of fragrance the following make:

The white lily of purity (Matt. v:8),
The crimson rose of love (Luke vii:47),
The pink carnation of tenderness (Eph. iv:32),
The sweet violet of humility (1 Pet. v:3),

12

BE WHAT YOU ARE

The blue forget-me-not of unselfish thoughtfulness (2 Tim.
i:16),
The mignonette of a sweet temper (Rom. xv:2),
And the maidenhair fern of an ever-green piety (1 Tim.
v:4).

*   *   *   *

The faces of some saints are like fresh flowers on a spring morning, while others resemble a damp fog on a November day. The latter chills, while the others cheer and gladden.

Be What You Are

"Ye are * * * if ye do" (*John xv:14*)

At Federal Hill, Baltimore, Colonel Warren gave orders to his guards that only officers in uniform were to be admitted to camp. One bright morning General Dix, who commanded the troops guarding the city, walked over from Fort McHenry in undress. Attempting to pass the line of sentries, in company with an aide, the old general was amused at finding a musket barring his passage, while the aide, with his glittering shoulder straps, was permitted to pass.

"Why do you stop me, my man?" inquired the general, quietly.

"My orders are to admit only officers in uniform," was the reply.

"But do you see that this is General Dix?" exclaimed the aide angrily.

"Well, between you and me, Major," said the sentry, his eyes twinkling with amusement, "I see very well who it is; but if General Dix wants to get into this camp, he had better go back and put on his uniform."

"You are right, sentry," remarked the general; "I'll go back and get my coat."

The soldier recognized that obedience to his superior's command was the law in the military realm. The same is true in the Christian life. We *prove* what we *are* by what we *do*.

There are seven things believers in Christ are seen to be, in John xv, and the consequent responsibility attached to each.

(1) We are *fruitful branches* through union with Christ (verse 5).

(2) We are *prevailing suppliants* by abiding in Christ (verse 7).

(3) We are *manifest disciples* by abundant fruit-bearing in Christ (verse 8).

(4) We are *faithful keepers* by obedience to Christ (verse 10).

(5) We are *true friends* by recognizing the claims of Christ (verse 14).

(6) We are *persecuted servants* by our identification with Christ (verse 20).

(7) We are *yoked witnesses* through our fellowship with the Spirit in our testimony to Christ (verse 27).

* * * *

To have the name of a saint and not to have the nature of one, is to be like the sign-post which points to the place, but never gets to the place to which it points.

Blessings in Disguise

"Thou could'st have no power at all against Me, except it were given thee from above" (*John xix:*11)

"There was given to me a thorn in the flesh" (2 *Cor. xii:*7).

"God gave me blindness," says Dr. Moon, "as a talent to be used in His service, that I might see the needs of those who could not see."

The ills of life will turn into angels of blessing if we remember God is in them. His permissions which mean great trial to us, lead us to places of benediction.

The bow of promise is seen in the dark cloud of judgment (Gen. ix:13).

BLESSINGS OF THE ATONEMENT

The stony pillow of Bethel is the forerunner of the ladder to the glory (Gen. xxviii:11, 12).

The binding of Moriah is followed by the raising from the dead (Heb. xi:17-19).

The seven years of service is rewarded by the acquisition of Rachel (Gen. xxix:28).

The backside of the desert is the prelude to the burning bush of revelation (Ex. iii:1, 2).

The fiery furnace reveals the succouring Saviour (Daniel iii:25) ;

And Gethsemane is crowned by Olivet (Heb. v:7; ii:9).

*   *   *   *

Heartaches are not pleasant while the ache is on, but they are heart-makers if rightly understood. The roll of the tides takes the roughness from the stones and makes them smooth.

Blessings of the Atonement

"The precious blood of Christ" (1 *Pet. i:*19)

"The only thing I want," said Bishop Hamilton in his dying moments, "is to place my whole confidence more and more perfectly in the precious blood." We may know more prefectly what the precious blood of Christ has done for us when we call to mind the following seven things:

(1) It *averts* the judgment of God against sin, as the blood of the paschal lamb did on the night of the Passover (Ex. xii:13; 1 Cor. v:7).

(2) It *converts* the one who believes in the Substitute, even as the blood of cleansing changed the position and condition of the cleansed leper (Lev. xiv:14; Rev. i:5).

(3) It *inverts* the position we once occupied to the world, for instead of being in it we are now separated from it, even as God said to Pharaoh of Israel: "I will put a redemption (margin) between thy people and My people" (Ex. viii:23).

(4) The blood of Christ *inserts* us in a new place, even as the blood of the covenant enabled Moses and the seventy elders to draw nigh and see the God of Israel (Ex. xxiv:5-10).

15

(5) It *asserts* that the blessings of pardon (Eph. i:7), peace (Col. i:20), power (Rev. xii:11), purity (1 John i:7), and paradise are secured in Him (Rev. vii:14).

(6) The blood of Christ *exerts* a powerful influence in its practical bearing, for it kills sin (Rom. vi:1-13), slays self (2 Cor. v:15), and overcomes pride (Phil. ii:5-8);

(7) And the blood of Christ *subverts* the powers of hell which have been conquered by His death, even as when the sacrificial lamb was offered by Samuel, and the Lord discomfited the Philistines in consequence (1 Sam. vii: 9, 10; Heb. ii:14; Col. i:14).

* * * *

The Blessing of Christ's atonement is the Blessing of every gospel blessing, for there is no blessing without it, and all blessing is secured by it.

Borrowing Misery

"I shall perish one day by the hand of Saul" (1 *Sam. xxvii*:1)

One advantage in riding through the country on a bicycle, is that one passes through many truly rural scenes. Besides this, one sees not only "sermons in stones" and "running brooks," and "good in everything," but pictures of gospel truth.

One thing the cyclist dreads, is a puncture, especially when he suddenly finds his tire down in a lonely country road, and after having carefully examined it, cannot locate the leaky part. Such was my experience some few miles out of York. What was to be done? There was no friendly cottage in sight, where a bowl of water could be obtained in order to find the escaping air in the tell-tale bubbles. In desperation the inner tube was put in the outside cover again, and the tire blown up. I rode on, expecting every minute to feel the rims of the wheel on the ground; but, to my agreeable surprise, the wheel kept up, and there was no need to touch it again in the run to London. Some cyclist friend will say: "Ah, the valve was leaking!" but it was not. Many evils in life are not so bad as they seem to be at first.

BRIGHT AND BURNING

(1) David exclaimed: "I shall now one day perish at the hand of Saul" (1 Sam. xxvii:1).

(2) The disciples cried out: "Master * * * we perish;" but instead of perishing they were "preserved by Him" (Mark iv:38).

(3) Paul was let down in a basket, and directly afterwards he was caught up into heaven (2 Cor. xi:33; xii:2).

(4) Joseph was cast into prison, but it was the prelude to his being led into the palace (Gen. xxxix:20; xli:40).

(5) John was banished to Patmos, but it became a paradise in the soul-ravishing view he had of Christ (Rev. i:9, 13-16) ;

(6) And Jacob found his stony pillow to be the place where the sunny path to heaven was seen (Gen. xxviii: 11-15).

*   *   *   *

To borrow misery is a sorry loan to get, for it is a loan which calls for a large interest, as well as being a fretting companion to torment.

Bright and Burning

"He was a burning and shining light" (*John v:35*)

"A cold firebrand and a burning lamp started out one day to see what they could find. The firebrand came back and wrote in its journal that the whole world was very dark. It did not find a place, wherever it went, in which there was light. Everywhere was darkness. The lamp when it came back wrote in its journal: 'Wherever I went it was light. I did not find any darkness in all my journey. The whole world was light.' The lamp carried light with it, and when it went abroad it illuminated everything. The dead firebrand carried no light, and it found none where it went."

The lesson of the allegory is, *we shall see around us what we are in ourselves.*

Ahab saw in Elijah an enemy, because he was an enemy of God (1 Kings xxi:20).

17

The Corinthians said Paul's "bodily presence was weak, and his speech contemptible," whereas they were sadly lacking in spirituality. If they had possessed his spiritual power, they would not have seen his bodily weakness (2 Cor. x:10; 1 Cor. iii:1).

Festus was lacking in spiritual reason; hence, he thought the apostle was mad (Acts xxvi:24, 25).

Very often the "mote" which is seen in another's eye is the reflection of the "beam" in our own (Matt. vii:4).

On the other hand, when the light of love is burning in the heart, many apparently unimportant things are found to have a heart of worth. Insignificant mites are mighty in value (Mark xii:42). A lad's five loaves and a few fishes are sufficient and abundant to supply the need of a hungry multitude (John vi:9). A little cloud is the harbinger of a great deluge of rain (1 Kings xviii:44); and a man, mean in appearance, like John the Baptist, is none the less a burning apostle of love, and a shining light of unmistakable testimony.

* * * *

Some who profess to be burning and shining lights to the Lord's glory, are ill-smelling lamps and a burning shame to their own disgrace.

Business of the Saint

"Follow thou Me" (*John xxi:22*)

Tradition tells of an old minister in Scotland, who, in discoursing on the word "follow," which was in his text, informed his hearers that he would speak of four kinds of followers.

"First," said he, "there are followers ahint; secondly, there are followers afore; thirdly, there are followers cheekie for chow, and sidie by sidie; and last o' a', there are followers that stand stane-still."

We smile at the old man's ignorance, in speaking of followers as before, beside, and standing still; but I am not sure whether he was not right after all, for we have known *professed followers* of the Lord Jesus who have run before their Lord, like Peter, when he cut off the ear of the servant of the high priest without his Lord's direction (Luke xxii:49).

BUSYBODIES AND HOW TO CURE THEM

There are also followers of the Lord who presume in placing themselves beside Him as if they were His equal,
like the man in the parable who took the uppermost
seat, and was placed in the lowest for his assumption
(Luke xiv:9);
and there are followers who stand still when they should
be following in the steps of their Lord, like Peter, when
he wanted to know what John was to do, instead of
obeying Christ's "Follow Me" (John xxi:22).
To follow Christ means
To imitate His example (1 Pet. ii:21),
To obey His Word (Matt. iv:20),
To take up His cross (Matt. xvi:24),
To deny the self-life (John xii:26),
And to be used in His service (John i:37).

*   *   *   *

The Best Business of heaven is to serve the Lord in the
business of earth. Earth's occupations are Heaven's opportunities to defeat Hell's machinations.

Busybodies and How to Cure Them

"Tattlers and busybodies" ("meddler," 1 *Pet. iv*:15 R. V.),
"speaking things which they ought not" (1 *Tim.*
v:13; 2 *Thess. iii*:11)

A native of Aniwa, named Titonga, recently gave the
following sound advice to his brethren: "I see many
things among us that are not right. There is often bad
talk. When you hear a whisper of scandal, you bend
forward your ear, and exclaim, 'Say that again: say it
again, that I may hear it well!' and then you take it and
put it in your heart, and go about looking for someone to
tell it to. You come to church and take the Word of
Jesus, and open it and read it and then you shut it and
leave it there. You go to school in the morning, and open
the Word of Jesus and read it; then you shut it and leave
it there. You go to your work and forget it. You do not
lay it up in your hearts. My friends, this is not right;
we must close our hearts and ears to bad talk, and open
our ears and hearts to the Word of Jesus."

DEVOTIONAL BIBLE STUDIES

If we give attention to pulling the beam out of our own
eye (Matt. vii:5),
build over against our own house
(Neh. iii:28),
cleanse ourselves from all filthiness
(2 Cor. vii:1),
keep our own hearts with all diligence (Pro. iv:23),
bridle our own tongue (Jas. iii:2),
look to our own spiritual welfare
(2 John 8),
and hearken to the voice of the
Lord Jesus ourselves (Luke
viii:35),
we shall have no time for "bad talk."

* * * *

To be a busybody is to be busy about the business of
other bodies, and to neglect the business which should
occupy the body who is minding the business of those
other bodies.

"But God———"

(*Acts xiii:30*)

Two significant words! When we leave God out of
our reckoning, difficulties will daunt us, temptations will
triumph over us, sin will seduce us, self will sway us, the
world will warp us, seeming impossibilities will irritate
us, unbelief will undermine our faith, Christian work will
worry us, fear will frighten us, and all things will wear a
sombre hue. When God is recognized as the One who
undertakes for us, then difficulties are opportunities to
trust Him, temptations are the harbingers of victory, sin
has no attraction, self is denied, unbelief is ignored, service is a delight, contentment sings in the heart, and all
things are possible.

(1) THE PARDONER OF SINS.—"Who can forgive sins *but
God* only" (Mark ii:7). He forgives sins for the sake
of Christ (1 John ii:12), through the blood of His
atonement (Eph. i:7), and He forgives fully (Ps. ciii:
3), freely (Rom. iii:24), and frankly (Luke vii:42).

20

(2) THE BESTOWER OF LIFE.—*"But God,* who is rich in mercy, &c." (Eph. ii:4, 5). The death of sin gripped us in its grasp, till the Lord in His grace quickened us by His Spirit. Now we have life from Christ (John v:25), life in Christ (Rom. viii:2), and Christ, in His life, in us (Gal. ii:20).

(3) THE KEEPER OF SAINTS.—*"But God* was with him" (Acts vii:9). Men may persecute, sin may tempt, the world may invite, the devil may harass, and the flesh may entice; but when God is with His own in His power, and they are with Him in their obedience, no evil can befall them; and no plague can come nigh their dwelling.

(4) THE ESTIMATOR OF HEARTS.—*"But God* knoweth your hearts" (Luke xvi:15). Men may deceive themselves with the veneer of profession, with the assertion of talk, and with the cloak of religion; but God weighs the motives, judges the heart, sees the reality, and estimates righteously.

(5) THE APPOINTER OF MEMBERS.—*"But God* hath tempered the body together" (1 Cor. xii:24). The word rendered "tempered together" means to "knit together," as the members of the body; to commingle, as the many drops of water make the stream. The word is a compound one: *"sun"* means together, the union of one thing with another; and *"kerannumi"* signifies to mingle. God has given to each member his place in the body, and it is the place of each member to keep in his own place, and not to displace any other member.

(6) THE CAUSE OF BLESSING.—*"But God* gave the increase" (1 Cor. iii:6). The word "to increase" is rendered "grow" in Matt. vi:28; Eph. iv:15; 1 Pet. ii:2; 2 Pet. iii:18. Man may plant and water, but God must cause the germination and growth. As man does his part, God fulfils His part. He can do without us, but He is pleased to do with us. He blesses our efforts, but our efforts are useless without His blessing.

(7) THE REVEALER OF TRUTH.—*"But God* hath revealed them unto us by His Spirit" (1 Cor. ii:10). The eye of man's perception cannot see the things of God, nor can the ear of his concentration locate them. They are only made known as we are living in the atmosphere of the Holy Spirit. for as we can only see and hear by means of the atmosphere, so we can only see and hear things of God by means of the illumination of the Spirit.

*   *   *   *

When God is in our reckonings we count and can count.

DEVOTIONAL BIBLE STUDIES

Calvary

"The place which is called Calvary" (Luke xxiii:33)

A man was explaining the City of Jerusalem and its vicinity. He described the situation of the city, the mount called Zion, the historic association of Olivet, the hallowed connections of Gethsemane, the silent waters of Shiloh, the grandeur of the tombs of the kings, the simplicity of the well of Jacob: when all of a sudden, a man who was intently listening to the lecturer, shouted *"Show us Calvary."* Calvary is the place which makes every other place in the Holy Land to be of interest.

As we look to the cross and remember the Christ who suffered there, we gladly say, "His death is

The *price* of our salvation (1 Cor. vi:20),
The *pass* into God's presence (Heb. x:19),
The *propitiator* of our guilt (Rom. iii:25),
The *peacemaker* for our reconciliation (Col. ii:20),
The *power* of our Christian life (Heb. xiii:12),
The *provider* of our blessing (Eph. i:7),
And the *plea* of our testimony (1 Cor. xv:1).

*   *   *   *

The Best Place in God's universe is Calvary. The place of a skull is the place where the skulls of a dead past are annihilated, and the skulls of dead sinners are vivified into living saints.

Carefulness

"If thou carefully hearken unto the Lord" (*Deut. xv:5*)

"Keep the door shut" was the imperative injunction of one of the officials as the train was slowly moving back into a railway station in England. An officious passenger would insist on standing near the door of a carriage and holding it open.

"It is all right," was the reply of the self-complacent young man, "I shall not fall out."

22

"Perhaps not," was the rejoinder, "but you might knock someone down by having the door open. Shut it!"

Sometimes Christians are equally thoughtless. They are quite concerned about their own safety, but they are not as equally solicitous of others' harm. "Do thyself no harm," was a wise word of Paul to the jailer (Acts xvi: 28), and it is a good rule to observe; but it is even more important to remember that "love worketh no ill to its neighbor" (Rom. xiii:10). The very first principle of vital godliness is, the believer is more concerned about other's weal than his own welfare. The child of God, as he lives up to his privileges, observes the following rules:

(1)   He denies himself (Luke ix:23).
(2)   He loves his brother (1 John iii:14).
(3)   He looks upon the things of others (Phil. ii:4).
(4)   He ministers to the need of those who are of "the household of faith" (Galatians vi:10).
(5)   He sympathises with those who are in sorrow (Rom. xii:15).
(6)   He allows others to be preferred before him (Rom. xii:10);
(7)   He seeks to please his Lord in all things (Heb. xiii:21).

*   *   *   *

To be careful with the thought of carefulness, is the believer's duty; but to be careful with the burden of anxiety is to the believer's damage.

Castaway

"Lest * * * I should be a Castaway" (1 *Cor. ix:27*)

"In the quarry, hard by the temple at Baalbek, in Syria, there is a tremendous block of stone, which, with labor that most present-day writers would call infinite—though there is nothing infinite in the work of man—has been hewn and squared. It is no less than 68 feet long, 14 feet broad, and 14 feet high. Yet, though so much trouble has been taken with it, *it was never built into the temple.*

As a company of the Lord's servants walked past it on one occasion, it seemed to lift its warning voice to them, saying, in the words of Paul, 'Lest by any means, when I have preached to others, I myself should be a castaway.' "

While we fully recognize that salvation is all of grace (Ephesians ii:8), and that eternal life is God's gift (Rom. vi:23), still it is possible

To lose the "full reward" (2 John 8),
For the crown to be taken by another (Rev. iii:11),
For the believer to be "ashamed" at Christ's coming (1 John ii:28),
To miss the abundant entrance (2 Peter i:11),
Not to obtain the "well done" (Matt. xxv:21),
To have the works burnt up (1 Cor. iii:15),
And to be disapproved as a servant of Christ (1 Cor. ix:27).

· * * * * *

To be faithful to the Lord is the sure way not to be disapproved by Him. If we honor Him by our devotion to Him, He will honor us by praise, honor and glory at His return.

Casting Away the Hindrance

"He casting away his garment, rose, and came to Jesus"
(*Mark x:50*)

"They told me," says Dr. Hedin, in recounting some of the legends related to him, in his travels in "The Big Sand" of Central Asia, "that there once existed a large town called Takla-makan in the desert, midway between the Yakand-daria and the Khotan-daria, but for ages it had been buried in the sand. * * * They reported, further, that the interior of the desert was under the ban of *telesmat* (an Arabic word meaning 'witchcraft,' 'supernatural powers'), and that there were towers, and walls, and houses, and heaps of gold tacks and silver jambaus (tack and jambau being Chinese coins). If a man went there with a caravan, and loaded his camels with gold, he would never get out of the desert again, but be kept there by the spirits. In that case, there was only one way in which he could save his life, and that was by throwing away the treasure."

How many there are who are weighted down with earthly things, which keep them in the desert of sin's condemnation and control.

"The cares of this life" (Luke viii:14).
Riches (1 Tim. vi:9).
Greed (Phil. iii:19).
Self-gratification (Heb. xii:16).
The world (2 Tim. iv:10).
Self-will (Jude 11).
And pride (Num. xvi:1; Jude 11).
Are some of the treasures which men have grasped at, and perished in consequence.
Men are not saved for what they give up, but they cannot have sin and the Saviour.
If they want the latter, they must part with the former, as the Thessalonians did, who "turned to God from idols, to serve the living and true God, and to wait for His Son from Heaven" (1 Thess. i:9, 10).
He that will save the treasure of the self-life will lose it, but he that will lose the self-life will find the treasure of the life which is eternal (John xii:25).

*   *   *   *

To be hindered by a hindrance is to be a hindrance as well as being hindered. When we hinder the Lord's work, we hinder God's people, as well as hinder ourselves by our hindrance.

Centralization

"Seek those things which are above" (*Col. iii*:1)

A young lady, in writing to a friend, said: "I want something, but I do not know what. My brain is not active enough to plan for itself. I have always lived in a rather narrow sphere, but feel sometimes as though I must strike out somewhere. My brain wants expanding, my thoughts need leading; but unless it is along an interesting path, my perseverance soon flags. Can you advise me?"

There will be no aimlessness in the heart and life, if the injunctions found in the following seven Scriptures are followed, for these seven S's are straight, sure, and settling:

"Seek" (Matt. vi:33).
"Set" (Col. iii:2; Ps. xvi:8).
"Separate" (2 Cor. vi:17).
"Strive" (Rom. xv:30).
"Save" (1 Cor. ix:22).
"Serve" (Rom. vii:6; Gal. v:13; Heb. ix:14).
"Show" (1 Tim. v:4; 2 Tim. ii:15; Heb. vi:11; James ii:18; iii:13; 1 Peter ii:9).
Look up the Scriptures carefully, ponder them thoughtfully, and practise them thoroughly.

*   *   *   *

When the heart is centred in the Lord and conserved for Him, we can converse with Him and He communicates His blessings to us.

Chain of Consequent Blessing

"Add to your faith" (*2 Peter i:5*)

Faith comes through the Word, joy comes through believing, patience comes through trial, power comes through prayer, victory comes through equipment, assurance comes through obedience, and glory comes through suffering. Note four of these.

(1) Faith Comes Through the Word. "Faith cometh by hearing, and hearing by the Word of God" (Rom. x:17). A God-given faith comes through the God-given Word and rests in the God-given Christ. Faith has no being apart from the Word, and no blessing either. The world's maxim is, "Seeing is believing" (Mark xv:32), but faith's axiom is "Believing is seeing" John xi:40; i:51; xx:29; 1 Peter i:8; 2 Cor. iv:17-18; v:7; Heb. xi:13-27).

26

CHAIN OF CONSEQUENT BLESSING

(2) Joy Comes Through Faith. "Joy and peace in believing" (Rom. xv:13). Joy is God-given in its source (Ps. xliii:4); strength-imparting in its blessing (Neh. viii:10); fruit-bearing is its accompaniment (John xv:11); the Spirit is its power (Rom. xiv:17; Gal. v:22); God is its sphere (Ps. xvi:11; Rom. v:11); Christ is its secret (1 Peter i:8); obedience is its minister (Acts viii:39); fellowship with the saints is its helper (Phile. 20); and persecution is its feeder (Acts v:41; xiii:52). But the essential thing in all, is to keep the wire of faith in connection with the main office—the Lord Himself (Phil. iv:1).

(3) Patience Comes Through Trial. "Tribulation worketh patience" (Rom. v:3). The patience spoken of is not sullen indifference, but calm endurance. It means holding out under pressure, and continuance under trial. Patience is the evidence of spiritual life (Luke viii:15), the companion of faith (2 Peter i:6), the precursor of happiness (Jas. v:11—the word "endure" is rendered "patience" in Rom. xii:12), the badge of love (1 Cor. xiii:7), the sign of the Spirit's strengthening (Col. i:11), the essential in the Christian race (Heb. xii:1), the acceptable offering (1 Peter ii:20), and the test of faith (James i:3). This grace, like every other, is found in the God of Patience (Rom. xv:5).

(4) Power Comes Through Prayer. "Tarry * * * until ye be clothed with power" (Luke xxiv:49, R. V.). Upper room tarrying brought the Spirit's triumphs. If we trace the effects of prayer through the Acts, we find it was the inceptor of Pentecost (i:14), the obtainer of renewed blessing (iv:31), the bringer of salvation (x:31), the opener of the prison (xii:5), the introducer to missions (xiii:3), the consoler in persecution (xvi:25), the comforter in sorrow (xx:36), the means of fellowship (xxi:5), and the healer of the body (xxviii:8). Prayer is not to be gauged by feeling, but by faithfulness; not by emotion but by promotion; not by noise, but by poise; not by words, but by worth; not by seeming effects, but by sanctified experience.

* * * *

There are three L's in which a heaven of blessing is found, namely: *Lean hard* upon Christ by faith (Canticles viii:5), *Look* up to Him by prayer (Psalm v:3), and *Listen to Him* by obedience (John x:27).

DEVOTIONAL BIBLE STUDIES

Childhood of Jesus

"The Child Jesus" (*Luke ii:43*)

A writer in a religious magazine, pictures a schoolboy exposed to the temptation of bad habits, pride, and dishonesty, to whom one evening, a loving, gentle angel appeared, and showed him some pictures. "He looked upon a boy at play, a lad about his own age, surrounded by other youths. They were all strong and happy, and the music of their merry laughter and their shouts could almost be heard. But amongst them all that Boy was pre-eminent, for His was a beauty beyond theirs, and where He was there could be no quarrelling, nothing but good-tempered enjoyment of the game. The picture faded, and in its stead Charlie saw a group of scholars seated at the feet of their teacher, and again the One amongst them, with thoughtful brow, listening more attentively than they all. Another picture showed the same Boy in a workshop, in ordinary dress, planing industriously a piece of wood, while the light streaming in at the open door shone on His face, and showed that, busy though He was, all His thoughts were moving in a higher sphere. Again, a picture showed Him with His mother, in happy, affectionate talk. Again, another represented the same Boy kneeling alone, praying to His heavenly Father with reverence and perfect child-like trust. As the last picture faded there was silence. Charlie had often seen pictures of Jesus Christ before, but never one that showed Him as He really was." And on his birthday night he "prayed with all his heart, 'O God, help me to make my boyhood like Thine; help me also to grow in favor with God and man.'" We have in Luke ii:44-52, seven pictures of the Lord Jesus in His childhood:

(1) The Supposed Presence (verse 44);
(2) The Sought Christ (verse 45);
(3) The Attentive Scholar (verse 46);
(4) The Precocious Boy (verse 47);

28

CHILDREN OF GOD

(5) The Conscious Son (verse 49);
(6) The Subjective Child (verse 51);
(7) The Growing Lad (verse 52).

*   *   *   *

Jesus was not only the Man of men, but the Boy of boys. He has passed through the experience of the latter, that He may help them in all their experiences.

Children of God

"Called the Children of God, and such we are" (1 *John iii:1,*
R. V.)

There are, as all the world knows (for it is a sharp and shrewd world), Christians who are "not summer, but winter painted green." Very disappointing are such Christians. Speaking of such, we may remind our readers of the boy who cried, "Hot mince-pies!" in the streets one frosty morning. A pedestrian, hearing the appetizing announcement, bought a pie; but, on setting his teeth into it, found it cold as a snow-ball. "I say, you boy, what do you mean by calling these hot mince-pies?" "That's the *name on 'em,*" replied the urchin.

It may be difficult sometimes to tell the true from the pretended Christian; but a little watching, a little touching, reveals the difference. "Are all Smyrna rugs alike?" asked a customer. "No," replied the shop-keeper; "some Smyrna rugs *are* Smyrna rugs; but most Smyrna rugs are not *Smyrna* rugs."

The progressive steps of a child of God and the marks of those who are truly the Lord's, are seen in the following Bible study:

> The Word of God recognises there are two families—the children of God, and the chidren of the Wicked One. Tares and Wheat, Dead and Living, Saved and Lost, Bound and Redeemed, out of Christ and in Him, Unrighteous and Righteous.

We become the children of God on the *Divine* side by the New Birth, and on the *Human* side by receiving Christ (John i:12, 13).

The proofs of sonship are as follows:

The *constitution* of sonship—life (John i:13).

The *right* of sonship—grace: "He gave" (John i:12, R. V.),

The *assurance* of sonship—the Spirit (Romans viii:16).

The *outcome* of sonship—heirship (Romans viii:17).

The *trait* of sonship—love (Eph. v:2),

The *proof* of sonship—holiness (Eph. v:8),

The *power* of sonship—blamelessness (Phil. ii:15),

The *evidence* of sonship—obedience (1 Peter i:14),

The *calling* of sonship—named "children" (1 John iii:1).

And the *manifestation* of sonship—likeness (1 John iii:10).

* * * *

The nature which makes us God's children shows itself in the likeness we bear to the Lord. "After its kind" is a fact in grace as well as in Nature.

Christ Crucified: the Theme of the Preacher

"We preach Christ crucified" (1 *Cor. i:*23)

Will you listen to the concessions of a Unitarian on the great truth of Christ's atonement? Thomas Starr King, a Unitarian, said: "The doctrine of the vicarious atonement is embodied by the holiest memories, as it has been consecrated by the loftiest talent of Christendom. It fired the fierce eloquence of Tertullian in the early Church, and gushed in honied periods from the lips of Chrysostom; it enlisted the life-long zeal of Athanasius to keep it pure; the sublimity of it fired every power, and commanded all the resources of the mighty soul of Augustine; the learning of Jerome, and the energy of Ambrose, were committed to its defence; it was the text for the subtle eye and analytic thought of Aquinas; it was the pillar of Luther's soul, toiling for man; it was shapen into intellectual proportions and systematic symmetry by the iron logic of Calvin; it inspired the beautiful humility of Fénélon; fostered the devotion and self-sacrifice of Oberlin; flowed like molten metal into the rigid forms of Edward's intellect, and kindled the deep and steady rapture of Wesley's heart. All the great enterprises of Christian history have been born from the influence, immediate or remote, which the vicarious theory of redemption has exercised upon the mind and heart of humanity."

Preaching Christ crucified we shall find it will be—

(1) *A Convincer* of sin, as seen on the Day of Pentecost (Acts ii:36, 37).

(2) *A Bringer of Blessing,* as evidenced in the lame man and Peter's words (Acts iii:13-19).

(3)) *A Means of Forgiveness,* as Peter emphatically states (Acts v:29-31).

(4) *A Procurer of Joy,* as witnessed in the result of the Eunuch's faith (Acts viii:29-39).

(5) *An Obtainer of the Spirit,* as was made known to Cornelius and those in his house (Acts x:39-44).

(6) *A Medium of Justification,* as Paul declared at Antioch (Acts xiii:38, 39).

(7) *An Imparter of Responsibility,* as the Apostle intimates to the elders at Ephesus, when He charges them to care for Christ's purchased possession (Acts xx:28).

* * * *

Christ crucified is the greatest theme in the universe, for it proclaims the greatest work ever performed by the greatest Person, and securing the greatest ends possible.

Christ Pre-eminent

"Not I, but Christ (*Gal. ii*:20)

"As you grow in your art," said Gounod to a young poet, "You will judge the great masters of the past, as I now judge the great musicians of former times. At your age I used to say, "I;" at twenty-five, I said "I and Mozart;" at forty. "Mozart and I;" now I say "Mozart."

The same thing is illustrated in the life of the believer who is growing in grace.

> At first the cry is, "What must *I* do" (Acts xvi:30),
> Then "that I may be found in Christ" (Phil. iii:9),
> Then "Christ liveth in me" (Gal. ii:20),
> And lastly, "Christ is all" (Col. iii:11).

* * * *

"Christ is our highest Orpheus, whose sphere-melody, flowing in wild, native tones, took captive the ravished souls of men, and still modulates and Divinely leads them."

Christ's Atonement

> "The life of the flesh is the blood, and I have given it to you upon the altar, to make an atonement for your souls: for it is the blood that maketh an atonement for the soul" (*Lev. xvii:11*)

Sir Walter Scott makes one of his characters, Old Mortality, to be occupied in re-chiselling the inscriptions on the tombstones of the Covenanters. Annually the old man visited the graves of the men who had laid down their lives for the sake of Christ and the Covenant, and removed the moss and dirt that might have gathered on their monuments. We may do something similar with the chisel of the pen in reproducing those epitaphs which speak of the "unseen things."

In Bunhill Fields cemetery there is the following epitaph on the tomb of an infant: "In memory of Westfield Lilley, son of Westfield and Sarah Lilley, who died June 2nd, 1798, aged one year and ten months.

> "Bold Infidelity, turn pale and die,
> Under this stone an *Infant's* ashes lie.
> Say,—Is it *Lost* or *Saved?*
> If Death's by *sin,* it sinned, for it lies here;
> If heaven's by *works,* in Heaven it can't appear.
> Ah, reason, how deprav'd!
> Revere the Bible! (sacred page) the *knot's unty'd;*
> It *died,* through Adam's *sin;* it *lives,* for Jesus died."

CHRIST'S BLOOD OF BLESSING

"Jesus died!" In the fact of Christ's atonement, as may be found in the following Scriptures, we find

The *antidote* for sin's ill (Rom. v:8),
The *severance* from sin's authority (Rom. vi:10, 11).
The *remover* of sin's condemnation (Rom. viii:34).
The *motive* for Christly action (Rom. xiv:15),
The *separator* from self's aggrandisement (2 Cor. v:14-16, R. V.),
And the *promise* of coming glory (1 Thess. iv:14; v:10).

*　　*　　*　　*

Christ's atonement is the expression of God's love in dealing with sin, and it is the extinguishing power to put it out. The fire of heaven consumes the flame of hell.

Christ's Blood of Blessing

"The blood of Jesus Christ His Son cleanseth us from all sin" (1 *John* i:7)

In the autobiography of the martyred James Chalmers, he recounts what gave him peace; he says: "I was pierced through and through with conviction of sin, and felt lost beyond all hope of salvation. Mr. Meikle came to my help, and led me kindly to promises and to light; and, as he quoted 'The blood of Jesus Christ His Son cleanseth us from all sin,' I felt that this salvation was possible for me, and some gladness came to my heart. After a time light increased, and I felt that God was speaking to me in His Word, and I believed unto salvation."

What a number have found, in the statement of fact that the blood of Christ cleanseth from sin, a furnisher of blessing.

(1) Verily His atoning blood is a *sin-remover* (Heb. ix:26),
(2) a *conscience-healer* (Heb. x:1-4),
(3) a *victory-provider* (Rev. xii:11),
(4) a *blessing-procurer* (1 Cor. x:16),

(5)   a *sin-killer* (1 Peter i:18, 19, R. V.),
(6)   a *self-displacer* (Gal. ii:20),
(7)   a *world-separator* (Heb. xiii:12),
(8)   a *love-inspirer* (2 Cor. v:14, 15).

*   *   *   *

To be cleansed by Christ means more than to have the pimples removed from the face of the life, it means the purification of the heart's affection, so that the bad blood which caused the pimples is removed.

Christ's Cross

"The cross of Christ" (*Philippians iii*:18)

In the Apocryphal Gospel of Nicodemus, the believing thief who was crucified with Christ, is represented as entering Paradise, "a miserable figure, carrying the Sign of the Cross upon his shoulders." And seeing him, all the saints said to him, "Who art thou? for thy countenance is like a thief's? And why dost thou carry a cross on thy shoulders?" In answer to them he said: "Truly have ye said that I was a robber and a thief in the world, doing all sorts of evil upon the earth. And for all these things the Jews crucified me along with Jesus. * * * And He gave me the sign of the cross, saying, 'Walk into Paradise carrying this.'"

We have no sympathy with a material cross, but we have the profoundest reverence for the glorious mediatorial significance of the cross, for by "the blood of the cross"

Christ has made peace for us (Col. i:20).
Has taken away the hindering law of ceremonies (Col. ii:14),
Reconciled Jew and Gentile to Himself (Eph. ii:16).
Through His "being obedient unto the death of the cross" He has reached the highest place in glory (Phil. ii:9).

34

CHRIST'S EXAMPLE, OR "IN HIS STEPS"

And believers find in the cross of Christ the power and
wisdom of God (1 Cor. i:18), therefore we may well
glory in it (Gal. vi:14).

    *   *   *

The heart of Christ beat in sympathy for the world in
the past eternity, and it broke in sacrifice for the world in
time on the cross.

Christ's Example

"I have given you an Example" (*John xiii*:15)

Huxley once wrote the following confession:—"No
human being, and no society composed of human beings,
ever did or ever will come to much unless their conduct
was governed and guided by ethical ideal!"

Where shall we find the highest example of "ethical
ideal?" In Christ, and in Him alone, for He, as He Himself says, left us an example for our following.

He is our Example in love (John xiii:34).
In humility (Phil. ii:5-8).
In self-denial (Rom. xv:2).
In helping each other (1 John iii:14-17).
In suffering wrongfully (1 Peter ii:21).
In serving each other (John xiii:15).
And in testimony (John xvii:18).

    *   *   *   *

"Christ is that ideal character present to the world in
Christianity, which, through all the changes of the centuries, has filled the hearts of men with an impassioned
love."

Christ's Example, or "In His Steps"

"Follow Me" (*John xii*:26)

An old Chinese woman, who had been brought to
Christ, brought her ancestral tablet to the missionary,
who had been the means of her conversion, and re-
quested that it might be burnt. The missionary responded to the request. A further request was made regarding the pot, in which the ashes of the ancestors were
preserved, that it might be destroyed. The missionary
suggested that the pot might do service to keep a plant in.

"No," said the woman, after thinking for a few minutes, "it belongs to the devil, and all that's connected with him must be destroyed." Whereupon she picked the pot up, and going outside the missionary's house, dashed it against the wall, and began, to sing in a cracked voice:

"Follow, follow, I will follow Jesus,
Anywhere, everywhere, I will follow on."

Following Christ is no child's play. Let us note some of the places to which He went, and see how they correspond to us as we follow Him. Following Christ we shall

(1)   Go beneath the waters of Jordan's judgment upon the self-life (Matthew iii:15; John xii:24-26);
(2)   We shall tread the wilderness of temptation (Matt. iv:1; 1 Peter iv:12);
(3)   We shall traverse the hill of Nazareth's persecution (Luke iv:29; John xv:18);
(4)   We shall encounter the Simon of misunderstanding (Luke vii:39; II Corinthians vi:9);
(5)   We shall pass through the Gethsemane of sorrow (Hebrews x:7; II Corinthians xii:8);
(6)   We may have to stand in the Gabbatha of scorn and suffering (John xix:13; 1 Corinthians iv:9-13);
(7)   And we shall go to the Golgotha of crucifixion (John xix:17; Gal. ii:20).

But everyone of these places has its compensation, for the "opened heaven" follows Jordan (Matt. iii:16; Heb. x:19); triumph is found in the wilderness (Luke iv:13, 14; Revelation iii:21), peace follows persecution (John x:39-42; xvi:33), faith grows stronger by trusting when misunderstood (Hebrews xii:2, 3; 1 Peter iii:16), angelic ministry is exercised in Gethsemane (Luke xxii:43; II Corinthians xii:9), reward comes to the endurer of suffering (Heb. ii:9-11; II Timothy ii:12), and glory is the outcome of Calvary's gory path (Luke xxiv:26; Rom. viii:17, 18).

*   *   *   *

To practice the precepts of the Christ in the ardour and willingness of love, we need the passion and potentiality of His sacrifical cross. The cross draws us to the Christ Who died on it, and the Christ makes any cross valuable.

Christ's Mastership

"For one is your Master, even Christ" (Matt. xxiii:8)

There are six different Greek words in the New Testament referring to our Lord that are translated "Master." One of these represents Him as the Overseer, another the File Leader, another the Teacher, another the Despot, the fifth the Supreme Owner, and the sixth the Initiated One. These words imply that He is different from us, in each relation, as represented by His name, and we are different from Him. Each name implies that something is supplied to us, and something expected from us. The names imply that (1) He is responsible for all needed provision; (2) it is our right and duty to look to Him for absolute guidance; (3) He is ready to fulfil His promise of instruction; (4) there must be complete submission to His will and command; (5) His rights as Owner can only be acknowledged by consecration to His service; and (6) He, being the One Who is initiated in the things of God, can lead us into their secrets. He watches over us, He leads us, He instructs us, He is our supreme Lord, He owns us, for He purchased us with His blood, and loves to teach us.

The following verses of Scriptures are where the different words are found.

The *Overseer* denotes Christ in His supreme authority, and is used of Him alone, and is only found in Luke's Gospel (Luke v:5; viii:24, 45; ix:33, 49; xvii:13).

The *File Leader* signifies Christ as the One Who leads and directs (Matthew xxiii:8).

The *Teacher* represents Him as the Instructor. Judas used this word, but he never called Him "Lord" (Matthew xxvi:25, 49).

The *Despot* speaks of Him as the One Who has absolute right and might (2 Tim. ii:21; 2 Pet. ii:1).

The *Owner* suggests the thought of possession and authority (Luke xix:16). The word is rendered *"owners"* in verse 33.

DEVOTIONAL BIBLE STUDIES

The *Initiated One* signifies Christ as the One Who is able to teach because He has been taught (Luke x:25; John xiii:13, 14).

*   *   *   *

Nothing is right in the life till Christ has the place of sovereignty in the heart. A Christ-possessed heart, means a Christ-reflected life. Only the Christ within can reproduce the Christ without.

Christ's purpose in dying

"He died for all, that * * * " (2 *Corinthians* v:15)

Some time since, Mr. Arthur Hacker put forth his strength in a highly-imaginative illustration of Malory's "Morte d'Arthur," picturing "The Temptation of Sir Percival," when the knight sheathed in armour, with helmet at his side, is seen seated in the enchanted wood, holding a wine-bowl in his hands, and having at his side a temptress, in the shape of a young but evil-looking woman. Close by Sir Percival is his good sword, *the hilt of which forms a cross, and gazing at this he is recalled to a sense of his duty.*

There are many practical lessons we may learn from the cross of Christ.

His death is the annuller of sin (Rom. vi:11),
The displacer of self (II Cor. v:14, 15),
The promoter of humility (Phil. ii:5-8).
The leader to righteousness (1 Peter ii:24),
The begetter of love (1 John iii:16),
The conqueror of Satan (Revelation xii:11),
And the harbinger of hope (1 Thessalonians iv:16).

*   *   *   *

Christ had a two-fold purpose in dying for us. He died to bring us to God in a lasting relationship, and He died to bring God to us in the sufficiency of His grace.

Christ's Substitutionary Death

"Christ suffered for sins once, the Righteous for the unrighteous" (1 *Pet. iii*:18, R. V.)

"My blood * * * shed for many unto the remission of sins"
(*Matt. xxvi*:28, R. V.)

That master of evangelical thought, Dr. Dale, has put
the subject in his own masterly way. He says: "In
every province of human thought we ascertain the Facts
first—make such of them—and try to explain them afterwards. We never deny the Facts because we find them
inexplicable. Some of the Facts about which we are most
certain, and with which we are most familiar, cannot be
explained. We cannot, for example, explain why we
see a mountain when the image of it is formed on the
retina; or why we hear a voice when vibrations are produced in the ear by the percussion of atmospheric waves.
Between the image on the retina and vision, between the
vibrations in the ear and sound, there is a gulf which no
speculation has ever been able to cross. The two classes
of phenomena—the impression on the physical organ on
the one hand, and consciousness on the other—are so
remote from each other, so unlike, that the relation between them cannot be traced. It may be that we shall
find ourselves unable to give any account of the relation
between the Death of Christ and the forgiveness of sin;
and yet the fact that the Death of Christ is the ground
of forgiveness, may be so certain to us as to be a great
power in life."

As we think of the work of Christ on the cross in the
broad outline of its comprehensiveness, it may be grouped
under the following seven points:

(1) The Death of Christ is *Generative in its Life.* "Except a corn of wheat fall into the ground and die, it
abideth alone: but if it die, it bringeth forth much fruit"
(John xii:24). "The Son of Man must be lifted up"
(John iii:14). His death was a necessity; hence, the
meaning and force of His *"must,"* for had He not gone
down into the dust of death, He would not have been
able to communicate to us His life. His death is our
life.

(2) The Death of Christ is *Substitutive in its Work.* Christ's own statement about the fact of His substitutionary work is conclusive and final. He says, in speaking of the great purpose for which He came into the world, that it was "to give His life a ransom for many" (Matthew xx:28). Dean Alford says of these words, they are "a plain declaration of the sacrificial and vicarious nature of the death of our Lord."

(3) The Death of Christ is *Protective in its Grace.* "Jesus, which delivered us from the wrath to come" (1 Thessalonians i:10). "We shall be saved from wrath through Him" (Romans v:9). "God hath not appointed us to wrath, but to obtain salvation through (R. V.) our Lord Jesus Christ" (1 Thessalonians v:9). In these verses there is an impending doom hanging over the sinner, which is averted through the action of Another. Mark the sentence, "Through our Lord Jesus Christ." The sense of the "through" is "by means of" Him. How? Because the stroke of Jehovah has fallen upon Him, as we read in Isa. liii:8: "For the transgression of My people was the stroke upon Him" (margin).

(4) The Death of Christ is *Inductive in its Blessing.* "Christ also suffered for sins once, the Righteous for the unrighteous, that He might bring us to God" (1 Peter iii:18, R. V.) He died to save us from hell and bring us to heaven; but what is of even greater moment He died to bring us *to God;"* or, as Rotherham renders it, "To introduce us to God." Yet there is more than introduction, there is *induction,* namely, bringing us to God and making us His children. Christ, in bringing us to God, brings us into the relationship of children, with all its privileges and responsibilities, and a great deal more.

(5) The Death of Christ is *Formative in its Power.* The Holy Spirit, in speaking of the believer being baptised into the death of Christ, speaks of it as that "Form of doctrine" (Rom. vi:17). The figure is that of a mould into which the metal runs and is shaped by it. The heart and life of the child of God are to be formed by the death of Christ. The death of the cross is to be the death of sin; and its munificent giving, its holy sacrifice, its Divine passion, its devoted service, its patient suffering, its self-effacement, and its God-glorifying spirit are to be ours.

(6) The Death of Christ is *Inspirative in its Motive.* The apostle, in speaking of the power which moved him in his life's service for Christ, says "The love of Christ constraineth us; because we thus judge, that One died for all, therefore all died" (II Corinthians v:14, R. V.) It was not love in a general sense which moved him, but the love as expressed in the death of His Lord. The fire which ignited his being was got from the altar of Christ's sacrifice.

(7) The Death of Christ is *Procurative in its claim.* The price which the Lord paid in order that He might procure us for Himself was the shedding of His precious blood. The price of His purchase is the right by which He claims us for Himself. "Ye are not your own, for ye are bought with a price: therefore, glorify God in your body, and in your spirit, which are God's" (I Cor. vi:19, 20). The claim of His call upon the whole of our nature is based upon the purchased price He gave for us in His death.

*   *   *   *

Sin has inoculated all mankind with its poison; but through identification with Christ's atonement, He, by the vitality of that death, transmits His life to us, and counteracts the virus.

Christ's Verilys

"Verily I say unto you" (*Matt. v:*18)

A little child, after praying her own little prayer by her bedside, was heard to say, "And now, dear Lord Jesus, I am *waiting* for You to speak to me."

We, too often, are in too great a hurry, to hear what the Lord has to say to us. Would we know what He says to us in some particulars, then let us ponder, pray over, and practise the thirty

DEVOTIONAL BIBLE STUDIES

"Verily I say unto you's" of Matthew's Gospel (Matt. v:18,
26; vi:2, 5, 16; viii:10; x:15, 23, 42; xi:11; xiii:17; xvi-
:28; xvii:20; xviii:3, 13, 18; xix:23, 28; xxi:21, 31;
xxiii:36; xxiv:2, 34, 47; xxv:12, 40, 45; xxvi, 13, 21, 34,
and further see the double "Verilys"—"Verily, verily I
say unto you"—in John's gospel.

* * * *

Christ's verities are backed by His verilys. The va-
lidity of His verities make us sure of the virtue of His
verilys. He says all that is worth saying, therefore, it is
not for us to do any saying, but it is our wisdom to do
all the believing.

Christ: the Balm for every Ill

"Is there no balm in Gilead? Is there no Physician there?"
(Jer. viii:22)

A well-known author, in describing a conversation between a doctor and clergyman, makes the doctor say:
"You fight the devil from the inside, and I fight him from
the outside. My chance is a poor one."

"It would be, perhaps, if you were confined to outside
remedies. But what an opportunity your profession gives
you of attacking the enemy from the inside as well!
And you have this advantage over us, that no man can
say it belongs to your profession to say such things, and
therefore disregard them."

"Ah, Mr. Walton, I have too great a respect for your
profession to dare to interfere with it. The doctor in
'Macbeth,' you know, could

> 'Not minister to a mind diseased,
> Pluck from the memory a rooted sorrow,
> Purge out the written troubles of the brain,
> And with some sweet oblivious antidote
> Cleanse the stuff'd bosom of that perilous stuff
> Which weighs upon the heart.' "

42

CHRIST: THE CARETAKER

"What a memory you have! But you don't think I can do that any more than you?"

"Do you know the best medicine to give, anyhow. I wish I always did. But, you see, we have no theriaca now."

"Well, we have. For the Lord says, 'Come unto Me, and I will give you rest.'"

"There! I told you! That will meet all diseases."

"Strangely, now there comes into my mind a line of Chaucer, with which I will make a small return for your quotation from Shakespeare; you have mentioned theriaca; and I, without thinking of this line, quoted our Lord's words. Chaucer brings the two together, for the word triacle is merely a corruption of theriaca, the unfailing cure for everything.

'Christ, which that is to every harm triacle.'"

Christ is the Rest for the weary (Matt. xi:28).
Christ is the Life for the dead (John x:10).
Christ is the Salvation for the lost (Luke xix:9).
Christ is the Liberator for the bound (Luke iv:18).
Christ is the Cleansing for the polluted (1 John i:7).
Christ is the Holy One for the sinful (1 Cor. i:30).
Christ is the All and in all (Col. iii:11).

* * * *

The only cure for fallen humanity is Divinity. The Christ of God does not patch up humanity, but through His atoning blood pardons the sinner who receives Him, and makes him a new creature.

Christ: the Caretaker

"He careth for You" (1 *Pet. v:7*)

I could not help thinking the words were a *good pillow* upon which to rest as I retired to bed, for they reminded me of the watchfulness of His care. When I got up in the morning, the words were still proclaiming their message, and spoke of the preparedness of His care to meet the difficulties of the day; hence they were a *strengthening cordial.* As I went out to do the Lord's work feeling its responsibility, the words had yet another message, for they reminded me of the sufficiency of His care to meet needs. Hence, they were a *gladsome encourager.*

Pondering the words still further, I could not help asking the question: *"How* does He care?" The following are some of the characteristcs of His care.

(1) He cares for us, as a *father* cares for his child, *providingly* (Romans viii:32).

(2) As a *mother* cares for her offspring, *affectionately* (Isaiah xlix:15).

(3) As a *gardener* cares for his garden, *attentively* (Isaiah xxvii:3).

(4) As the *eye-lid* cares for the eye, *instantly* (Deuteronomy xxxii:10).

(5) As a *friend* cares for a friend, *faithfully* (Prov. xvii:17).

(6) As a *keeper* cares for his charge, *watchfully* (Psalm cxxi:4-8).

(7) And as a *banker* cares for the treasure deposited with him, *secretly* (Col. iii:3).

* * * *

He who *looks up* to God in prayer will always find He *looks down* to provide for the need which prompts the the petition.

Christ the Chiefest, or Better than the Best

"The chiefest" (*Canticles v:*10)

One was asked whether he did not admire the admirable structure of some stately building; *"No,"* said he, *"for I have been at Rome. where better are to be seen every day."* So says the true-hearted believer when the fair and attractive things of earth are presented to him, and are compared with Christ. He is better than the best, and richer than the richest. Mark what the Holy Spirit says of the things which belong to Him.

(1) His love is unknowable (Eph. iii:19).
(2) His riches are unsearchable (Eph. iii:8).
(3) His joy is unspeakable (1 Peter i:8).
(4) His ways are untrackable (Romans xi:33).
(5) His grace is inexhaustible (II Cor. ix:8).
(6) His peace is unfathomable (Philippians iv:7).
(7) And He Himself is unsurpassable (Ex. xv:11).

*   *   *   *

The superlative of Christ's perfection is beyond all question, as one has said, "Christ is the mightiest among the holy, and the holiest among the mighty, who lifted with His pierced hands empires off their hinges, turned the ·stream of time into new channels, and still governs all the ages."

Christ: the Emancipator from Sin

"He looseth the prisoners" (Ps. cxlvi:7)

A little fun at the Birmingham Post-office led to a remarkable sequel. Among the postal packets, was a parcel containing a pair of handcuffs, which were being sent from Derby to a manufacturer in Birmingham, to be fitted with a key. The paper covering of the package had, during transit, been badly torn, with the result that when the handcuffs reached the Birmingham sorting-office, they were exposed to view. They were an object of curiosity, and presently one of the clerks jocularly clasped one of the cuffs round the wrist of his left hand. To his dismay, there was no key to unfasten it, and he, therefore, went to the central police-station. Here a key was found, but, as the officer was turning it, it broke off in the cuff. The situation, at first comical, had now become really serious. The broken key would have to be drilled out, or the handcuff filed through, before the clerk could be released from his unpleasant encumbrance. But it was Sunday, and no place of business was open. The clerk therefore returned to the post-office and explained his plight to his superintendent, by whom he was ordered to go to Derby by the first train the next morning, explain the whole circumstances to the owner of the handcuff, and apologise; and then return to Birmingham, and proceed to the manufacturer and have the handcuff taken off.

Sinners often play with sin, like the man with the handcuffs, and find presently they are unable to give it up, for it has got them, and holds them firmly in its grasp, until a power outside of themselves gives them release.

> Christ is the Great Emancipator. He delivers from the *penalty of sin* by His atoning death (1 Peter ii:24).
> He delivers from the *power of sin* by His risen power (Colossians ii:12, 13).
> He delivers from the *pollution of sin* by His in-dwelling presence (John xv:4, 5).
> He delivers from the *pauperism of sin* by the riches of His Grace (Ephesians ii:7).
> He delivers from the *pleasure of sin* by the pleasures in His right hand (Psalm xvi:11, R. v.).
> He delivers from the *principle of sin* by His operating love (1 John iii:6).
> And He will deliver from the *presence of sin* at His glorious return (Phil. iii:20, 21).

*　　*　　*　　*

He who plays with sin will find that sin will not play with him. It will hold and hurt. Then Christ alone can heal and deliver.

Christ: the Fortress

"The Lord is my Rock and my Fortress" (2 *Sam. xxii*:2)

In carrying on a war, the first thing wanted is a strong castle to retreat to. When the Duke of Wellington entered on the famous Peninsular Campaign, in

CHRIST: THE FORTRESS

which he drove Bonaparte's armies back to France, he built a stupendous fortification at Torres Vedras forty miles in circuit. Six hundred cannon were mounted on 150 towers; while every jutting rock bristled with weapons of defence. No such fortress was ever seen before. Massena, the French general, thought he was sure of Wellington and his troops, and came down with 80,000 men, like a whirlwind, expecting to drive them all into the sea. All at once they saw before them this appalling entrenchment stretching right across their path. Immediately they came to a halt, while their general rode to-and-fro for days in hope of finding some weak point at which he might enter. But all in vain. Torres Vedras was impregnable. He shook his head, and with shame gave orders for a retreat.

Now, the Lord is our "Torres Vedras"—our FORTIFICATION. No weapon formed against this Fortress can prosper. In it we may hold out against a siege for a whole lifetime. Iniquity shall never be our ruin if we do but cleave to Christ, for He is the

(1) *Strong Fortress* for safety in time of peril (2 Sam. xxii:2);

(2) *Sheltering Fortress* for preservation from our enemies (Ps. xviii:2);

(3) *Sure Fortress* to keep from perplexity and doubt (Ps. xxxi:3);

(4) *Settled Fortress* for habitation (Ps. lxxi:3);

(5) *Supreme Fortress* for excellence, for none can do, or be, like Him (Ps. xci:2);

(6) *Suitable Fortress,* for He can meet the need of each and all (Ps. cxliv: 2);

(7) *Succouring Fortress* in the time of affliction (Jer. xvi:19).

* * * *

Christ is our hiding and abiding place. Hiding in Him is our safety and peace; and abiding in Him is our sanctification and satisfaction.

DEVOTIONAL BIBLE STUDIES

Christ: the Keeper

"Unto Him that is able to keep you from falling" (*Jude* 24)

The natives òf India used to say that when Sir Henry Lawrence looked twice to heaven, and then to earth, he knew what to do. The 121st Psalm stands out in striking contrast to the previous one, where the Psalmist is in distress and loneliness, as he is surrounded by enemies. But now we find him rising from the earth and his own despair to the height of the Lord's preserving care. Like the brave general above named, he knows what to do, for the Lord is his Constant Keeper. The Lord is seen in no less than nine different characters. We behold Him as the Almighty Helper (verse 2); as the Sure Upholder (verse 3); as the Constant Keeper (verse 3); as the Vigilant Watchman (verse 4); as the Assuring Preserver (verse 5); as the Sheltering Protector (verses 5 and 6); as the Absolute Guardian (verse 7); as the Personal Sustainer (verse 7); and as the Unfailing Friend.

(1) *Almighty Helper* (verse 2). If we look to the marginal reading of verse 1, he asks the question, "Shall I look to the hills?" but comes to the conclusion that his help comes from Him who made the hills.

(2) *Sure Upholder* (verse 3). "He will not suffer thy foot to be moved."

(3) *Constant Keeper* (verse 3). "He that keepeth thee will not slumber."

(4) *Vigilant Watchman* (verse 4). "He that keepeth Israel shall neither slumber nor sleep."

(5) *Assuring Preserver* (verse 5). "The Lord *is* thy Keeper."

(6) *Sheltering Protector* (verses 6 and 7). "The Lord is thy Shade," &c.

(7) *Absolute Guardian* (verse 7, R. V.). "The Lord shall keep thee from *all* evil."

48

CHRIST: THE LIFTER-UP

(8) *Personal Sustainer* (verse 7). His personal thought of us in our personal need is seen if we ponder the seven "Thys" and three "Thees," all of which are wrapped up in "He shall keep thy soul."

(9) *Unfailing Friend* (verse 7). "The Lord shall keep * * * for evermore" (R. V.)

* * * *

Christ keeps us for Himself from the world; He keeps us in Himself from sin; He keeps us by Himself from Satan; and He keeps us with Himself for fellowship.

Christ: the Lifter-Up

"Thou hast lifted me up" (*Ps. xxx*:1)

The biographer of Bismarck says of him. "Bismarck always disliked England and everything English; naturally from his point of view, for the constitutional monarchy and parliamentary system were in irreconcilable antipathy to his whole theory of government. The two systems are in fact the negation of each other. The British system is an expansion of that noble verse in the 'Te Deum:' 'Govern them and lift them up for ever.' The true end of government is always to lift up the governed. The despotic idea of goverment is just the reverse: 'Govern them and keep them down for ever.' Of that idea Bismarck was the most perfect incarnation of our era, and naturally, therefore, Britain was always to him an object of intense dislike." Certainly the lifting up is the Christian act, for practical Christianity is a lifting up of the whole being.

> Christ is ever doing what He did to Peter's wife's mother, of whom we read, "He came, and took her by the hand, and lifted her up" (Mark i:31).
> The Lord is the "Lifter-up." This is one of His titles (Ps. iii:3).
> He lifts up from the dunghill of sin, and sets us among the princes of His power (1 Sam. ii:8).
> He lifts up from the gates of death's despair, and makes us partakers of His life (Ps. ix:13).

49

He lifts us up from the hatred of our enemies and keeps us
in safety (Ps. xviii:48, xxvii:6, xxx:1).
He lifts up those who are in the enemy's power, and makes
them free in His liberty (Mark ix:27);
And He lifts us up in the time of our weakness, and makes
us strong for His service.

*   *   *   *

Love's siftings often precede His liftings. He sifts
to get rid of the chaff, and He lifts to gladden our hearts.

Christ: The Precious One

"Unto you therefore who believe He is precious" (1 *Pet.* ii:7)

"Christ is precious, is He not?" I said to an aged saint,
who was very feeble and ill; in fact, she was wandering
a good deal, as we could tell by her incoherent talk; but
the mention of Christ's name touched a responsive chord
in her nature, for she immediately replied: "He is precious, if we make Him so."

The benefit of anything is the use we make of it. It
is the bread we eat which satisfies our hunger, and not
the bread in the baker's shop. It is the money which
is invested that gains interest, and not that which the
miser hoards up.

The same is true with regard to spiritual things.

It is the hand of the diligent which maketh rich (Prov.
x:4).
Those who take the water of life get their soul-thirst
quenched, and their soul's need met (Rev. xxii:17).
Those who receive Christ are made the children of God to
their eternal making (John i:12.)
Those who believe on Christ possess eternal life to their
own joy and peace (John iii:36).
Those who obey Christ show that they are His by their
obedience, to their assurance and power (John x:27).
Those who hearken to Christ are they upon whom condemnation shall never come (John v:24).
Those who surrender to Christ by whole-hearted consecration, are those to whom He surrenders Himself to their
comfort (Song of Sol. ii:16).

CHRIST: THE REST-GIVER

Those who lean on the Beloved by prayerful trust, find He
gives them the consciousness of His love to their triumph (Song of Sol. viii :5) ;
And those who walk with Him in the hour of strife, find
He honors them in making them walk with Him in
white to their honor (Rev. iii :4).

*   *   *   *

Christ is not only precious apart from us, but to us
is the preciousness (see R. V. Margin of 1 Pet. ii :7), for
He imparts Himself to us.

Christ: The Rest-Giver

"Come unto Me * * * I will give you rest" (*Matt. xi :28*)

In Newport Church, in the Isle of Wight, lies buried
the Princess Elizabeth (daughter of Charles the First).
A marble monument, erected by Queen Victoria, records
in a touching way, the manner of her death. She lan-
guished in Carisbrook castle during the wars of the Com-
monwealth—a prisoner, alone and separated from all the
companions of her youth, till death set her free. She was
found dead one day, with her head leaning on her Bible,
and the Bible open at the words, "Come unto Me, all ye
that labor and are heavy laden, and I will give you rest."
The monument in Newport Church records this fact. It
consists of a female figure reclining her head upon a
marble book, with the text engraven on it.

She had found, as many another has found, that Christ,
and Christ alone, is the One who can give rest.

He gives *rest from a guilty conscience,* through faith in
His precious atonement, for He has put away sin by the
sacrifice of Himself (Heb. ix :26).
He gives *rest from fear of judgment,* for there is "no condemnation to them who are in Christ Jesus" (Rom.
viii :1).
He gives *rest from the fear of death,* for by His death He
has rendered powerless him who had the authority of
death (Heb. ii :14).

51

He gives *rest from anxiety,* as we are careful for nothing, thankful for anything, and prayerful in everything (Phil. iv:6, 7).

He gives *rest from the evil of unbelief,* as we are diligent to enter unto His rest (Heb. iv:3).

He gives *rest from a disturbing heart,* as we are found yoked with Him in the will of God (Matt. xi:29);

And He gives *rest from defeat,* as we are environed with His presence, for His rest is on every side (2 Chron. xiv:7).

Who would not have this many-sided blessing of rest? Come and rest. Take His yoke and be blest. Believe and enter into His rest.

Rest, weary soul!
The penalty is borne, the ransom paid,
For all thy sins full satisfaction made!
Strive not to do thyself what Christ has done,
Claim the free gift, and make the joy thine own;
No more by pangs of guilt and fear distrest.
Rest, sweetly rest!

*   *   *   *

To rest in Christ is be rested. The rest of faith brings the restedness of blessing.

Christ: the Rise or Fall of all

"This Child is set for the falling and rising again of many"
(*Luke ii*:34)

Trapp says, "Nothing so cold as lead, yet nothing so scalding if molten; nothing more blunt than iron, and yet nothing so keen if sharpened; the air is soft and tender, yet out of it are engendered thunderings and lightnings; the sea is calm and smooth, but if tossed with tempests it is rough beyond measure. Thus it is that mercy abused turns to fury; God, as He is a God of mercies, so He is a God of judgment; and it is a fearful thing to fall into His punishing hands. He is loath to strike; but when He strikes, He strikes home. If His wrath be kindled but a little, yea, but a little, woe be to all those upon whom it lights; how much more when He is sore displeased with a people or a person?"

CHRIST: THE SIN-BEARER

Christ is one of two things to all. He is either the Stone
on which we are broken to penitence and salvation, or
He is the Stone to grind in pieces to punishment and
condemnation (Luke xx:18).
The pillar of cloud was light to Israel and darkness to the
Egyptians (Ex. xiv:20).
The ways of the Lord are to walk in for our blessing,
or ways to stumble in to our hurt (Hosea xiv:9).
God is a Consuming Fire to purify His people (Mal. iii:3),
and a Burning Fire to scorch His enemies (Mal. iv:1-6).
Christ is life to those who receive Him (John iii:36), while
He is wrath to those who reject Him (Rev. vi:16).
Christ is the Chief Corner Stone to those who rest on Him
in faith for salvation (1 Pet. ii:6), while He is a Stone
of Stumbling to those who will not have Him (1 Pet.
ii:8).
Christ is precious to those who believe (1 Pet. ii:7), while
He is despised by those who neglect Him (Isa. liii:3).
When Christ comes He brings eternal rest for His people,
but He gives eternal destruction to those who have not
obeyed the gospel (2 Thess. i:6-8).
Has not all this a voice for us? Offended mercy is very
wroth.

*   *   *   *

Men's misconceptions of truth arise from a misapprehension of Christ. If we would know the truth about
Him, we must know Him about Whom the truth speaks.

Christ: The Sin-Bearer

"He bore our sins" (1 *Pet. ii:24*)

A missionary in charge of one of the native
Churches in China, was examining a number of candidates for Christian baptism. After having put sundry questions to a woman who had applied for Church
membership, he asked, "Had Jesus sin?" (This is one of
the questions in the Catechism, which enquirers are encouraged to learn. The book, of course, gives a negative
answer.) Somewhat to the missionary's astonishment,
she replied, "Yes." The question was repeated in a way

likely to elicit a negative reply, but she answered emphatically, "He had sin." The candidate was next asked if he (the examiner) had sin, to which she rather hesitatingly replied, "No." The missionary soon put her right on that point, and further asked how it came about that Jesus, the great living God of heaven, could have sin. "Why, *He had mine!*" was the unhesitating reply. I fancy that our friend, just won from heathenism, was a deeper theologian than the missionary at first thought. True, she could not read her Bible, but she knew that "The Lord hath laid on Him the iniquity of us all," and that He "bare our sins in His own body on the tree."

"Yes, all the griefs He felt were ours,
　　Ours were the woes He bore;
Pangs, not His own, His spotless soul
　　With bitter anguish tore.

"He died to bear the guilt of men,
　　That sin might be forgiven;
He lives to bless them, and defend,
　　And plead their cause in heaven."

(1) DECLARATION.—"Christ died for *our sins* according to the Scriptures" (1 Cor. xv:3).

(2) CONSTERNATION.—"*Our sins* testify against us" (Is. lix:12). See also Neh. ix:37; Dan. ix:16.

(3) PROPITIATION.—"Propitiation for *our sins*" (1 John ii:2).

(4) MANIFESTATION.—"He was manifested to take away *our sins*" (1 John iii:5).

(5) IDENTIFICATION.—"When He had by Himself, or for Himself (representatively), purged *our sins*" (Heb. i:3).

(6) EMANCIPATION.—"Loosed us from *our sins* by His own blood" (Rev: i:5, R. V.).

(7) SEPARATION.—"Gave Himself for *our sins*, that He might deliver us out of this present evil world" (Gal. i:4).

*　　*　　*　　*

Relying on the finished work of Christ we are safe, responding to His Word we are sure, and resting in His will we are happy.

Christ: the Unchanging One

"Jesus Christ the same" (*Heb. xiii:8*).

An incident was related by Schuyler Colfax regarding Abraham Lincoln. It was during the dark days of 1863, on the evening of a public reception given at the White House. The foreign legations were there gathered about the President.

A young English nobleman was just being presented to the President. Inside the door, evidently overawed by the splendid assemblage, was an honest-faced old farmer, who shrank from the passing crowd until he and the plain faced old lady, clinging to his arm, were pressed back to the wall. The President, looking over the heads of the assembly, said to the English nobleman: "Excuse me, my lord, there's an old friend of mine."

Passing backward to the door, Mr. Lincoln said, as he grasped the old farmer's hand: "Why, John, I'm glad to see you. I haven't seen you since you and I made rails for old Mrs.——, in Sangamon county, in 1847. How are you?"

The old man turned to his wife with quivering lips, and without replying to the President's salutation, said: "Mother, he's just the same old Abe!"

So say we of Christ.

His love is the same, for it is *"everlasting"* (Jer. xxxi:3).
His keeping is the same, for it is *constant* (1 Pet. i:5).
His power is the same, for it is *enduring* (Heb. xiii:5).
His ministry is the same, for *"He ever liveth"* (Heb. vii:25).
His pleasures are the same, for they are *lasting* (Ps. xvi:11).
His promises are the same, for they are *sure* (2 Cor. i:20).
He Himself is the same, for He is *immutable* (Mal. iii:6).

* * * *

The Best Way to look at God's dark providences is to look through them, and see the bright and sympathetic Face of the watching Friend on the other side.

DEVOTIONAL BIBLE STUDIES

Clouds

"The clouds are the dust of His feet" (*Nahum i:3*)

Clouds and no sunshine are good for cyclists. There were not more than five or six hours of sunshine during the time I was cycling to London. The heavens were overshadowed with clouds, and yet there was only one sharp and short shower. The cloudiness of the weather had its distinct advantages, for there is nothing so fatiguing as the sun scorching down upon one when cycling. There are many angel faces seen in the clouds, as the artist realized when he painted the famous picture entitled "Cloudland," which seems at first sight to be only a mass of clouds, but on closer observation, angel faces are seen looking out upon you. The following are a few of the things which we may find in the clouds of life.

(1) The bow of promise (Gen. ix:13);
(2) The glory of the Lord's presence (Ex. xvi:10);
(3) The rain of His blessing (1 Kings xviii:44);
(4) The covering of His protection (Ps. cv:39);
(5) The strength of His power (Ps. lxviii:34);
(6) The dew of His grace (Prov. iii:20);
(7) And the word of His testimony (Ps. xcix:7; Matt. xvii:5).

*   *   *   *

Clouds are not clogs to hinder us, they are bringers of showers to bless us.

Commendation's Ministry

"I praise you" (1 *Cor. xi:2*)

"In those books, *Mrs. Wiggs of the Cabbage Patch* and *Lovey Mary*, I find a woman who always wore the garment of praise. Mrs. Wiggs went about seeking to eulogise, embodying the very spirit of her Master. When Lovey Mary was leaving the Cabbage Patch, she said, 'You all bluffed me into being good. You began to

brag about me, and then I wanted to be good more than
anything in the world.' Mrs. Wiggs had done it. And
she did it also with her children. 'I have always found
compliments better than switches.'"

The Apostle Paul often found it essential to rebuke the
saints, but he was never forgetful to remember their
good points.

> He could "thank God" that the "faith" of the saints in
> Rome was "spoken of" (Rom. i:8);
> He appreciated the fact that the saints in Corinth came
> "behind in no gift," and were found "waiting for the
> coming of the Lord Jesus" (1 Cor. i:7);
> Although Paul had sharp words to say to the Galatian
> saints because of their legal spirit, he none the less
> recognized they "did run well" (Gal. v:7);
> He thanked God for the "fellowship in the gospel" of the
> saints at Philippi, and was confident of their continu-
> ance, and was encouraged by their prayers (Phil.
> i:3-6, 19);
> He could praise God because he had "heard of" the "faith
> in Christ" of the Lord's people at Colosse, and of their
> "love to all the saints" (Col. i:4);
> His thankfulness is most pronounced as he contemplates
> "the work of faith, the labor of love, and patience of
> hope" of the Thessalonian believers (1 Thess. i:3);
> And he was moved and grateful for Timothy's sympathetic
> "tears," and for Philemon's "prayer" (2 Tim. i:4;
> Philemon 22).

* * * *

To be an encourager of God's saints is to be a helper
indeed and in need, but to be a damper to discourage
His people is to join hands with him who ever seeks to
hinder the saints.

Concentration

"This one thing" (*Phil. iii*:8-14)

Mr. Spurgeon once related how in going through the
famous factory at Sevres he noticed an artist painting a
very beautiful vase. He says: "I looked at him, but he

did not look at me. His eyes were better engaged than in staring at a stranger. There were several persons at my heels, and they all looked and made observations, yet the worker's eye never moved from his work. He had to paint the picture upon that vase, and what benefit would he get from noticing us, or from our noticing him? He kept to his work. We would fain see such abstraction and concentration in every man who has the Lord's work to do. 'This one thing I do.' Some frown, some smile, but 'this one thing I do.' Some think they could do it better, but 'this one thing I do.' How they could do it may be their business, but it certainly is not mine. Remember it does not matter much about its appearing to be a somewhat small and insignificant affair, for as much skill may be displayed in the manufacture of a very minute watch as in the construction of the town clock; in fact, a minute object may become the object of greater wonder than another of larger dimensions."

Concentration is the secret of success in anything, but especially in the Christian life. The "one thing" of Paul's concentration, like the hub in which the spokes of the wheel are held, centralises many things. The following seven things are in the hub of the "one thing:"

(1) The *"I count"* of renunciation (verse 8);
(2) The *"I may"* of acquisition (verse 10);
(3) The *"I * * * know"* of initiation (verse 10);
(4) The *"I might"* of elevation (verse 11);
(5) The *"I follow"* of determination (verse 12);
(6) The *"I do"* of concentration (verse 13);
and (7) the *"I press"* of consecration (verse 14).

* * * *

To concentrate one's being on Christ is to be consecrated to Him, for concentration is the soul of consecration. When the heart is occupied with Him, the heart is occupied by Him.

Conditions Fulfilled: Blessing Assured

"If ye be willing and obedient, ye shall eat the good of the land" (*Is. i:19*)

"I WISH I 'ad *them*," said a little ragged maiden, as she stood looking into a shop window, which was radiant with exquisite jewels, and pointed to a cluster of wondrous beauty. These words she uttered to her brother, who was standing with protective arm around her.

I have heard believers in Christ wish they had certain blessings of the Gospel, but they fail to get them, because they fail to exercise the grace of faith.

> The blessing of *purity* comes to those who have the indwelling Christ (Eph. iii:16, 17);
>
> The jewel of *power* is possessed by those who are possessed by Christ, the power of God, through waiting upon Him (1 Cor. i:24; Acts i:4);
>
> The jewel of *peace* is enjoyed by those who are careful for nothing, prayerful in everything, and thankful for anything (Phil. iv:6, 7);
>
> The jewel of *patience* is obtained by looking to and following the Lord Jesus (Heb. xii: 1, 2; xi:13);
>
> The jewel of *perception* comes to those who are taught by the Holy Spirit (1 Cor. ii:10; Eph. i:17, 18);
>
> The jewel of *principle* operates in those who are ruled by the truth (Ps. cxix:29, 30);
>
> And the jewel of *progress* belongs to those who grow in grace (2 Pet. iii:18).

*   *   *   *

Some seek blessings that they may have the comfort of the blessings they seek, and they miss it; while others are found in the path of obedience, and find that the blessing of the Lord seeks and finds them.

59

Conditions Fulfilled: Blessing Secured

"If * * * ye shall" (*Isa. i:*19)

The following notice was put on a corridor dining car of a Midland train: *"This carriage is intended only for the use of passengers desiring to lunch on the journey."* The diners had an advantage over the non-diners. The only condition for the more comfortable carriage was the payment for the lunch. The privilege was to the payer. If God's people are prepared to pay the condition attached to God's promise they shall receive privileges which are otherwise missed.

> The *"take"* of Christ's yoke is essential to the *"find"* of His rest (Matt. xi:29);
>
> The *"if"* of abiding is necessary to answered prayer (John xv:7);
>
> The *"tarry"* of prayer is requisite to obtain the enduement of power (Luke xxiv:49);
>
> The *"keepeth"* of Christ's commands is the condition attached to the manifestation of His grace (John xiv:21);
>
> The *"put on"* of God's panoply is prerequisite to the standing against the assaults of the enemy (Eph. vi:11);
>
> The *"beholding"* of the Lord's glory is the precursor of the transfigured life (2 Cor. iii:18);
>
> and the *"come out"* of separation must precede the Lord's coming into the heart and life to dwell and walk in the believer (2 Cor. vi:17, 18).

*   *   *   *

Conditions fulfilled are the sure precursors of securing the promises of God to the full. If we ful-fil by our obedience, He will fill full with His blessing.

Confession of Sin

"None that doeth good" (*Rom. iii:*12)

King Frederick VI. of Denmark, while travelling through Jutland, one day entered a village school, and found the children lively and intelligent, and quite ready

CONFIDENCE TOWARD GOD

to answer his questions. "Well, youngsters," he said, "what are the names of the greatest kings of Denmark?" With one accord they cried out: "Canute the Great, Waldemar and Christian IV." Just then a little girl, to whom the schoolmaster had whispered something, stood up and raised her hand. "Do you know another?" asked the king. "Yes; Frederick VI." "What great act did he perform?" The girl hung her head, and stammered out: "I don't know." "Be comforted, my child," said the king; "I don't know, either."

Everyone who has come into the light of God's holiness, measured himself by the rule of God's law, and compared himself with the perfection of the Lord Jesus must

Confess with Job, "*I am vile*" (Job xl:4);
Cry out with Isaiah, "*I am undone*" (Isa. vi:5).
Own with the bride, "*I am black*" (Song of Sol. i:5).
Say with David, "*I am a worm*" (Ps. xxii:6).
Write with Paul, "*I am carnal*" (Rom. vii:14).
Pray with Peter, "*I am a sinful man*" (Luke v:8).
And Confess with the prodigal, "*I am no more worthy*" (Luke xv:21).

* * * *

Confession is more than asking for forgiveness, it is the naming of the sin in humble penitence. Brokenness of heart about the sin, and a breaking from the sin confessed are the traits of true confession.

Confidence Toward God

"If our heart condemn us not, then have we confidence toward God" (1 *John* iii:21)

"When Clifton Johnson was travelling in Ireland, he sat down one day in a cottage, to talk with an old woman. As they were having their 'dish of discourse,' there came a clap of thunder, and the old woman at once spread out her hands in supplication, crying:

DEVOTIONAL BIBLE STUDIES

" 'God bless and save us! And save his honour, and save the people and all of us!'

"For the space of half an hour the thunder was frequent, and each time she prayed. Then she told Mr. Johnson this story, which has a good moral in its defining of the proper spirit which should belong to prayer:

" 'There was a man, and he was working in a field, and it came on to thunder, and he put his head in a hole in the wall, and he said, "God save whet's out o'me!" But he ought to have prayed for the whole of him; for he no sooner said that than the wall fell and took his head clean off.

" 'It was telled to me that this was a judgment on the crathur, because it is not right to pray *small*, just for yourself. But you should pray *large*—to save us all—pray big and open-hearted. But that may be only a story, sir.' "

"That may be only a story," but it has its lesson, for if he had prayed wholly for himself, the whole of himself would have been preserved. The fact is, if we are to pray wholly, we must have a whole-hearted confidence born of a whole-hearted consecration.

An uncondemning heart is the secret of boldness in approach to God in prayer. Among the conditions which were requisite for a man to be a priest under the Levitical economy, was that he was to be perfect; no one who was lame, blind, that had a flat nose, that had any superfluous growth, that was broken-footed or broken-handed, that was crookbackt, a dwarf, or that had a blemish in his eye, a scurvy or scabbed person, or broken in any way, was allowed to approach and "offer the bread of his God" (Leviticus xxi. 17-21): nor "come nigh to offer the offerings of the Lord." The Lord looks not now on the outward appearance, but on the heart. These things were written for our learning, though, and have a lesson for us, for those who have the halt of hesitation in obedience to God, those who are blinded by unbelief, those who have

62

CONSCIENCE

the brokenness of backsliding, those who have the crookedness of compromise, those who are stunted in their spiritual growth, those who have the scurvy of fretfulness, and those who have the scabs of discontent, cannot have the wholeness, which is requisite in order to approach God with boldness, so that they may prevail in prayer.

*   *   *   *

Confidence in God's Word, is faith's authority; confidence toward God, is faith's boldness; and confidence with God, is faith's joy.

Conscience

"A Conscience" (*Acts xxiv:16*)

"Bessus, a native of Pelonia, in Greece, being seen by his neighbors pulling down birds' nests, and destroying their harmless young, was severely rebuked for his cruelty. His excuse was that their notes were insufferable to him, as they never ceased twitting him for the murder of his father. Poor birds, they were innocent enough in the matter, but it was a guilty conscience which muttered its ceaseless reproaches in his ears." Every sound is to the guilty conscience an accusing voice and a death-knell; but, where the conscience is clear, the twitter of the birds, the music of the waves, and the tolling of the bells are voices which quiet our hearts, and make us say—in truth —with Shakespeare's Wolsey in reply to Cromwell, who asks

"How does your grace?
                    Why, well;
Never so truly happy * * *
I know myself now; and feel within me
Above all earthy dignities,
A still and quiet conscience."
Conscience was the *Voice* to charge Joseph's brethren with their sin (Gen. xliv:16).

63

Conscience was the *Spectre* to haunt Saul for his disloyalty
(1 Sam. xv:20).

Conscience was the *Troubler* to disturb Ahab for his greed
(1 Kings xviii:17, 18).

Conscience was the *Prosecutor* to charge David with his
iniquity (2 Sam. xii:7).

Conscience was the *Handwriting* to condemn Belshazzar for
his profanity (Dan. v:22, 23).

Conscience was the *Arresting Hand* to detain Achan because
of his coveteousness (Josh. vii:24).

Conscience was the *Iron* which branded Cain with his crime
(Gen. iv:15).

Conscience was the *Whip* which lashed Judas for his unholy betrayal of Christ (Matt. xxvii:3-5).

*　　*　　*　　*

A conscience that is adjusted by the compass of God's
Word is the only conscience that is reliable.

Consciousness of the Divine

"Before Me" (Gen. xvii:1)

We know very little about Tennyson's inner religious
life. His biography is remarkably silent concerning his
religious experiences; but a favorite niece of his, who had
many walks and talks with her uncle, has related more of
his inmost religious life than the world has ever before
known, and proves that the great poet, though so reticent
concerning his inner life, was, in the deepest sense, a comrade of the Quiet Hour. As they were walking together
on the beautiful downs on the Isle of Wight, with the
sounding sea ever in their ears, and God's bright skies and
great plains above and about them, he said to her: "God
is with us now on this Down, just as truly as Christ was
with the two disciples on their way to Emmaus. We cannot see Him, but the Father, and the Saviour, and the
Spirit are nearer, perhaps, now, than then, to those who
are not about the actual and real presence of God, and
His Christ with all who yearn for Him."

CONTENTMENT

"I said," writes the niece, "that such a near actual presence would be awful to most people."

"Surely the love of God takes away, and makes us forget all our fear," answered Tennyson. "I should be sorely afraid to live my life without God's presence, but to feel that He is by my side now, just as much as you are—that is the very joy of my heart."

"And I looked on Tennyson as he spoke, and the glory of God rested on his face, and I felt that the presence of God overshadowed him."

The Lord's desire and command are plainly inculcated as we ponder the following passages of Scripture in connection with the words, "Before Me."

(1) GOD'S APPRECIATION.—"Thee have I seen righteous *before Me*" (Gen. vii:1).

(2) GOD'S COMMAND.—"Walk *before Me*, and be thou perfect" (Gen. xvii:1).

(3) GOD'S CLAIM.—"Thou shalt have no other gods *before Me*" (Ex. xx:3).

(4) GOD'S EXPECTATION.—"None shall appear *before Me* empty" (Ex. xxiii:15; xxxiv:20).

(5) GOD'S VERDICT.—"Thy way is perverse *before Me*" (Num. xxii:32).

(6) GOD'S MANDATE.—"Keep silence *before Me*" (Isa. xli:1).

(7) GOD'S CARE.—"Thy walls are continually *before Me*" (Isa. xlix:16).

* * * *

To recognize the presence of the Lord by faith is to realize His company to our joy.

Contentment

"Godliness with contentment is great gain" (1 *Tim. vi:6*)

In the *Earthly Paradise* there is the story of a poor Roman scholar, who, by reading the writing on an image, and watching the shadow it cast on the ground discovered the way into a hall full of treasure. He gathered all he could carry, thinking joyfully of the palace such wealth would build. As he turned to go, he saw on the floor a wonderful green stone, and stooped to lift it, imagining that its price would purchase half the world. The stone was fixed to the ground, and as he struggled to move it, he saw the figure of an armed knight that stood near,

"Pointing against the ruddy light
A huge shaft ready in a bow,"

begin to move the bowstring to his ear. The arrow struck a dazzling carbuncle, by which the hall was lighted, and all was instantly dark. The scholar groped in vain for the door by which he had entered, and at last perished miserably by the side of his treasure.

The story is a parable of the thirst for something more, which wears away so many lives. Contentment is rare now, and very old-fashioned.

Contention and contentment are the same in the contents of their first two syllables, but what a difference in their contents as a whole. The Greek words *"arkeo"* and *"arketos"* give a chain of Scriptures which tell of the soul and secret of contentment. The words are rendered *"enough," "sufficient," "suffice,"* and *"content."*

(1) A DARK PAST.—"The time past of our life may *suffice* us" (1 Pet. iv:3).
(2) A DIVINE SAVIOUR.—"Show us the Father, and it *sufficeth* us," &c. (John xiv:8).
(3) A GLORIOUS ASSURANCE.—"My grace is *sufficient* for thee" (2 Cor. xii:9).
(4) A HAPPY COMPANIONSHIP.—"It is *enough* that the disciple be as his Lord" (Matt. x:25).
(5) AN IMPERATIVE COMMAND.—"Be *content* with such things as ye have" (Heb. xiii:5).
(6) A NEEDFUL REMINDER.—"*Sufficient* unto the day is the evil thereof" (Matt. vi:34).
(7) A CONTENTED CONCLUSION.—"Having food and raiment let us therewith be *content*" (1 Tim. vi:8).

*　　*　　*　　*

Contentment in the Lord is one way to prove we are consecrated to Him.

Continuance in Prayer

"Continue in Prayer" (*Col iv:2*)

Fletcher's whole life was a life of prayer; and so intensely was his mind fixed upon God, that he sometimes said: "I would not move from my seat without lifting up my heart to God." "Whenever we met," says Mr. Vaughan, "if we were alone, his first salute was, 'Do I meet you praying?' And if we were talking on any point of Divinity, when we were in the depth of our discourse he would often break off abruptly, and ask, 'Where are our hearts now?' If ever the misconduct of an absent person was mentioned, his usual reply was, 'Let us pray for him.'" Oh! for a like spirit of constancy in prayer.

Again and again we read in the Acts, of the believers continuing in prayer, but there was not only continuance, there was intensity and strength, too.

The forerunner of Pentecost is found in those named, who "with one accord *continued stedfastly* in prayer" (Acts i:14, R. V.);

The feeder of the Church's life is indicated in the announcement that the believers were "day by day, *continuing stedfastly* with one accord in the temple" (Acts ii:46, R. V.);

The essentiality is described in the apostles' declaration, when they said "we will *continue stedfastly* in prayer" Acts vi:4, R. V.); and the Spirit's injunction is still "*continue stedfastly* in prayer" (Col. iv:2, R. V.).

Constancy is the soul of the Christian life, it is the continual treading which makes the beaten track, it is constant use that makes the strong arm, it is repeated practice that makes the musician perfect, it is continued rubbing that makes the vessel bright, it is the persistent study that wins the prize, it is the running water that makes a channel, and it is the plodder who prevails. The same is true with stedfast prayer, it is a *track-maker* to the throne of grace, it is a *nerve-invigorator* in Christian service, it is a *praise-inciter* in temple worship, it is a *life-brightener* in the spiritual walk, it is

DEVOTIONAL BIBLE STUDIES

a *blessing-bringer* in the realm of grace, it is a *soul-deepener* in the things of God, and it is an *inspiraiion-giver* to enable us to continue in the heavenly race.

* * * *

If we would *"grow up"* into Christ in all things, we must *"go out"* from the world of sin (Genesis xii. 1), and *get up* to the Bethel of prayer (Genesis xiii:3, 4).

Contraband

"The voice is Jacob's voice, but the hands are the hands of Esau" (*Gen. xxvii:22*)

A Chinese trader was the scene of a humorous smuggling incident upon her arrival at Sydney from the East recently. The Customs officials made an unusually extensive search for contraband opium and cigars, and one of them became suspicious of the attitude of a sick sailor, who lay in his bunk with a "broken leg." Sharply interrogated, the invalid whined out in English, "Doctor says, no touchee me; no movee." The official, however, proved inexorable, and amid choice imprecations in florid Cantonese, the sailor was tenderly removed to another bunk. A search revealed the cause of illness, which consisted of a wholesale consignment of boxes of cigars, neatly packed in rows, as a foundation to the mattress.

Something very similar is often found among professing Christians. They are so comfortable in their sloth and self-sufficiency, that they exclaim against any special effort to disturb them; but when the Lord comes with His searchingness, then

He brings to light the contraband of the want-of-love, as He did in the case of the Church in Ephesus (Rev. ii:4);
The contraband of the want-of-firmness, as with the Church in Pergamos (Rev. ii:14);
The contraband of the want-of-separation, as with the Church in Thyatira (Rev. ii:20);
The contraband of a mere profession, as with the Church in Sardis (Rev. iii:1);

68

COUNTING THE COST

The contraband of self-sufficiency, as with the Church in
  Laodicea (Rev. iii:17);
The contraband of unholy alliance, as with Jehosaphat
  (2 Chron. xviii:1);
And the contraband of self-dependence, as with Peter (Luke
  xxii:33).

*　　*　　*　　*

The unrighteous thing is more unrighteous when it is
covered up than when it is made known. To be a walking
lie, while we profess to be a living saint, is worse than
bad.

Counting the Cost

"Count the Cost" (Luke xiv:28 R.V.)

"I want you to spend fifteen minutes every day praying for foreign missions," said the pastor to some young
people in his congregation. "But beware how you pray,
for I warn you that it is a very costly experiment." "Costly?" they asked in surprise. "Aye, costly," he cried.
"When Carey began to pray for the conversion of the
world it cost him himself, and it cost those who prayed
with him very much. Brainerd prayed for the dark-
skinned savages, and, after two years of blessed work, it
cost him his life. Two students in Mr. Moody's summer
school began to pray the Lord of the harvest to send forth
more servants into His harvest; and lo! it is going to cost
America five thousand young men and women, who have,
in answer to this prayer, pledged themselves to the work.
Be sure it is a dangerous thing to pray in earnest for this
work; you will find that you cannot pray and withhold
your labor, or pray and withhold your money; nay, that
your very life will no longer be your own when your
prayers begin to be answered."

It is always a costly thing to give oneself wholly over
to the Lord, to be used as He wills in His service.

69

It cost Elijah much persecution, for he was hounded by the woman Jezebel, who eagerly sought his life (1 Kings xix:2);

It cost John the Baptist his head (Matt. xiv:3-10);

It cost Paul and Silas pain and imprisonment (Acts xvi:23);

It cost Stephen his life (Acts vii:60);

It cost the Apostle John banishment to the Isle of Patmos (Rev. i:9);

It cost Paul desertion (2 Tim. iv:16);

And it cost Christ the cross (Phil. ii:8).

*　　*　　*　　*

Counting the cost is only the investment on our part: the interest God gives more than compensates for any loss, or cost. Faith looks not back at its giving up, but it ever looks to its gain in Christ (Phil. iii. 8).

Crimson Lights

"The Blood of the Lamb" (*Rev. vii:*14)

While passing the World's Fair at St. Louis, in the night train, the thousands upon thousands of electric lights on all the buildings made a magnificent display; and, as I was looking, the lights on the Festal Hall changed to a deep crimson. This set me thinking that, amid all the wonders of God's creation, and all His works in providence, there was one fact which stands out in deep carmine fact, namely the blood of Christ's crimson atonement.

The atonement of Christ's death is

The *sin-cleanser* of the sinner's conscience (1 John i:7).

The *self-annuller* of the old life (Gal. ii:20);

The *soul-sanctifier* of the saint's life (Heb. xiii:12);

The *service-inspirer* of the believer's work (2 Cor. v:14);

The *victory-giver* in the warrior's conflict (Rev. xii:11);

The *magnet-drawer* to the Church's communion (1 Cor. x:16);

And the *song-incentive* of Heaven's praise (Rev. v:9).

*　　*　　*　　*

The carmine fact of Christ's death is the death of every sin, and the life of every virtue, as well as the inspiration to all service.

70

Crucifixion with Christ

"Christ crucified" (1 *Cor.* i:23)

"A destitute out-of-work, who recently came into the hands of the Church Army at their new Labor Home, lately a police-station at Bow, was found to have a representation of the Crucifixion tattooed on his back. He explained that he had had it done many years ago as a protection against flogging! It seemed that he had been in the Army, and that there is, or was, a notion prevalent amongst soldiers that no officer would dare to order a man to be flogged whose flesh bore this symbol, nor any soldier to carry out such an order. The man himself fully believed the story, and it would be interesting to know whether, in the old flogging days, the notion was generally held in the army."

Not the representation of the Crucifixion tattooed on the person will prevail with heaven.

But (1) Faith in the Crucified, who died "for" us (1 Cor. i:13);

    (2) Identification with Christ crucified will conquer self (Gal. ii:20);

    (3) Oneness with Him will separate from the world (Gal. vi:14);

    (4) Crucifixion with Christ will stultify the flesh (Gal. v:24);

    (5) Christ crucified is the secret of holiness (Rom. vi:6);

    (6) Christ crucified reveals the power and wisdom of God (1 Cor. i:23, 24);

    (7) Christ crucified is the one theme of the true evangeliser (1 Cor. ii:2).

*   *   *   *

Self-crucifixion is the effort of self in endeavoring to put itself to death; but crucifixion with Christ means we believe we are dead with Christ in His death.

DEVOTIONAL BIBLE STUDIES

Dead by the Death of Another

"Ye are become dead to the law" (*Rom.* vii :4)

An illustration of how the law has no claim upon a
dead man is that of a well-known debtor, who saw no
possible way of paying his debts, which he owed almost
entirely to one man, a benevolent, though just, individual.
In his extremity, the debtor adopted the ruse of dying,
and his wife rapidly made it known that the great stress
of this debt on her husband's mind had killed him. His
creditor, touched, and, perhaps, somewhat stricken by
reason of previous hardness in worrying for payment,
visited the bogus widow, and, gazing upon the face of
the dead man, told the weeping woman not to worry
about the debt, which he would entirely forego. "I'll
give you a receipt for the full amount," he said, to pacify
her: and he did it. The next day, the extraordinary
news passed through the town that the dead man had
wonderfully come to life; and, as a matter of fact, he was
about again, pretending convalescence, in the course of a
few days.

Since Christ has died for the believer, he is, in the
death of Christ,

Dead to sin's penalty (Rom. vi:7);
Dead to sin's authority (Rom. vi:11);
Dead to the world's attraction (Gal. vi:14);
Dead to self's life (Gal. ii:20);
Dead to the flesh's pursuits (Gal. v:24);
And dead to the law's claim (Rom. vii:4).

* * * *

Baptized into Christ's death means the death of self.
Baptized into the Body means to be dominated by the
Head, thus energised by His power.

Dead with Christ

"For ye are dead" (*Col.* 3:3)

In the Supreme Court of California some time ago, a
man named McIntyre was brought into Court from the
jail at St. Quentin, to answer a charge of murder. It

72

appeared from his defence that he was serving a life
sentence at St. Quentin, to which he had been subjected
for murdering a man named Renowden, in Santa Clara
County. He had been tried, convicted, and sen-
tenced for Renowden's murder, and he claimed that he
was, in consequence, legally and civilly dead, and that in
bringing him up for trial on another charge the authori-
ties had blundered. He claimed that being dead, in law
for the murder of Renowden he could not be subject to
prosecution on trial for any other crime. The plea is a
novel one, but it seems probable that the Court will pro-
nounce it valid. The claim of being dead to the law
while yet alive is that of the Christian, but in his case
it is not his own death that he pleads, but that of Christ,
his Divine Substitute. "Likewise reckon ye also yourselves to be dead unto sin, but alive unto God through
Jesus Christ our Lord" (Romans vi:11).

Believers are dead with Christ:

> To sin's penalty, for Christ has borne it (Rom. vi:7, mar-
> gin).
> To law's claim, for Christ has answered it (Rom. vii:4).
> To sin's power, for Christ has broken it (Rom. vi:2; 1 Pet.
> ii:24).
> To Satan's claim, for Christ has annulled it (Heb. ii:14).
> To self's living, for Christ has transfixed it (Gal. ii:20).
> To the old man's habits, for Christ has nailed him and them
> to the cross (Col. iii:3-9).
> To the world's pursuits, for Christ has doomed them (Col.
> ii:20).
> To the flesh's lust, for Christ has crucified it (Gal. v:24).

*   *   *   *

Faith makes true in the life, what God says is true
for us in Christ. He says we are dead with Christ, and
Faith believes it, and has no ear for sin, no hand for its
service, and no feet to walk in its ways.

Death in the Pot

"There is death in the pot" (2 *Kings* iv:40)

The manager of a Woolwich beerhouse died recently
in Guy's Hospital from exhaustion following delirium

tremens, after suffering from lead colic.

He told the house surgeon that he had been in the habit of drinking the first draught of beer drawn from the pipes each morning. The doctor explained that this beer, having been in the pipes all night, would have absorbed lead, and thus lead would get into the man's system. There was the same danger from water.

How often danger is lurking where it is least expected.

> In the house of honored preferment Joseph found the trap of impurity (Gen. xxxix:7);
>
> After the paradise of revelation Paul was conscious of the tendency to the inflation of pride (2 Cor. xii:7);
>
> In the tent of hospitality Sisera found the cruel nail of Jael (Judges iv:18-21);
>
> In the sphere of honored service the man of God out of Judah fell into the snare of flattery and became the disobedient prophet (1 Kings xiii:14-22);
>
> In the mount of ardent devotion to God there lies the valley of discouragement near, as is evidenced in the contrast between Elijah on Mount Carmel and under the juniper tree (1 Kings xviii; xix:4);
>
> In the place of privilege there often stands the arbour of slumber, as was seen when the disciples were with Christ in the Garden of Gethsemane, and yet they slept (Mark xiv:33-37);
>
> And after the opened heaven of God's acknowledgment there often follows the wilderness of temptation (Matt. iii:16; iv:1).

* * * *

When sin is in the heart, its poison will penetrate to every part of our nature, for out of the heart are the issues of life.

Devices of the Devil

"Not ignorant of his devices" (2 *Cor.* ii:11)

After Admiral Dewey had conquered the Spanish fleet at Manila, the Spanish revenue cruiser *Callao,* which had been among the Southern Islands for sixteen months, knowing nothing of the war, sailed into the harbor with the Spanish flag flying and asked for the Admiral of the Spanish fleet. Several shots fired at her, convinced her that something was wrong. She hauled down her flag, and hoisted the white flag. A boat's crew of Americans boarded her and hoisted the Stars and Stripes.

The Spaniards were caught because they were ignorant of the war. A great many believers are caught by the great enemy of souls, because they are ignorant of his devices.

> Thus Peter was caught in the trap of self-confidence (Matt. xxvi:35, 69-75);
>
> Moses was caught in the gin of self-action (Num. xx:11);
>
> David was caught in the snare of fleshly-lust (2 Sam. xi:4);
>
> Jacob was caught in the net of deceitfulness (Gen. xxvii:18-20);
>
> The disciples were caught in the meshes of self-aggrandisement (Luke ix:46);
>
> John was caught in the maze of sectarianism (Luke ix:49);
>
> And the sons of Zebedee were caught in the quicksands of un-Christlikeness (Luke ix:52-56).

*   *   *   *

Filled with the Spirit, armed with God's armour, and initiated by God's Word, we shall not be ignorant of Satan's doings and devices, but we shall avoid the one and conquer him in the other.

Devil: Giving no Place to

Neither give place to the devil" (*Eph.* iv:27)

In the closing examination of a theological seminary, the professor gave the students a paper containing two subjects, *"The Holy Spirit and the Devil,"* and told them to write half-an-hour on each of the subjects.

One of the students wrote steadily for one hour on the Holy Spirit, and wrote at the bottom of his manuscript, "I have no time for the devil."

The child of God should have no time to listen to the devil's lies as Eve did (Gen. iii:1-6).
No time to go off into some by-path to be entrapped by the devil's "snares" (1 Tim. iii:7);
No time to be off guard to be overcome by the devil's "wiles" (Eph. vi:11).
No time to be "beguiled" by his baits (2 Cor. xi:3);
No time to be caught by his "devices" (2 Cor. ii:11);
No time to give "place" to his leadings (Ephes. iv:27);
And no time to be discouraged by his buffetings (2 Cor. xii:7).

* * * *

Keep out of the devil's lap of the world, if you would avoid the slaps of his wounding. He will rob you of the locks of your power, and make you grind in the prison-house of failure if he gets you asleep, as he did Samson (Jud. xvi:19-21).

Difficulties

"I leaped over a wall" (*Ps. xviii:29*)

"There are twenty hills between here and the place of your destination," said a friend as he met another going in the opposite direction on his bike. It was enough to make one *ill* to think of those *hills,* and it *ill* became him to cause those *hills* to rise before us. We thought as we walked up the long *hill* out of Grantham, if the twenty *hills* are all like this, we shall be *ill* before we get over the *hills*. But we found the hills were not so bad after all, for they made a good switchback, and relieved the monotony of a dead level. We could not help thinking we had borrowed misery in wondering how we were to rise above the rises of the way, for the up-and-down was rather a relief and a change, than a *tiresome* difficulty. Many an imaginary difficulty has been an inspiriting delight; and what seemed to be irksome in the distance, was not bad when we came near.

DOUBLE CENTRE

The red sea of difficulty (Ex. xiv:13-22);
The Saul of persecution (1 Sam. xxvii:1);
The fret of some thorn in the flesh (11 Cor. xii:9);
The loneliness of some Isle of Patmos (Rev. i:9);
The prison of man's hate (Acts xii:3, 4);
The fierce fire of trial (1 Peter i:7);
And the temptations of the devil (Matt. iv:11) have only
  brought the Lord near in the help of His hand, in the
  heart of His love, in the strength of His grace, and
  in the vistr of His glory.

Hardship is not the worst ship in which to sail on the
ocean of life, especially if we have *fellowship* with the
Lord.

Double Centre

"Therefore....He hath poured forth this" (*Ac.* ii:33, *R. V.*)

One has said, "Jesus died on the Cross to make freedom
from sin *possible*. The Holy Spirit dwells within me to
make freedom from sin *actual*. The Holy Spirit does *in*
me what Jesus did *for* me. The Lord Jesus draws a
cheque for my use. The Spirit cashes that cheque, and
puts the money into my hands. Jesus does in me now by
His Spirit what He did for me centuries ago on the cross
in His person.

Now these two truths, or two parts of the same truth,
go together in God's plan, but, with some exceptions,
have not gone together in man's experience. That ex-
plains why so many Christian lives are a failure and a
reproach. The Church of Christ has been gazing so
intently upon the hill of the cross with its blood-red
message of sin and love, that it has largely lost sight
of the ascension mount with its legacy of power. We
have been so enwrapt with that marvellous scene on
Calvary—and what wonder!—that we have allowed our-

selves to lose the intense significance of Pentecost. That last victory shout—'it is finished'—has been crowding out in our ears its counterpart—the equally victorious cry of Olivet—'all power hath been given unto Me.' "

> Passover and Pentecost are intimately connected (Lev. xxiii:4-21; John vii:37-39).
>
> Christ's baptism was typical of His death and resurrection, and Pentecost is forecast by the abiding Spirit upon Him (Matt. iii:13-17).
>
> The cleansed leper was not only sprinkled by blood, but he was also anointed with oil (Lev. xiv:1-18).
>
> Christ not only showed unto His disciples the marks of His passion, but He also gave an infusion of His life, in the Upper Room (John xx:19-22).
>
> Christ not only says, "come unto Me," but He also says, "Take My yoke upon you." Both are requisite for the double rest (Matt. xi:28, 29).
>
> Sealed with the Spirit speaks of God's possession (Eph. i:13, R. V.), but filled with the Spirit declares we are God-possessed (Eph. v:18).
>
> Christ as our Harbour means justification (Rom. iii:24, 25), but Christ as our Holiness is Joy (1 Cor. i:30; Rom. xv:13).

*   *   *   *

There is a great difference between possessing the Holy Spirit and being possessed by Him. In the former case He is possessed as the Seal marking us as God's property, but in the latter He is reigning in the heart as Sovereign.

Effectiveness of the Holy Spirit

"The Same God" (The Holy Spirit)) *"worketh"* (effectually worketh) "all in all" (1 *Cor. xii*:6)

The late A. J. Gordon of Boston in speaking of the need of the Holy Spirit, said:

"The blind man does not need more light, but more eyes; the deaf man does not need more sound, but more hearing; and the Christian does not need more of the

EFFECTIVENESS OF THE HOLY SPIRIT

Spirit, but more of the inspiration; that is, the inbreathing of the Spirit. Suppose I go to a man who is sick with pneumonia, and the nurse says, "Oh, sir, he needs more air." "But the windows are open wide, he has all the air there is. Do you not see it is not more air that he wants, but more lungs?" Now the Spirit is *spiritus,* the breath of God, the breath of Jesus Christ, if I may say it, and you and I are the cells in those lungs. If the lungs get closed up, you will have a consumptive Church, a feeble Church, an asthmatic Church, a Church which is full of weakness and failure, simply because it does not take in more of the Spirit. It is not that you need more of the Holy Spirit, but the Holy Spirit needs more of you."

When He has His own way in us, He effectually worketh in and through us.

The Greek word, variously rendered (given in italics) in the following passages, signifies to work effectually, that is, to accomplish the desired end.

(1) GOD'S EFFECTUAL WORK FOR US.—"*Working* of His mighty power, which He *wrought* in Christ." &c. (Ephesians i:19, 20).

(2) SPIRIT'S EFFECTUAL WORK IN US—"The power that *worketh* in us" (Ephesians iii:20; Phil. ii:13; Colossians i:29).

(3) WORD'S EFFECTUAL WORK UPON US—"Which also *effectually worketh*" (1 Thessalonians ii:13).

(4) RIGHTEOUS MAN'S EFFECTUAL PRAYER—"The *effectual fervent prayer,*" &c. (James v:16).

(5) CHRIST'S EFFECTUAL MINISTRY—"Works *do show forth* themselves in Him" (Matthew xiv:2).

(6) BELIEVER'S POWER TO EFFECTUALLY WORK OUT HIS SALVATION—"God which *worketh* in you both to will and *to do* of His good pleasure" (Phil. ii:13).

(7) WORKER'S SECRET OF EFFECTUAL SERVICE—"He that *wrought effectually* in Peter, the same was *mighty* in me" (Gal. ii:8).

*　　*　　*　　*

To lift up holy hands in prayer is the way to secure the lifting up of God's hands in power.

DEVOTIONAL BIBLE STUDIES

"Enter in"

(John x:9).

"Enter into" (*Ezekiel xliv*:16)

"While walking in London," a Christian worker relates, "I was accosted by a French pastor, who said, 'Excuse me, were you not in Paris some time ago?'

"I replied, 'Yes.'

"Then he enquired: 'Did you not, in one of your addresses, say that *"the latch was on our side of the door"?*'

" 'Yes,' I replied, 'I believe I did say so.'

" 'Well,' he answered, 'I always thought it was on the Lord's side, and I kept knocking, knocking until I heard your words—*I lifted the latch.* Since then, everything has been changed to me. My work, congregation, Church, all changed.' "

What a difference would be made in the lives of God's people if they would only use the hand of faith to lift the latch of God's promise, and enter through the door of love into the fulness of God's grace! What would the blessings be?

(1) *Safety in the hour of trial,* for being in the chamber of His love no ill could touch us (Isaiah xxvi:20).

(2) *Peace amid trouble,* for while calamity overtakes the wicked, the merciful are resting (Isaiah lvii:2).

(3) *Privilege of prayer,* for being near the Lord we can tell Him all (Matthew vi:6).

(4) *Pasture after salvation.* Having entered into the fold of grace, and thereby finding salvation, we feed upon His grace, whether in the sanctuary, or in the field of labour (John x:9).

(5) *Rest of sanctification.* Canaan's rest is a type of the rest of faith which comes through obedience to the Divine Word (Hebrews iv:3).

(6) *Liberty of access.* Liberty to enter into and to remain in the holiest is through the blood of Christ (Hebrews x:19).

(7) *Responsibility in service.* To keep God's charge is the saint's responsibility (Ezekiel xliv :16).

*   *   *   *

To limit the Holy One by unbelief is to proclaim a sad want of grace in the heart. To measure the Almighty by our limitations is to place ourselves in the place of privations.

Evidences of Christianity

"Ye are our Epistle" (2 *Corinthians* iii:2)

"Benjamin Franklin tried to convince the farmers of his day, that plaster enriched the soil. All his philosophical arguments failed to convince them, so he took plaster, and formed it into a sentence by the roadside. The wheat coming up through those letters was about twice as rank and green as the other wheat, and the farmer could read for months, in letters of living green, the sentence, 'This has been plastered.'"

The contention of Franklin was proved by the more luxurious growth of the wheat. The same thing is brought out in the Christian life. It is not the say of profession, but the saintliness of practice which shows the reality of faith in Christ.

> *Obedience proves love's existence,* as Christ says, "If ye love Me, ye will keep My commandments" (John xiv:15, R. v.).
> *Love demonstrates life.* Love is the fruit of life. Life's vitality is seen in love's action. Regard for our brethren shows our relationship to the Lord (1 John iii:14-19).
> *The savour of godliness proves the existence of grace.* Grace, like salt, is always pungent (Col. iv:6), for it tells by its manner of living in what school it has been taught (Titus ii:11-13).
> *Fruit evidences union.* Grapes prove the vine. Apples, the apple-tree. Figs, the fig-tree. The tree is known by the fruit (John xv:5; Matt. vii:16).

DEVOTIONAL BIBLE STUDIES

Good works show the new birth. Good works do not bring
life, but life brings good works. Being "in Christ Jesus"
is God's workmanship, but we are there for "good
works" (Eph. ii:10). As the watch is made to keep
time, so the Christian is made for good works.

Continuance proclaims discipleship. Christ ever says to
those who believe on Him, "If ye continue in My Word,
then are ye My disciples indeed" (John viii:31).

And the *legible character of a consecrated life tells the Spirit's
inner workings.* The epistle without speaks of the
Writer within (II Corinthians iii:2).

*   *   *   *

Healthfulness and happiness are plants which grow in
the soil of holiness, and the flowers which bloom on them
are usefulness and love.

Failure and Success

"In Adam * * * In Christ" (I *Cor. xv:22*)

An old colored man called on a judge, asking for advice. "What I'se gwine to inculcate, judge, is dis. What
mus' I do to change mah prognomen? When I find dat
I'se weighed down wif ah prognomen dat's bound to kill
mah trade, what mus' I do?" "You wish to change your
name?" inquired the judge. "And why?" "Cause mah
name is Failure. Yes, sah, dat's mah name. I'se a white-
washer, and dat name jes' queers me." "Very well, uncle.
Why not use the first letter of your name?" suggested the
Court. "Dat's wuss," groaned the old man. "I'se tried
dat. I had a big sign painted 'A Failure,' and mah trade
left me." "The initial letter does make an unhappy combination," agreed the Judge. "But I'll tell you what to
do. Use your first name, and then people will not notice
the last name so much." "Dat's der mos' discimmoding
of all, sah. It's downright scand'lous. Mah first name is
Adam, sah."

"Adam," is the representation of the greatest failure
in the world, for, as Thomas Boston says, "God made

FAITH AND WORKS

Adam captain of the ship of humanity, and he ran us on to the rocks and made shipwreck of us."

What a difference between the first and last Adam. Mark the contrast.

First Adam.	Last Adam.
Sin (Romans v:12).	Righteousness (Rom. v:19).
Death (1 Cor. xv:22).	Life (1 Cor. xv:22).
Banishment (Gen. iii:24).	Nearness (Eph. ii:13).
Condemnation (Rom. v:18).	Justification (Romans v:9).
Curse (Genesis iii:17).	Blessing (Galatians iii:14).
Shame (Genesis iii:11).	Glory (John xvii:10).
Poverty (Ephesians ii:12).	Riches (11 Cor. viii:9).
Sorrow (Genesis iii:16).	Joy (Romans v:11).
Defeat (Ephesians ii:2).	Victory (1 John v:5).
Enmity (Romans viii:7).	Peace (Col. ii:20).
Bondage (Gal. iii:22).	Liberty (Galatians v:1).

*   *   *   *

A Christian is "a man in Christ" (2 Cor. xii), which means he is no longer in the Adam of failure, in the self of sin, and in the world of condemnation.

Faith and Works

"Faith without works is dead" (*Jas. ii:26*)

A traveller in the West Indies says there are two things for which the islands are noted—hurricane and sugar-cane. During a hurricane, a negro householder, who found his cabin in danger, made a rope fast to it, and sent all the members of his family to haul away upon it to windward. He, being a pious man—especially in hurricane times—took to praying.

"Oh, Lor', we know that we're all weak," he said. "We know that nothin' that we can do is of any use before Thee—— If yo' don't keep haulin' at that rope I'll use it on yo' backs, yo' lozy bones," he added to his family, and then went on praying.

The combination of his ejaculation, while it may not impress one as very polite, at least evidenced his belief in honest effort and earnest supplication. They should ever go together.

Loves proves its affection by its sacrifice (1 John iii:16-18).

Hope evidences its reality by its purity (1 John iii:3).

Repentance shows its genuiness by its works (Matt. iii:8).

Holiness reveals its character by its likeness to the Lord (1 Pet. i:15-17).

Conversion manifests its worth by turning to God from idols (1 Thess. i:9).

Patience demonstrates its character by its endurance (Jas. v:7, 8).

Faith unfolds its reliability by its faithfulness (Gal. v:22, R. V.).

*   *   *   *

Faith walks with God in the path of obedience, and finds joy warbling in the heart in consequence.

Faithfulness

"Be thou faithful unto death" (*Revelation ii:10*)

Many are the incidents of the civil war in America, but one of the most pathetic and striking illustrations of faithfulness, is found in the negro lad who was given the custody of a pair of cavalry boots by an officer in the Confederate Army. One day an attack was made on the supply train where the lad was, and an officer rode up and demanded those boots for himself. The negro lad simply clasped the boots with both arms. The officer enraged at the noncompliance with his request, ran his sword through the lad's body, and attempted to drag the boots from him, but with a death-grip the lad gripped the boots the tighter, and his master found the colored lad dead with the boots clasped in his arms. After the war was over, there was to be seen in the hall of the house of the officer, a cabinet containing a pair of blood-stained cavalry boots, and over them the simple but speaking inscription, "Tobe's boots." He was faithful to his trust, even unto death.

FAITH ILLUSTRATED AND FOLLOWED

There is nothing so much appreciated by our Lord as faithfulness. Faithfulness is the

(1) *Mark of stewardship,* for a steward must be "found *faithful*" (1 Corinthians iv:2).

(2) Faithfulness is the *stamp of a genuine believer*—"What part hath he that **believeth* with an infidel?" (11 Cor. vi:15).

(3) Faithfulness is the *qualification of a true minister*—"a *faithful* minister of Christ" (Colossians i:7; iv:7, 9).

(4) Faithfulness is the *summary of the Christian Life*—"He that is *faithful* in that which is least is *faithful* also in much" (Luke xvi:10).

(5) Faithfulness is the *certificate of trustworthiness* in the things of God—"If ye have judged me *faithful*" (Acts xvi:15); "commit to *faithful* men" (2 Tim. ii:2; 1 Tim. iii:11).

(6) Faithfulness is the *fulfilment of the Lord's command*—"Be thou *faithful*" (Revelation ii:10).

(7) And faithfulness always *calls forth the Lord's commendation*—"Well done, good and *faithful* servant" (Matthew xxv:21, 23; Luke xix:17; Galatians ii:9; Ephesians vi:21; Col. iv:9; 1 Timothy i:12; Hebrews iii:2; 1 Peter v:12; 111 John 5; Revelation ii:13).

*Same word in the Greek.

*   *   *   *

To truly recognize the faithfulness of our Lord is to respond to Him in faithfulness. Faith feeds upon God's faithfulness, and becomes faithful and full.

Faith Illustrated and Followed

"Looking unto Jesus the Author and Perfecter of faith."
"Considering the issue of their life, imitate their faith"
(*Heb. xii:2; xiii:7,* R. V.)

"In a crisis of British foreign affairs, a huge ladder had been erected for decorative purposes against the Nelson column in Trafalgar Square, London. 'What are they doing?' asked one of the crowd. 'They're gettin' him down. They'll be wantin' him soon,' said another. So with our national ideals, our memories of great men—in

85

peace they tower above our heads as objects of our admiration, far off, unpractical, but beautiful; in days of trouble we take them down for use."

The above was related by a well-known writer at a meeting in London. Are there not too many "ideals" and "memories" lying dormant in the minds of God's people? The men in the crowd suggested, by their "They're gettin' him down," and "They'll be wantin' him soon," something practical and powerful. Who is the "Him," who shall make our memories mighty factors to move us as those of yore, and shall make the statues of ideals into practical personages, warm with the health of life to do exploits? Who, indeed! None other than the Lord Jesus Himself.

> He is the *Physician* to heal every malady (Matt. ix:12).
> He is the *Potter* to mould us after His image (Rom. ix:21).
> He is the *Preserver* to keep away every ill (Job vii:20).
> He is the *Power* to strengthen us in trial (I Cor. i:24; II Cor. xii:8, 9).
> He is the *Potentate* to reign over our our entire nature (I Tim. vi:15).
> He is the *Prince* to lead on in the Divine life (Acts iii:15).
> And He is the *Portion* to satisfy the deepest longing of the heart (Lamentations iii:24).

*　　*　　*　　*

The *sublimity* of faith is seen in its *simplicity,* for the faith which honors God by its trust is honored by God to its triumph.

Faith, or Down to My Boots

"Your faith to Godward is spread abroad" (I *Thessalonians i*:8)

"I believe it down to my boots," said an aged saint to me, as we were talking about the will of God.

She had remarked, "He does everything according to the purpose of His will."

FAITH'S SIMPLICITY

Whereupon I asked her, "Do you believe that?"

With a look of intense feeling and soul vehemence she replied, "I believe it down to my boots."

Her faith was thorough, there was no break in it. When we believe after that fashion God can do something for us.

It is good to *"have faith in God"* (Mark xi:22), for that brings us into communication with Him.

It is better to be *"strong in faith"* (Romans iv:20), for that keeps us from staggering.

It is best to be *"full of faith"* (Acts vi:5; xi:24), for that allows no room for doubt or fear.

It is better than the best to possess *"the full assurance of faith"* (Hebrews x:22), for then there is an abundance of confidence in the Lord.

Yea, we may go a step further and have *"great faith"* (Matthew xv:28), *"so great faith"* (Matthew viii:10).

And a *"faith which worketh by love,"* to bring blessing to others (Galatians v:6).

Such a faith is God-honouring in its confidence, Christ-exalting in its obedience, and Spirit-glorifying in its responsiveness.

* * * *

Having faith in God you will have none in yourself. There is no room for self, if God has the room.

Faith's Simplicity

"The man believed the Word that Jesus had spoken unto him"
(John iv:50)

A beautiful story is told about Abraham Lincoln. During the Civil War, a father came to him to beg for the life of his boy who was condemned to be shot, and he stood weeping at the door of the President's house, not one hour only or one day only; day after day he knocked, with tears, until Lincoln could stand it no longer. He had received telegrams from the seat of war that he was not to pardon that boy, but at last the great-hearted President said, "General or no general, discipline or no discipline, I am going to pardon that man's son." The father was brought in to hear the news, but when he saw Lincoln smile, his own expression of hope changed to terror. "Mr. President," he said, "you are only saying that to get me to go away, and you will have my boy shot when I am gone." Said Lincoln, "Go away, old man; if your son lives till I have him shot he will be as old as Methusaleh." I would like you to take the word of Christ as simply as that old man took the word of his President.

> Faith's simplicity is strikingly illustrated in the Gospels, where people simply believed Christ's Word and were blessed.
>
> The Centurion believed Christ's Word for the healing of his servant (Matt. viii:8, 13).
>
> The man with the withered hand showed his faith in Christ's Word by stretching forth his hand (Matt. xii:13).
>
> The blind men responded to Christ's Word when He asked them if they believed He could heal them by saying "Yes Lord" (Matt. ix:28, 29).
>
> The Syrophenecian woman took a puppy's place in accepting Christ's Word about her and got a children's portion (Matt. xv:26-28).
>
> The ten lepers showed their faith in Christ's Word in going their way to the priests as He directed (Luke xvii:14).
>
> Zacchaeus demonstrated his faith in Christ's Call by receiving Him joyfully and acting as a saved man (Luke xix:5-9).
>
> The Dying thief's silence after Christ's response to his request speaks of his faith in the Lord's assurance (Luke xxiii:42, 43).

*　　*　　*　　*

To regulate our minds and ways by the regulator of God's truth, is to prove we are in unison with the Sun of God's nature. The time-keeper does not regulate the sun.

Faith's Storehouse

"I hope" (trust) "in Thy Word" (*Ps. cxix*:114)

"I do not trust either Pope or Councils," said Luther before the Emperor at Worms; "since it is manifest that they have often erred and contradicted themselves. My conscience is held by the Word of God. I cannot, and will not, retract anything, for to act against conscience is unsafe and unholy. So help me God."

> The Word of God is the *anchor* to keep us steady in the storm of temptation (1 John ii:14).
> The *bolt* to fix us to the Rock of Ages in the hour of trial (1 Thess. i:6).
> The *nail* to keep us firm in the time of persecution (Rev. iii:8).
> The *pivot* to keep us true in the day of witness-bearing (Acts iv:31).
> The *pin* to hold us steady in the aggressive warfare of the Gospel (Acts xix:20).
> The *hawser* to keep us to the moorings of God's holiness (John xvii:17).
> And the *staple* to hold us fast to the Lord (Psalm cxix:67).

*   *   *   *

The unseen is the seen to faith (Hebrews xi:1-13), for it has confidence in the Unseen, love to the Unseen, and joy from the Unseen (1 Peter i:8).

Faith's Towardness

"Faith toward our Lord Jesus Christ" (*Acts xx:21*)

Mr. Oncken, in the early days of his preaching at Hamburg, was brought up before the burgomaster many times and imprisoned. This magistrate one day said to him in very bitter terms, "Mr. Oncken, you see that little finger?" "Yes, sir." "As long as that little finger can be held up, sir, I will put you down." "Ah," said Mr. Oncken, "I do not suppose you see what I see, for I discern not a little finger, but a great arm, and that is the arm of God, and as long as that can move you will never put me down."

Faith always looks beyond the human and the present to the eternal and Divine. Faith is never occupied with itself. Its *Object* is the Lord Jesus Christ. It rests in

Him as *"Jesus,"* and finds salvation from sin's desert and dominion; it receives Him as *"Christ,"* and experiences His sanctifying touch and influence; and it submits to Him as *"Lord"* by allowing Him to dominate the heart and conduct. Faith is like the ivy which clings to the oak, and lives upon it. It has no power to stand nor thrive of itself; so the believer says,

> "Strong Son of God, Immortal Love,
> Whom we, that have not seen Thy face,
> By faith, by faith alone, embrace."

Faith is represented under many different similies.

Faith is the *feet* which come to Christ in response to His "Come unto Me" (Matt. xi:28).

Faith is the *hand* which receives "the gift of God" (John i:12).

Faith is the *sense* which tastes and sees that the Lord is gracious (1 Pet. ii:3).

Faith is the *eye* which looks to Christ and proves the truth of His "Look unto Me and be ye saved" (Isaiah xlv:22).

Faith is the *touch* which comes in contact with Christ and finds the healing power of His grace (Mark v:29-34).

Faith is the *ear* which hears His voice and obeys His word (John x:27).

And Faith is the *heart-throb* which beats in response to the Spirit's quickening life (Rom. xv:13).

*   *   *   *

To delight in the Lord means whole-hearted obedience to Him; and this makes Him to delight in us. To love Him in our obedience is to find His love our comfort.

Faith's Walk

"We walk by faith, not by appearance" (*2 Corinthians v:7, R. V., Margin*)

John Wesley writes in his diary: "My brother Charles among the difficulties of our early ministry used to say, 'If the Lord would give me wings I would fly.' I used to answer, 'If the Lord bids me fly I would trust Him for the wings.'" All God bids us do, He virtually promises to help us do.

90

FAITH'S WALK

(1) *The way of faith is not the way of sight.* That is, it is not the looking for *evidences,* either in our own feeling, or in the circumstances that attend us. True faith does not ask for these things. It rests on something altogether apart from them.

(2) *The way of faith is not the way of effort.* That is, when we are trusting another to do a thing for us, we have ceased to try to do it for ourselves, and real faith is confidence in God, that He is working in our behalf. So, instead of bringing worry and effort into our hearts, it brings *rest.*

(3) *The way of faith is the way of reliance upon the Character and Promise of Another—upon God and His Word.* Faith looks to God to work, as He has said He would; and refuses to undertake for itself, except to fulfil those conditions that God may have laid down with His promise. Indeed, the largest part of faith's struggle, often, is to *keep from interfering* on its own behalf—to *keep from helping God out,* as it were. Unbelief cannot and will not wait for God to work, but must rush ahead to help itself. Thus it fails to receive from God; for "He worketh for him that *waiteth for Him*" (Isa. lxiv:4, R. V.) Faith, on the contrary, is willing to endure trial, and to wait long, if need be, till God is ready to interpose on its behalf. It knows that "He is faithful who has promised," and "though the vision tarry, it will wait for it, for it will surely come."

A great part of faith's work, therefore, is *fighting unbelief, refusing* to look at those things that dishearten, and destroy confidence. Satan is ever ready with temptations to doubt. Often, too, the circumstances about us are such as would in themselves utterly discourage us. God often "waits to be gracious" until our self-hopes and efforts are done. He is the real faith—to *hold on,* in the midst of these untoward things, until, in His good time, *God works.*

(4) *Faith's victory consists in holding fast to God's promise, until He sends help.* Faith has *all things* promised to her (Mark ix:23). If she will but *stand,* and *trust God* and *wait,* she can have anything she needs or asks. Let her but refuse *to doubt,* refuse to move, or *question,* or give back in any wise, and the triumph will surely be hers, in due season.

(5) *The way of faith is God's way with His people.* He has no other. "*Without* faith it is *impossible* to be well-pleasing unto Him" (Hebrews xi:6, R. V.)

He who is infinite, trustworthy, asks that we trust Him, could He ask less? When our Lord Jesus was on earth, He always asked to be believed. He rejoiced at faith, and always wrought for it, but was astonished at unbelief (Mark yi:6; iii:5).

"Let him take hold of *My Strength*," says God, by Isaiah, but it must be by *faith* alone. May God Himself teach us this blessed *way* of *faith*, whether in our work, our spiritual experience, or our still more direct dealing with God in prayer. We must learn to *trust*, and to go on *believing* against all obstacles. "Behold, God is my salvation. I will *trust*, and *not be afraid*, He *knoweth* them that *put their trust in Him*" (Isaiah xii:2; Nahum i:7).

* * * *

Faith and obedience are synonymous terms, when we trust we obey, and when we obey we trust.

Fasten Your Grips

"Take fast hold" (*Prov. iv*:13)

"I pray you to fasten your grips," C. H. Spurgeon once said. "This sentence I met with in one of those marvellous letters which Samuel Rutherford left as a priceless legacy to the Church of God in all ages. Truly he hath dust of gold. I thought it would make a capital text for a prayer-meeting address, and so I jotted it down. It gripped me, and so I gripped it, in the hope that it might grip you, and lead you 'to fasten your grips.' But do not imagine that I have taken a text from Rutherford because I could not find one in the Bible, for there are many passages of Scripture which teach the same lesson. As, for instance, that exhortation, 'Lay hold on eternal life;' or that other, 'Hold fast that thou hast;' or that other, 'Hold fast the form of sound words.' The things of God are not to be trifled with, 'lest at any time we let them slip:' they are to be grasped, as Jacob seized the angel, with, 'I will not let thee go.' Faith is first the eye of the soul wherewith it sees the invisible things of God, and then it becomes the hand of the soul, with which it gets a grip of the substance of 'the things not seen as yet.' A man has two hands, and I would urge you to take a double hold upon those things which Satan will try to steal from you. Take hold of them as the limpet takes hold upon the rock, or as the magnet takes hold of steel. Give a life grip—a death grip: 'I *pray you to fasten your grips!*'"

There are several things we are exhorted to "Hold fast."

(1) FAITHFULNESS—"*Holdest fast* My name" (Rev. ii:13).

(2) CONFESSION—"Let us *hold fast* our confession" (Heb. iv:4, R.V.).

(3) HOPE—"Let us *hold fast* the confession of our hope" (Heb. x:23, R. V.).

(4) TRUTH—"*Holding fast* the faithful Word" (Titus i:9).

(5) PATTERN—"*Hold fast* the pattern of sound words" (2 Tim. i:13).

(6) GOOD—"*Hold fast* that which is good" (1 Thess. v:21).

(7) CONTINUANCE—"*Hold fast* till I come" (Rev. ii:25).

* * * *

When we hold Christ by our faith, He holds us by His power. The grace of His grip makes us grip His grace with grace.

Fear Not, or the Attention of Grace

"Fear not! Ye are of more value than many sparrows" (*Luke xii:7*)

The closing days of the late Dr. Vince were somewhat pathetic. It is recorded that during his last illness, in the early morning, he seated himself in a chair in his bedroom and looked through a bay-window. Turning to his wife, he said: "My dear, I fear I cannot possibly recover from this illness, and when I am gone what will become of you —what shall you do? I know my people will be kind to you out of love to me." She tried to comfort him, but he was very low. In a few moments three or four loud taps were heard, which made both of them look up, and there was a sparrow with a worm in its mouth tapping against the window pane. He at once repeated the Master's words: "Are not two sparrows sold for a farthing? and one of them shall not fall to the ground without your Father." His countenanced brightened; he no longer seemed depressed. To him it was a messenger of comfort, and who could doubt that the message from on high was sent to solace him in his affliction?

The careful attention of the Lord to details is aptly expressed when we remember, He

(1) Names His sheep (John x:3).
(2) Numbers our hairs (Matthews x:30).
(3) Counts our steps (Job xxxi:4).
(4) Books our thoughts (Malachi iii:16).
(5) Bottles our tears (Psa, lvi:8).
(6) Takes our hands (Isaiah xli:13).
And (7) Supplies our need (Philippians iv:19).

* * * *

The parasites of fear, doubt, questioning, and unbelief cannot live in the warm sunshine of God's love and the fresh air of the Spirit's presence.

Fellowship with Christ

"Called unto the fellowship of His Son" (1 *Cor. i:9,* R. V.)

Rumor says, on one occasion Queen Victoria, in speaking of the late Prince Consort, said: "He was such an one that I would have gladly walked barefooted round the world with him."

FINDINGS OF THE SPIRITUAL LIFE

To be with Christ is the cry of the new-born soul, as is evidenced in the delivered demoniac, who prayed that he might be *"with Him"* (Luke viii. 38):

It is *the prelude to seeing* Christ's glory, for Peter and the other two disciples were said to be *"with Him"* ere they saw His glory (Luke ix:32).

It is *the place of honour,* for the disciples were said to be *"with Him"* before He instituted the Last Supper (Luke xxii:14).

It is *the secret of witness-bearing,* as the people owned, for they took knowledge of the early disciples that they had been *"with Jesus"* (Acts iv:13).

It is *the power that separates from sin,* for we are said to be "dead *with Christ*" (Romans vi:8).

It is *the keeping-place* of our life, for it is said to be hid *"with Christ"* (Col. iii:3).

And it is *the hope of the coming glory,* for we shall for ever be *"with the Lord"* (1 Thess. iv:17; v:10; Colossians iii:4).

*　　*　　*　　*

Fellow*ship* is a good ship in which to sail; for in that ship Christ is owned as Captain, and all obey His authority; hence, there is oneness among the fellows.

Findings of the Spiritual Life

"I rejoice at Thy Word as One that findeth great sport" (*Ps. cxix:162*)

Someone has said, "All men adopt as their motto, 'Win gold.'" But men are distinguished from each other by the practical ending of that motto.

The vain man says, "Win gold, and wear it."

The generous man says, "Win gold, and share it."

The miser says, "Win gold and spare it."

The prodigal says, "Win gold, and spend it."

The usurer says, "Win gold, and lend it."

The fool says, "Win gold, and end it."

The gambler says, "Win gold, and lose it."

The wise man says, "Win gold, and use it."

(1) THE FINDING OF PRAYER, through the seeking of faith —"Seek, and ye shall *find*" (Matthew vii:7).

(2) THE FINDING OF REWARD, through the renunciation of self—"He that loseth his life for My sake shall *find* it" (Matthew x:39).

(3) THE FINDING OF HEART REST, through being yoked with Christ—"Ye shall *find* rest" (Matthew xi:29).

(4) THE FINDING OF PASTURE, through the going in and out of fellowship—"Shall go in and out and *find* pasture" (John x:9).

(5) THE FINDING OF FISH, through following the Lord's instructions—"Cast on the right side of the ship, and ye shall *find*" (John xxi:6).

(6) THE FINDING OF HELP, through coming to the throne of grace—"*Find* grace to help in time of need" (Hebrews iv:16).

(7) THE FINDING OF COMMENDATION, through endurance under trial—"Might be *found* unto praise." &c. (1 Peter i:7).

* * * *

The proof of walking in God's way is found in obeying His Word.

Flies

"Corrupted by reason of the Swarm of flies" (*Ex. viii*:24)

When the sun shines the flies sting, and they are most persistent in their patronage of your face, and think nothing of walking along the bridge of your nose, digging their forceps into the surface of your skin, and resent any hand that seeks to remove them with the buzz of opposition. Many have found, when the sun of prosperity is shining, flies which have stung them to their hurt.

Solomon was stung by the fly of licentiousness (1 Kings xi:1-6).

Hezekiah was bitten by the fly of pride (Isa. xxxix:1-6).

Saul was poisoned by the fly of self-will (1 Samuel xv:22, 23).

Jeshurun was blighted by the fly of unbelief (Deut. xxxii:15).

Demas was infected by the fly of worldliness (II Timothy iv:10).

FORGETFULNESS

Lot was contaminated by the fly of self-seeking (Genesis xiii:10-13).

And Jehoshaphat was stung by the fly of unholy alliance (II Chronicles xviii:1).

*   *   *   *

The believer who sins against the love of God will soon find God, in his love, smiting the believer.

Forgetfulness

"Hath forgotten" (2 *Pet. i*:9)

The antiquary, Dr. Stukeley, is said to have called one day by appointment upon Sir Isaac Newton. Newton, however, was in his study, where no one dared disturb him. The dinner hour arrived, and the man-servant brought in a portion of a boiled fowl for his master. Hungry himself, and knowing the irregular habits of the philosopher, Stukeley took the liberty of appropriating the dish, covering it up afterwards, and telling the servant to prepare another for Newton. An hour or so passed, and the author of the "Principia" made his appearance. Lifting the cover from the dish of chicken eaten by his friend, he exclaimed, "See what studious people are; I forgot that I had dined."

Believers are apt to forget things they should remember. The Lord says, if we fail to add to our faith the things which He enjoins, we forget the obligation we owe to Him in that He cleansed away our old sins (II Peter i:5-15).

If this passage is pondered, it will be found "these things" of the Christian graces are referred to five times.

"These things" are the soil of fruitful knowledge (verse 8).

The lack of "these things" causes short-sightedness and a duller memory (verse 9).

The doing of "these things" prevents falling, and secures an abundant entrance into the kingdom. (verses 10, 11).

It is necessary to be constantly reminded of "these things" (verse 12).

And to have them repeated to us (verse 15).

*   *   *   *

We cannot help exercising our faith when we remember God's promise, "I will never leave thee" (Hebrews xiii:5).

Frankincense

"This is thankworthy" (1 *Peter ii*:19)

Count Tolstoi, in defending his belief in non-resistance, says: "You can show by your peaceable behaviour that you are not governed by the barbarous impulse of retaliation, and your adversary will not continue to strike a man who neither resists nor tries to defend himself. It is by those who have suffered, not by those who have inflicted suffering, that the world has been advanced." The Count's statement is but the reflection of what we find in the New Testament. Peter, in his first letter, has a good deal to say of *Christ's sufferings for us* (1 Peter ii:21-23; iii:18; iv:1); and he has also much to say of *our suffering for Him*. There are at least seven phases of this profitable, if not always palatable, truth:

(1) *The essence of suffering* is to "endure grief, suffering wrongfully" (ii:19).

(2) *The spirit in which suffering is to be taken* is "to take it patiently," for this is "acceptable with God" (ii:20).

(3) *The cause of our suffering* is to be "well doing" and "for righteousness' sake," then we are said to be "happy," or blessed (ii:20; iii:14).

(4) *The betterness of suffering* for "well doing," as we are in the line of God's will, is definitely expressed (iii:17).

(5) There is *an important* "as" *to recognize in suffering,* that is, to "suffer *as* a Christian" (iv:15, 16).

98

(6)   There is *an act in all suffering* never to be omitted, namely, to "commit" the keeping of ourselves to the "faithful Creator" (iv:19).

(7)   And there is *the end of suffering*, when it comes to an end—"the God of all grace, who called you unto His eternal glory in Christ after ye have suffered a little while, shall Himself perfect, stablish, strengthen you" (v:10, R. V.).

*   *   *   *

Did you ever hear the proverb: "The itch of disputing is the scab of the Church?" Think of it, and as a Christian, act on Eph. iv:1-3.

Freshness

"My glory was fresh in me" (Job xxix:20)

The American invasion is fertile of stories, and one of the most recent is this from *The Country Gentleman:* An enterprising Yankee came over to England and decided to open a shop in Birmingham. He obtained premises next door to a man who also kept a shop of the same description, but was not very pushing in his business methods.

The methods of the Yankee, however, caused the older trader to wake up; and, with the spirit of originality strong upon him, he affixed a notice over his shop with the words, "Established fifty years," painted in large letters. Next day the Yankee replied to this with a notice over his store to this effect: "Established yesterday; no old stock."

We have known some Christians who were living on the mouldy fare of a past experience.

> We need always to be anointed with the "fresh oil" of the Spirit (Ps. xcii:10);
> To feed upon the new manna of His Word of Promise (Num. xi:8);
> To listen with the ear of attention every morning to the voice of the Lord's instruction (Isa. l:4);

DEVOTIONAL BIBLE STUDIES

To have the garden of our being watered with the water
of life "every moment" (Isa. xxvii:3);
To have the renewing of God's power for the stress of life
"day by day" (II Cor. iv:16);
To have the lamp of our testimony fed by the oil of truth
and the attentive ministry of our great "High Priest"
(Lev. xxiv:3, 4);
And the "always abounding in the work of the Lord" (I
Cor. xv:58).

*   *   *   *

If we would *retain* the Spirit's *power,* then we must
maintain the Spirit's grace by *prayer.*

Fruit

"Your fruit unto holiness" (*Rom. vi:22*)

A barber, who practiced his art in a large Yorkshire
village, had a rival. The man was an earnest Christian
and local preacher. He noticed, in a recent week, a
great increase of customers, and on making inquiry,
learnt that the practitioner at the other end of the village
was ill. At the end of the week the barber made a
calculation, and all he had taken above his average he
took to his brother of the razor, with the warm expression
of his Christian sympathy. Is Christianity played out?
Verily, no! The Christianity was not "played out" in
the sense of being *non est,* but it was "played out" in
very reality in the sense of practicality, even as the sailor
plays out the rope to the helping of a vessel in distress. After all, what constitutes Christianity?

What, indeed, but Christ-like action.
Helping the widows (Acts vi:1).
Clothing the naked (Acts ix:39).
Visiting the sick (Matt. xxv:36).
Caring for the afflicted (James i:27).
Housing the homeless (Luke x:34).
Feeding the hungry (Luke xiv:13).

FRUIT-BEARING

And living as Christ did (1 John ii:6), are the soul, the
essence, the backbone, and the sap of Christianity.
Where these are lacking, there may be the Inanity of
profession, but not the practice of Christianity.

* * * *

Divine grace makes us Divinely human.

"As we are Thy children true,
We are more truly men."

Fruit-bearing

"His fruit was sweet to my taste" (*Can. ii:3*)

A curious feature of the Boer war has been the discovery of jam by the British soldier. To judge from
Mr. Brodrick's printed reply to a question in the House
of Commons, jam has leapt from the rank of a household delicacy to the position of a military necessary,
without which a campaign can hardly be conducted with
success. 34,582,762 pounds of jam were consumed during the war by the Army, most of it manufactured in
England, the rest of it in the Colonies. It is com-
puted that in the year 1900 alone, thirty train-loads of
jam, at 300 tons to a load, were sent to the front; and
that the Army consumed more than half its own weight
of jam in that time.

Nearly thirty-five million pounds of jam! Tommy
Atkins should be sweet by now. The fact of T. A.
taking so much jam, suggests the thought that we must
be sweetened to be sweet. How true this is in the
spiritual realm. The blessing of the Lord in any one
particular communicates its nature to the receiver.

Thus the grace of Christ is our power (II Cor. xii:9).
The joy of the Lord is our strength (Neh. viii:10).
The gentleness of Jehovah makes us great (Ps. xviii:35).

DEVOTIONAL BIBLE STUDIES

The peace of Christ gives us calm (John xiv:27).
The Word of God sanctifies (John xvii:17).
The presence of Jesus causes us to be glad (John xx:20).
And the beauty of the Lord makes us beautiful (Ps. xc:17).

*   *   *   *

The *foliage* of a beautiful life is found in the *rootage* of God's grace.

Fulness of Blessing

"Full with the blessing of the Lord" (*Deut. xxxiii:23*)

Sometimes the condition of a church and community, is like that of famine-stricken Leyden, when it was besieged by Philip's Polish army. Within the beleaguered town death reigned. Its brave defenders were starving by thousands. Succour was waiting for them in the Dutch fleet which could not reach the city. But the heroic Hollanders sluiced the dykes and let in the sea, and as the rescuing fleet swept in, they flung the loaves of bread to the overjoyed crowds which thronged the canals of Leyden. Then pouring into the great Protestant cathedral, they made its arches ring with thanksgiving unto God, their Deliverer.

If the sluices of our heart's faith are open to the Lord, by whole-hearted consecration to Him, then the water of the Spirit's power will come pouring into our life, and we shall know the blessings which are treasured up for us in the ships of Christ's precious promises. The river of God is full of water (Psalm lxv:9), and there are many tributary streams which go to make up its fulness.

> Filled with the Spirit means fulness of life to vitalise, for "the trees of the Lord are *full* of sap" (Ps. civ:16);
> Fulness of power to strengthen as Micah says, "I am *full* of power by the Spirit of the Lord" (Micah iii:8);
> Fulness of grace to bless, as illustrated in Stephen, who is said to be "*full* of grace" (Acts vi:8, R. V.);

GAIN OF GODLINESS

Fulness of joy to gladden, for the Lord desires that our
    joy "should be *full*" (John xv:11; xvi:24; 1 John i:4);
Fulness of His Word in testimony, as Elihu says, "I am
    full of matter; the Spirit within me constraineth me"
    (Job xxxii:18);
Fulness of wisdom in work, as seen in Joshua, who was
    "*full* of the Spirit of wisdom" (Deut. xxxiv:9);
And fulness of holiness in life, like the hands of the High
    Priest on the day of atonement, which were to be "*full*
    of sweet incense" (Lev. xvi:12).

*　　*　　*　　*

Holiness is the root of happiness. The latter can no
more be had without the former, than plants can be had
without roots.

Gain of Godliness

"Godliness with contentment is great gain" (1 *Tim. vi*:6)

A gentleman was once talking to Thomas Maunt, a
pious waterman on the river Thames, and, having ascer-
tained that he never labored on the Sabbath, and was dependent upon his labors for a living, he said: "Well, as
your gains have been so small, you could not lay much
up. Have you not been anxious, as you have proceeded in
life, lest, from the very nature of your employment, exposed as it is to dangers and all weathers, you should be
laid up by illness, and have nothing to support you?"

"No, sir; I have always believed in God's providence.
I think I am just fitted for the situation which He has
appointed to me; and that which He has fixed is best. I
am, therefore, satisfied and thankful. I endeavor to do
the duty which falls to me, and to be careful of my earn-
ings. I have always had enough, and I have no fear for
years to come."

"Yet, my friend, if illness were to come, and you had
not a provision made for the supply of your need in helpless old age, ought this not to give you some uneasiness?"

DEVOTIONAL BIBLE STUDIES

"No, sir; that's not my business. Future years are not my business. That belongs to God; and I am sure that, doing my duty in His fear now, and being careful in what He entrusts to me, He will supply my need in the future in the way which He shall think best."

No one can over estimate the worth of contentment.

Contentment is a blessing-bringer (Heb. xiii:5);
It is a mind-tranquilizer (Phil. iv:11);
It is a satisfaction-finder (1 Tim. vi:8);
It is a gain-getter (1 Tim. vi:6);
It is a dispute-expeller (Luke iii:14);
It is a trust-expresser (Isa. xxvi:3);
It is a life-adjuster (Matt. vi:33);
And it is a God-acknowledger (Prov. iii:6).

*   *   *   *

To count up our mercies is to find ourselves wholly occupied. To ponder our miseries is to be sorely distracted.

Given Up

"I gave them up" (*Ps. lxxxi:12*)

The manager of a cotton mill received a complaint from the girls in the weaving-room, that they could not make the bobbin boys hear them call for more bobbins. Having bought several bells, he instructed the boys to answer these when rung by the girls. For a time all went well. No matter where the boys were the bells were heard above the clatter of the looms. But by-and-bye the girls began to complain that the boys were getting careless, and hindered them more than before; while the boys answered that the girls did not ring loud enough. The manager therefore went to the room, and experimented by ringing the bell again and again; and yet, although the bobbin boy was not far off, he paid no attention. Suddenly it flashed across the manager's mind that the bells must be at fault. On inspection, he found that the girls had been in the habit of snatching up the bells by the metal instead of the handles, and they had thus covered the bells with oil from the machinery. The bells were accordingly cleaned, and all went well. To how many people has the clear voice of conscience become a dull sound? Not at once, but gradually, till the voice ceases to be heard. The Lord never gives up any to judgment till they have first given themselves up to sin. The following are illustrations:

(1) Pharaoh and the Egyptians—"Gave their life over," &c. (Ps. lxxviii:50).

(2) Israel in the Land—"He gave His people over" (Ps: lxxviii:62).

(3) Israel in the Wilderness—"I gave them up" (Ps. lxxxi:12).

(4) Israel and Idolatry—"God . . . gave them up to worship the host of heaven" (Acts vii:42).

(5) The Heathen—"God gave them up" (Rom. i:24, 26, 28). Three times, it is said, God gave them up. They gave themselves up to sin, and God gave them up to judgment in consequence.

*   *   *   *

Sin cannot *prevail* over us as long as we *avail* ourselves of the grace that is in Christ.

Gladness

"Be glad in the Lord, and rejoice, ye righteous" (*Ps. xxxii:11*)

Madame De Krudener sought all her happiness in worldly pleasures, till profound melancholy seized her which nothing could relieve. One day, a shoemaker waited on her in compliance with her orders. A single glance at his countenance showed her that he was as happy as she was miserable. She could not forbear asking, "My friend, are you happy?"

To which he replied, "I am the happiest of men, Madame." His looks and his words greatly impressed her; nor could she rest till she had sought and found the secret of his joy.

DEVOTIONAL BIBLE STUDIES

He was a devout Moravian, and gladly seized the opportunity to preach Christ to her. She also received the "anointing," and to the close of her life served the Lord with gladness, diffusing in her turn the same saving aroma to others.

There are many ministers to the believer's gladness in Christ. Let us consider—in the light of the Greek word *chairo* ("to rejoice")—seven feeders to the river of joy which flows through the nature of God's children.

(1) RECONCILIATION.—"It was meet that we should make merry and be *glad*" (Luke xv:32), is the rebuke of the father to the elder son; who grumbles at the rejoicing occasioned by the prodigal's return. We are glad in the Father's gladness in being welcomed to His heart, hearth, and home, for they speak of His love, and care, and protection, and the joy He has in blessing us.

(2) REGISTRATION.—"*Rejoice,* because your names are written in heaven" (Luke x:20). Love inscribed our names in the Lamb's book of life. This registration, not only tells of the security of the believer in Christ, but it also proclaims the individual interest He takes in each believer, as Billy Bray used to say, "The Lord knows my name, and where I live."

(3) REDEMPTION.—"He went on his way *rejoicing*" (Acts viii:39). The eunuch had found release from sin's penalty and power; hence, joy filled his heart after he had confessed his faith in Christ as his Emancipator. The meaning of the word Redemption is being "set at liberty by virtue of a price paid." This is aptly illustrated in the experience of the eunuch.

(4) RECIPROCATION.—"*Rejoice,* inasmuch as ye are partakers of Christ's sufferings" (1 Pet. iv:13). Thus the apostle comforts the suffering saints; Christ bids us do the same (Matt. v:13), and the early Christians exemplify it (Acts v:4). The keen edge of suffering is removed where there is this mutuality in suffering; yea, He suffers in us (Col. i:24; Acts ix:4), and we bear His marks (Gal. vi:17).

(5) REFLECTIONS.—"I *rejoiced* greatly that I found of thy children walking in truth" (11 John 4; 111 John 3). The consistent life of a believer as it corresponds with the truth brings a four-fold benefit, for it honours the God of Truth to His glory, it strengthens the walker in truth to his betterment, it influences others to a corresponding action, and gladdens those who are going the same way.

(6) RECOGNITION.—"When he came, and had seen the grace of God, was *glad*" (Acts xi:23). Barnabas recognised the working of God's grace in the conversion of those who had believed in Christ at Antioch. As the flowers, in their variegated beauty, proclaim the properties of the artistic sun; so, wherever the sun of God's grace shines into the heart, its properties are seen in the graces of the Spirit which adorn the life.

(7) RECOLLECTION.—"Then were the disciples *glad,* when they saw the Lord" (John xx:20). The cause of their gladness was the uplifted hands of Christ. What a host of recollections would crowd into their minds as those pierced hands were shown to them, for those hands not only reminded them of His living Presence, but of His consummated work on Calvary. We may well be glad in having *Him,* for He is the *secret* of joy, the *spring* of gladness, the *substance* of rejoicing, and the *source* of all blessing.

* * * *

If we are *clinging* to the Lord with a whole *heart,* we shall soon be *singing* to Him with soul *art.*

God-in-ness, the Secret of Godliness

"In God the Father" (1 *Thess.* i:1)

Two of the most devoted saints who have moved among the Roman Catholics were Archbishop Fénelon and Madame Guyon. The former, in writing to the latter, gives us an illustrative comment of what it is to find our joy and our all in God alone. Madame Guyon had been a great help and stimulus to Fénelon, and he recapitulates in a letter to her what he understood her to mean, and mentions six points, which I may summarize as follows:

(1) The subjection of the natural appetites and propensities by the grace of God through faith.

(2) Ceasing to rest on inward sensibility. "When **we** lose our inward happiness, we are very apt to think **we** lose God; not considering that the moral life of the soul does not consist in pleasure, but in union with God's will."

(3) "Entire crucifixion to any reliance upon our virtues whether outward or inward." Ceasing from what God makes us, and resting in Him alone.

(4) Acquiescence in the will of God in trying providences. "The blows which God sends upon us are received without the opposition which once existed, and existed oftentimes with great power."

(5) A new life of love in God Himself, and finding in Him all the blessings of His grace.

(6) Life in union with God. "It is not enough to be merely passive under God's dealings. The spirit of entire submission is a great grace; but it is a still higher attainment to become *flexible;* that is to say, to move just as He would have us move."

God-in-ness is the secret of the godly life, by God-in-ness we mean making God our Home, so that we know something of dwelling in the secret place of the Most High. There are two words which frequently occur in the New Testament, namely, *"In God."* The whole host of the redeemed, described as the Church, is said to be *"in God,"* for He is the Sphere in which they are blessed, and in which they are to move (1 Thess. i:1; ii:2, 3).

The Object of the believer's confidence, and the attitude of the believer's life, should be to trust *"in God"* (2 Cor. i:9; 1 Tim. iv:10; v:5; vi:17; Titus iii:8; 1 Peter i:21; iii:5).

The security of the believer's life, amid the storms and stress of his earthly pilgrimage, which keeps him steady, is the assuring knowledge that his life is "hid with Christ *in God"* (Col. iii:3).

The one soul-lifting and inspiring thing, when trial comes, sorrow, tears, and circumstances are clouded, yea, at all times, is to "joy *in God"* (Rom. v:11).

That which gives wing to thought, fervour in service, and courage in testimony, is to be "bold *in* our *God"* (1 Thess. ii:2).

The element in which the child of God is to move is the love of God; for, as we love each other, we prove God dwells in us, and we *"in God"* (1 John iv:15, 16).

And as we look out on life's horizon, we are cheered by the remembrance that Christ is coming; our barque is thus kept steady by the anchor of hope, for our "hope" is *"in God"* (1 Peter i:21).

*   *   *   *

Paul said, "I have learned the secret" (Philippians iv: 12, R.V.). How many there are who are not content to learn the secret.

God, not Hills

"Shall I lift up mine eyes to the hills?" (margin *Ps. cxxi*:1).
"Unto thee lift I up mine eyes (*Ps. cxxiii*:1)

All the difference in the world is made to us by the standpoint from which we look. If we look to the hills of our surroundings, we shall be disappointed; but if we look to the Lord, we shall be delivered.

A traveller, as he passed through a large and thick wood, saw a part of a huge oak which appeared mis-shapen, and almost seemed to spoil the scenery. "If," said he, "I were the owner of the forest, I would cut down that tree." But when he had ascended the hill and taken a full view of the forest, the same tree appeared the most beautiful part of the landscape. "How erroneously," said he, "I have judged while I saw only a part." "This plain tale," says Dr. Olin, "illustrates the plans of God. We now see but in part. The full view, the harmony and pro-portion of things, are all necessary to clear up our judg-ment."

The right attitude is to look at the things of earth from the standpoint of heaven. What does this mean?

(1) *Safety from the world.* Lot looked to the Sodom of the world and got entangled in it; Abraham looked to the Lord and got the reward of faith (Gen. xiii:14, 15).

(2) *Deliverance from the fear of man.* The unbelieving spies saw the sons of Anak, and felt they were "grass-hoppers" (Num. xiii:33); while Isaiah the seer, sees "the inhabitants" of earth to be "grasshoppers" (Isa. xl:22).

(3) *Rest in adversity.* Looking at our circumstances, we say, with Jacob, "all these things are against mē" (Gen. xlii:36); but believing the Word of the Lord, we shall say "all things work together for good" (Rom. viii:28).

(4) *Victory in conflict.* David, in his own strength, was almost defeated by a giant (2 Sam. xxi:15-17); but when he went against Goliath, in the name of the Lord, he got the victory (1 Sam. xvii:45-50).

(5) *Confidence in trial.* The servant of Elisha seeing only the Syrian host was dismayed, but the man of God, knowing of the inner circle which encompassed him, rested in calm assurance (2 Kings vi:15-17).

DEVOTIONAL BIBLE STUDIES

(6) *Guidance in perplexity.* Looking around, we shall say with Job: "I looked for good, then evil came unto me; and when I waited for light, there came darkness" (Job xxx:26); but counting upon the Lord, and seeking His direction, we shall be able to bear a like testimony to the Psalmist, who said: "They looked unto the Lord and were lightened" (Ps. xxxiv:5).

(7) *Supply in need.* Counting upon human resources, we shall often have to say, with Haggai, we "looked for much, and, lo, it came to little" (Haggai i:9); but looking at the Source of all blessings, then we shall find our need met, as the lame man did, when he obeyed the "look on us" of the apostles, and they in turn "directed him to the Lord Jesus" (Acts iii:4-6).

*   *   *   *

What is God? God *is* God. He is the only answer to the question. Who can describe the smell of the violet? If what He has made is beyond description, how much more He Who made it?

God's Best

"The best gifts" (1 Cor. xii:31).

In looking round a room in Brooklyn I saw the following lines on an illuminated text card:

> "God has His best things for the few
>   Who dare to stand the test,
> He has His second choice for those
>   Who will not have His best."

The words set me thinking of those of God's saints, for whom He wanted His best, and they, by their hesitation or unbelief, preferred a "second choice."

Abram was called at the first to go direct to Canaan, but he made a second choice in staying at Haran for a time, till the Lord spoke to him again. How significant is the past tense of Genesis xii:1. "The Lord *had* said unto Abram" (Gen. xi:31; xii:1-3); also "when his father was dead" of Acts vii:4, plainly indicating that death had to snap the bond which caused him to tarry in Haran.

GOD'S CARE

Lot appears to have been only a second rate believer. He seems to have started wrong. Meaningful is the statement that "Lot went with Abram" (Gen. xii:4), while the latter went with God, in response to His call. Again, Lot "lifted up his eyes, and beheld all the plain of Jordan," &c., while Abram, who did not look, was bidden by the Lord to "look" at Heaven's expanse, as He gave him Heaven's promise (Gen. xiii:10-14).

God wanted Moses to go at His bidding and speak to Pharaoh; he hesitated, and complained he could not speak, and passed the honour on to Aaron—thus Aaron got the best blessing, and Moses the second choice (Ex. iv:14-16); the same thing is illustrated again when the Spirit was distributed among the seventy elders for administration purposes, instead of resting on Moses alone (Num. xi:11-17).

The Children of Israel made the second choice of wandering in the wilderness, instead of entering the Promised Land. They saw many things of the Lord's doings, but they would have had a greater blessing if they had entered into His rest (Heb. iii:11).

Martha made the second choice of being cumbered with service, while Mary had the Lord's rest in sitting at His feet (Luke x:39-42).

Moses and Elijah, when transfigured on the Mount with Christ had fellowship with Him in conversing about His death; While the disciples were concerned about the place where they were found, and said: "It is good to be *here*," certainly the *better* was to be with *Him*. God's best is always given to those who seek it by self-abandonment to His will and whole-hearted faith (Luke ix:31-33).

*　　*　　*　　*

The best way to have the true Martha activity of service is to have the Mary attention of stillness. Worship before work.

God's Care

"He careth for you" (1 *Peter* v:7)

God is great in great things, but He is very great in little things. A party of tourists were at the Matterhorn, and admiring the proportions of the beautiful mountain, when it was remarked, that God was not only seen in the

III

lofty snow-clad mountain, but also in the beautiful mosses found in its crevices. A gentleman of the party produced a pocket microscope, and, having caught a tiny fly, placed it under the glass. He reminded the company that the legs of the household fly in England were naked, then called their attention to the legs of this little fly, which were thickly covered with hair. The God Who made the lofty mountains rise, attends also to the comfort of the tiniest of His creatures, even to providing for them socks and mittens to keep them warm.

All around, wherever we look, we see God is a God of detail. He is careful over the little things, which reminds us at once of His personal love for us, and His personal interest in all that concerns us.

> "Among so many, can He care?
> Can special love be everywhere?"
> I asked. "My soul bethought of this,
> In just that very place of His,
> Where He hath put and keepeth you,
> God hath no other thing to do."

When we ponder the Word of God, we are assured again and again of His personal, loving interest in us.

(1) He numbers the hairs of our head—"Even the very hairs of your head are all numbered" (Luke xii:7).

(2) He bottles the tears of our sorrow—"Put Thou my tears into Thy bottle" (Ps. lvi:8).

(3) He records the thoughts of our meditation—"A book of remembrance was written before Him, for them that feared the Lord, and that thought upon His name" (Mal. iii:16).

(4) He orders the steps of our walk—"The steps of a good man are ordered by the Lord" (Ps. xxxvii:23).

(5) He hears the cry of our supplication—"Before they call, I will answer; and while they are yet speaking, I will hear" (Isa. lxv:24).

(6) He looks after our interests in all things—"All things work together for good to them that love God" (Rom. viii:28).

GOLGOTHA

(7) And He supplies every need of our requirement—"My God shall fulfil every need of yours," &c. (Philippians iv:19, R. V.)

* * * *

The child cannot define its mother *scientifically*, but it knows the mother's love and care *intuitively*. The child of God cannot explain the *unsearchableness* of Jehovah, but he does know His *unquenchable* love.

Golgotha

"He bearing His cross went into a place called * * * Golgotha"
(*John* xix:17)

There are many interesting legends in the Apocryphal lives of Christ, and many illustrations of truth, even as the gems of priceless worth are found in the soil of earth.

"Among these, may be instanced the history of the cross, which was first a branch of the tree of life, and, being planted by Seth, 'flourished and became a great and beautiful tree.' Solomon ordered it to be used for the building of the temple, but 'the workmen could find no place where it could be used, it always was found too long or too short,' and it was cast aside. It then became a bridge over a pool of water.

" 'When the Queen of Sheba was about to cross the pool she saw in the Spirit that the Saviour of the world should be suspended upon that beam, and, through respect, she adored instead of walking over it.' Solomon, conceived, perhaps, as representing the secular spirit in Judaism, ordered it to be 'buried in the bowels of the earth,' but the place where it was buried became the pool of Bethesda, and with its reappearance on the surface in the fulness of days this legend closes."

In the legend may be found many facts of the truth of the gospel, namely,

DEVOTIONAL BIBLE STUDIES

The cross of Christ has a past, for its actuality is proclaimed in the pierced Christ of the prophetic Word (Ps. xxii:16);

The cross cannot be adapted to the temple of men's erections, for it is a stumbling block and foolishness to them (1 Cor. i:18);

By means of the death of the cross a bridge is made, which brings blessing from God to us and enables us to come to Him (Eph. ii:16);

We glory in Him who bore the cross, and bow in adoration before Him as the Lamb who was sacrificed upon it (Rev. v:8, 9);

The cross is the House of Mercy (Bethesda), whose healing waters cure the malady of sin (1 John i:7);

And it will ever rise above the earth, yea, will light heaven, for the slain Lamb is the Light of earth, and the glory of heaven (Rev. xxi:23).

*   *   *

Christ went to the place of a skull for us, that He might give us a place in the many mansions.

Good Out of Evil

"Out of the eater came forth meat" (*Judges xiv*:14)

Science told us one time, "that as rain, and mist, and haze of any kind obviously interfere with the passage of light, so must rain or fog, of all sorts, deaden sound. This was formerly regarded as self-evident. It is now known to be absolutely untrue. It has been proved over and over again, that when the sky is thickest, when all view is lost, and danger may be at hand, and unsuspected, then it is that Nature comes to our aid in her own way. It is just then that sounds lend us their readiest warning; that the approaching train may be heard a mile further than usual; that the horse's footfall, the rattle of the wheels, the shout of the human voice—all such sounds ring out with unwonted clearness."

Does not the above also illustrate, not only the blundering of man, but the over-ruling of the Lord in making the things which take from us in one way, to minister to us in another?

GOOD WORK

Thus Joseph would never have reached the place of power
in Egypt, had he not been put in the place of desertion
in the pit (Gen. xxxvii:24);

The three Hebrew young men would never have enjoyed the
special warmth of the Lord's presence, had they not had
the heat of the fiery furnace (Dan. iii:21).

Samson would not have been satisfied with the honey found
in the lion, had he not had the lion to overcome (Judges
xiv:5);

Esther would never have been the means of blessing to her
people, had it not been for the wicked plotting of Haman
(Esther ix:24, 25);

The martyr's painful death made it possible to receive the
crown of life (Rev. ii:10);

Paul's thorn in the flesh brought the sufficient grace of God
(2 Cor. xii:7);   •

And Christ's cross was the precursor to His throne (Luke
xxiv:26).

* * * *

Many a bad beginning has had a good ending through
Divine mending. The bow of God's blessing is seen by
faith in the dark cloud of man's blunder.

Good Work

"Prepared unto every good work" (2 *Tim.* ii:21)

In the Freshwater Church there is a marble tablet,
about thirty inches square, fixed into the wall by the lec-
tern. On this plain, simple tablet there is the following
in memoriam to Lionel Tennyson, signed "A. T." It
was almost unnecessary to place the poet's initials under
these lines, for no one could mistake the Tennysonian
art of loading a slight song with a large burden of meaning:

"Truth for truth is truth he worshipt, being true as he
was brave;

Good for good is good he follow'd, yet he looked beyond
the grave.

Truth for truth, and good for good! The good, the
true, the pure, the just!

Take the charm 'for ever' from them, and they crumble
into dust."

DEVOTIONAL BIBLE STUDIES

Among all ranks and degrees in Freshwater, Lionel Tennyson is remembered with esteem, admiration, and affection. Boatmen, cabdrivers, laborers, lodging-house keepers, all regarded his death as a personal loss.

(1) ABOUNDING—"Abound to every *good work*" (2 Cor. ix:8).

(2) FRUIT—"*Fruitful* in every *good work*" (Col. i:10).

(3) STABLISHED—"Stablish you in every *good * * * work*" (2 Thess. ii:17).

(4) DILIGENCE—"Diligently followed every *good work*" (1 Tim. v:10).

(5) PREPARATION—"Prepared unto every *good work*" (2 Tim. ii:21).

(6) READINESS—"Ready to every *good work*" (Titus iii:1).

(7) PERFECTION—"Make you perfect in every *good work*" (Heb. xiii:21).

(8) COMPLETION—"He which hath begun a *good work* in you, will perform it" (Phil. i:6).

*　　*　　*　　*

Warm hearts, willing hands, and wise heads are needed in the Lord's work. If the wise head guides the willing hands, and both are influenced by the warm heart of love, then we shall be among God's superlatives.

Greatness of the Lord

"Thine, O Lord, is the greatness" (1 *Chron.* xxix:11)

Little Tommy (who has never been out of Whitechapel before): "Oh! oh! oh!" Kind lady: "What's the matter, Tommy?" Little Tommy: "Why, what a big sky they've got 'ere, miss!"

What exclamations there would be on the part of God's children, if they only knew

The fullness of the "*great love*" with which they are loved Ephes. ii:4).

The freedom of the "*great salvation*," in which they are saved (Heb. ii:3).

The might of the "*great power*" of the Holy Spirit (Acts iv:33).

116

HARD PLACES

The meaning of the ministry of the *"great High Priest"* Heb. iv:14).

The care of the *"great Shepherd"* for His sheep (Heb. xiii:20).

The stimulus of the *"great and precious promises"* (2 Peter i:4).

And the glory of the *"great city"* (Rev. xxi:10), methinks they would exclaim, "What a big sky of blessing God has for me."

* * * *

"Man's holiness is much-ado-about-nothing." God's holiness is Christ-in-everything.

Hard Places

"Thou hast shewed Thy people hard things" (*Ps.* lx:3)

"It is related of a New England farmer that he put all his combativeness into a rough farm in Massachusetts, and made it one of the best. Once a friend said, 'I should think that with your love of farming you would like to have a more productive soil to deal with—in some Western State for instance.'

"I should hate farming in the West," he said, vigorously. "I should hate to put my spade into the ground where it did not hit against a rock."

There are many rocks—hard places—that the Christian meets as he uses the spade of daily toil in turning over the soil of life.

Every hard place has its compensation, even as the blows of the sculptor chips away the stone to find "the angel" in the marble. The following are but a few instances of some of the hard places and the compensations found in them.

    (1) The *pit of persecution* was a hard place to Joseph, but he found that it was a step to the palace of influence (Gen. xli:41).

    (2) *The stony pillow of loneliness* at Bethel, Jacob found was the foundation of the way cast up to heaven (Gen. xxviii:12, 17).

(3) *The Red Sea of difficulty* was the precursor of the Lord's delivering grace (Exod. xiv:21-28).

(4) *The Zarephath of trying circumstances* was the opportunity for the Divine supply (1 Kings xvii:9-16).

(5) *The desert of discouragement* was the forerunner of the angel's visit to Elijah (1 Kings xix:5).

(6) *The wilderness of temptation* was the place of victory to Christ (Matt. iv:11);

(7) And *the Bethany of sorrow* brought the comfort and sympathy of Christ to the family that He loved (John xi:35, 43, 44).

*   *   *   *

Difficulties met *with* God, always prove to be blessings *from* Him. The clouds bring the showers.

Every *letting down* in a basket of trial, is the precursor to the *lifting up* to the heaven of revelation (see 2 Corinthians xi:33; xii:12).

Heart Disease

"Pride of thine heart" (*Jer. xlix*:16)

Students of physiology at an American University have dissected the heart of the mammoth elephant, Jumbo, who met his death some years ago. This wonderful piece of anatomy has been in Dr. Wilder's possession for some time, preserved in a barrel of alcohol. It is the largest heart in existence, weighing thirty-six and a half pounds, and measuring twenty-eight by twenty-four inches. The wall of the artery is five-eighths of an inch thick, and that of the ventricle three inches thick.

God has dissected man's heart, and He says of it, that it is,

Stout with pride (Isa. ix:9),
Rebellious (Jer. v:23),
Uncircumcised (Jer. ix:26),
Deceitful (Jer. xvii:9),

118

HEART KEEPING

Stony (Eze. xi:19),
Unclean (Matt. xv:19),
Impenitent (Rom. ii:5),
And hard (Mark xvi:14).

* * * *

Pride blinds the mind, curses the soul, warps the judgment, stifles the conscience, and dulls the moral sense.

Heart Keeping

"Keep thy heart with all diligence, for out of it are the issues of life" (*Prov. iv:23*)

A very poor countrywoman was handing to an agent of the Bible Society her "mites," kept in a jug. More than half-a-crown had been gathered in her poverty, chiefly in farthings and half-pence. Not liking to take the money, the agent said: "Are you sure, Mary, that you gave this out of your heart?" "No, sir; indeed, it is out of the jug." "Yes, but did it first come out of your heart?" "Nay, nay, sir, for it was never there." If Christ can keep the heart free from the love of money, He can keep it free from any other sin.

There are some things which should not be in the heart, namely,

Impurity (Eph. v:3),
Love of money (1 Tim. vi:10),
Unbelief (Heb. iii:12),
Pride (Ps. ci:5),
Love of the world (1 John ii:15),
Envy (James iii:14),
And doubting thoughts (Luke xxiv:38).

* * * *

Keep in the good company of the Lord's presence, and the company will keep you good.

DEVOTIONAL BIBLE STUDIES

Hell's Defeat

"He shall crush thy head" (*Gen. iii:15, Rotherham*)

The strange beauty of the Apocryphal Gospels at their best, is perhaps best seen in the story of the "Descent into Hades," or, in English mediæval speech, the "Harrying of Hell." A singular dialogue takes place between Satan and "Hades," in which the latter is represented as in great fear—"the snatching away of Lazarus beforehand seemeth to me to be no good sign, for, not like a dead body, but like an eagle, he flew out of me." And in speaking of Christ's descent into Hades, he says, "And I think He is coming here to raise all the dead." Then a great light streamed into Hades, that had been dark since the Creation. And "our holy father Adam"—this is surely a beautiful touch of poetry—gazed "wondering greatly on the multitude of his descendants." Then all the saints followed the Lord, "and He led them all into the glorious grace of Paradise."

However much we may disagree with the description of Christ's descent into Hades, of this we may be sure,

> He has destroyed by His death the authority of him who had the power of death (Heb. ii:14).
> He has taken away the strong man's armour (Luke xi:22).
> He has seized the spoil from the strong (Is. liii:12). Lowth's rendering.
> He has stripped principalities of powers (Col. ii:15 correct reading).
> He now holds the keys of Hades and death (Rev. i:18).
> He led in ascensional glory "a multitude of captives" (Eph. iv:8, margin);
> And we are now come to the "spirits of just men made perfect" (Heb. xii:23).

*   *   *   *

If we *arm* ourselves with the armor of God, we shall be preserved from Satanic *harm*.

If we are subject to Satan's *shaking* in temptation, let us look to the Lord, then we shall find it will turn to our *making*.

HOLY CARELESSNESS

Holding On

"Hold fast" (*Heb. iv:*14)

"Hold on there," shouted the conductor, as the street car jerked off, in starting on its journey.

"It is all very well to tell us to hold on," observed one of the passengers, "but there is nothing to hold to." Every strap was held by some passenger, and those who crowded on to the car later had no strap to hold to, to keep them steady.

The following things we are exhorted to hold fast:

(1) *The Name of Christ,* which means faithfulness to Him (Rev. ii:13);

(2) *The Experience of His Grace,* which means communion with Him (Rev. ii:25);

(3) *The Place to which we have Attained,* which means reward from Him (Rev. iii:11);

(4) *The Gospel of Salvation,* which means assurance by means of Him (1 Cor. xv:2, R.V.);

(5) *The Good of Grace,* which means progress in Him (1 Thess. v:21);

(6) *The Confidence of Faith,* which means endurance through Him (Heb. iii:6);

And (7) *The Confession of our Lord's Coming,* which means appreciation of Him (Heb. x:23, R.V.).

* * * *

To "hold the fort" of a consecrated life, there is a needs be to be held by the consecrating Christ.

Holy Carelessness

"We are not careful to answer thee" (*Dan. iii:*16)

"If He does not care to take me out, I do not care to go out. It's not that I'm good; it's only that I don't care for anything He doesn't care for. What would it be that all men acquitted me, if God did not trouble Himself about His children."

DEVOTIONAL BIBLE STUDIES

Thus remarked one who had been imprisoned falsely, and who was being condoled with by a friend. Many of God's children have had to suffer wrongfully.

Joseph in prison (Gen. xxxix:20);
The three Hebrews in the furnace (Dan. iii:21);
Daniel in the lion's den (Dan. vi:16);
Peter imprisoned (Acts xii:4);
Paul and Silas in jail (Acts xvi:23);
James beheaded (Acts xii:2);
And last, but not least, Christ Himself (John xix:18).
The special recipe for God's children, who are suffering wrongfully, is found in 1 Peter ii:19-22.

* * * *

Turn your *care* into *prayer*, and you will find that your prayer places you under God's care, and He will kill your care.

How to be Happy

"Happy is that people whose God is the Lord" (Elohim is Jehovah—*Ps. cxliv*:15)

"I was very happy. I sought comfort from the unknown source of my life. He gave me to understand His Son, and so I understood Himself, and was comforted." The secret of all happiness is the Lord Himself.

Many want blessing *from* Christ, and they miss *it*, because they miss *Him*.
When the Lord is our *Salvation*, we are happy in being saved (Isa. xii:2);
When He is our *Sanctification*, then we are happy in His holiness (1 Cor. i:30);
When He is our *Strength*, then we are happy in His power (Ps. lxxxiv:5);
When He is our *Supply*, then we are happy in His fulness (Phil. iv:19);
When He is our *Shelter*, then we are happy in His protection (Ps. lxi:3);

122

HUMILITY

When He is our *Satisfaction,* then we are happy in His love
(Ps. lxv:4);
And when He is our *Sphere,* then we are happy in our en-
vironment (John xv:10, 11).

*　　*　　*　　*

To see the bleeding Christ is to behold a blessing
Saviour. We cease to be blessed when we cease to bless.
There is no sanctification where there is no sacrifice.

Humility

"Humble yourselves in the sight of the Lord" (*Jas. iv*:10)

The frog was wondering how he could get away from
the cold clime in which he found himself during the winter. He got into conversation with some wild geese, and
they suggested he should migrate with them. The difficulty was, how it could be accomplished, seeing the frog
had no wings. "You leave it to me," said the frog, "I've
got a splendid brain." After due deliberation, he got the
geese to pluck up a strong reed, and, when they had done
it, he suggested the following. The geese were to each
of them hold one end of the reed, and he would hold on
to the middle with his mouth. In due time, the geese and
the frog started on their migratory journey. When they
were somewhat on their way, they were passing over a
village, and the villagers turned out to see such an unu-
sual sight as that of two geese with a reed in their mouths
and a frog holding on in the middle by his mouth, and
they cried, "Oh! how wonderful, whoever could have in-
vented such a device?" This remark made the frog so
self-conscious, and puffed him up with such a sense of his
importance, that he could not help opening his mouth,
and exclaiming, "I did it!" His self-advertisement was
his undoing, for the moment he opened his mouth he let
go his hold, and fell to the ground to his death. Pride
will always meet with a fall; while the Lord always
crowns the queen of graces—humility—with His blessing.

DEVOTIONAL BIBLE STUDIES

The following are reasons why we should be humble and humble ourselves:

(1) Because sin has humbled us. Our individual body is called "the body of our *humiliation*" (Phil. iii:21, R.V.).

(2) Because Christ was humbled for us on the cross—"His *humiliation*" (Acts viii:33).

(3) Because it is following in the steps of Christ—"He *humbled* Himself" (Phil. ii:8).

(4) Because it evidences we know the great secret of contentment—"I know how to be *abased*,* &c.," (Phil. iv:12).

(5) Because the Lord commands it—"*Humble* yourselves" (1 Peter v:6).

(6) Because it shows we are obedient, for "*humility*" (Acts xx:19) and "*lowliness*"* are the garments of grace (Eph. iv:2; Phil. ii:3; Col. iii:12; 1 Peter v:5).

(7) Because it shows we are yoked with Him, who is "meek and *lowly** in heart" (Matt. xi:29).

(8) Because the Lord has promised grace and salvation to the humble (Jas. iv:6; 1 Pet. v:5; Luke i:52; Matt. xxiii:12).

The same word or a cognate one signifies humility.

*　　*　　*　　*

Meekness is that quality which defies without defiance the irritations of the world; and the secret of meekness is found in being in the will of God with the Meek and Lowly in heart.

Ignorance

"If thou hadst known" (*Luke xix:42*)

A little girl said in a grammar lesson, "The saddest thing in all her experience was the subjunctive mood in the past perfect tense: 'If I had known, if thou hadst known, if he had known, if they had known.'"

Then she made the comment, "Why did they not know, why did not someone tell them?" "Christ used the subjunctive mood when He wept over Jerusalem and said, 'If thou hadst known,'" etc. That, indeed, was a sad case.

IGNORANCE OF THE UNSAVED

Ignorance is a soul-destroyer (II Pet. iii:5).
Ignorance is a blessing-robber (Acts iii:17).
Ignorance is a God-denier (Acts xviii:30).
Ignorance is a peace-disturber (Luke xxiv:16).
Ignorance is a power-preventer (John i:26).
Ignorance is a progress-retarder (Rom. x:3).
And Ignorance is a mind-darkener (I Pet. i:14).

* * * *

If we would be *sensitive* to the Spirit's *leading*, then we must be *responsive* to the Spirit's *teaching*.

Ignorance of the Unsaved

"They know not" (*Job. xxiv:*16).

"Men are four:
He who knows not, and knows not he knows not,
  He is a fool; shun him.
He who knows not, and knows he knows not,
  He is simple; teach him.
He who knows, and knows not he knows,
  He is asleep; waken him.
He who knows, and knows he knows,
  He is wise; follow him."

The man who "knows not" is in the worst condition of all, for he is

(1) WITHOUT LIGHT—"*They know not* the light" (Job. xxiv:16).

(2) WITHOUT PERCEPTION—"*They know not,* neither will they understand" (Ps. lxxxii:5).

(3) WITHOUT PEACE—"The way of peace *they know not*" (Isa. lix:8).

(4) WITHOUT THE LORD—"*They know not* Me, saith the Lord" (Jer. ix:3; Micah iv:12).

(5) WITHOUT RIGHT—"*They know not* to do right" (Amos iii:10).

125

(6) WITHOUT KNOWLEDGE OF CHRIST AND HIS MISSION—
"*They know not* Him that sent Me" (John xv:21).
"*They know not* what they do" (Luke xxiv:16).

(7) WITHOUT GUIDANCE—"Ye * * * err, because *ye know not* the Scriptures" (Mark xii:24).

*   *   *   *

Not to know the Lord, whom to know is life eternal, is to want the eternal life which comes through knowing Him.

Imitators

"Imitators of God as beloved children" (*Eph. v*:1, R. V.)

John Wesley was once travelling with a general who was angry with his servant. On the man's asking for forgiveness for his offense, the general replied:

"I never forgive!"

"Then, sir," said Wesley quietly, "I hope you never sin!"

The manner and method of our actions toward others are to be based on the Lord's dealings with us.

> We are to forgive as the Lord has forgiven us (Eph. iv:32).
> We are to be perfect in graciousness towards the unthankful, even as the Lord is (Matt. v:44-48).
> We are to be willing, to give our lives for the Lord's people, even as the Lord has given Himself for us (1 John iii:-16).
> We are to serve others as the Lord serves us (John xiii:14).
> And believers in Christ are to love each other even as Christ has loved them (John xiii:34).

*   *   *   *

Holiness is not Christ *and* me, but Christ *in* me. Every place is hallowed ground where He is found.

Jesus Only

"Saw no man, Save Jesus only" (*Matt. xvii*:8)

In going about New York with some English friends on one occasion we saw many curious intimations. *"Never closed"* was the intimation regarding a café. Night and day a meal could be obtained. How like the Throne of Grace: its provision and help are always obtainable. On a motor beer wagon, we read on its tailboard, *"Danger, keep off the beer barrels."* The warning, I presume was to boys who might be inclined to swing on behind. There is danger not only in the barrels, but in the liquor they contain. Happy are all those who keep from the danger. A Mr. Strovinsky announced outside his café, *"Dinners served to strictly orthodox friends only."* Whoever the "orthodox friends" were, they found an exclusive brother who would minister to their needs alone. The announcement caused me to tell my friends the following incident: A hall in the West End of London, where an exclusive sect of Christians met, had the following announcement outside of it, "JESUS ONLY." A storm of wind and rain played havoc with the notice, and tore a piece of the calico away, so that it read, "US ONLY." It is a sorry thing when believers are so inflated with conceit and self-religiosity that they think they are right and everybody else is wrong. JESUS ONLY is right enough when it is applied to *Him,* but it is bad when He is used as a stalking-horse for our own notions. Jesus only is well when it means

Resting on the *only foundation* (1 Cor. iii:11),
Being saved through the *only name* (Acts. iv:12).
Coming to the Father through the *only way* (John xiv:6).
Listening to the *only Son* (Matt. xvii:5).
Following the *only Shepherd* (John x:4).
Drinking the *only living water* (John iv:14).
And feeding upon the *only* satisfying bread (John vi:35).

*　　*　　*　　*

Christianity is not a system of dogmas, it is summed up in a person, as Gladstone said, "Christianity is Christ."

127

DEVOTIONAL BIBLE STUDIES

Joy-filled

"These things write we unto you that, your joy may be full"

(1 *John* i:4)

A lady overpowered with joy after listening to the Word of God said, "I feel like a cat in cat-nip." "Cat-nip!" exclaimed the preacher; "I don't know what you mean." It was then explained that cats love to roll in a certain herb, which they eat when sick; and that they are so pleased when they find themselves in cat-nip that they roll and gamble for very joy. It was a very expressive way to denote her joy.

> Certainly the child of God has every reason to be joyful.
> His sins are forgiven (1 John ii:12).
> His peace is made (Col. i:20).
> His life is hid (Col. iii:3).
> His inheritance is kept (1 Pet. i:4).
> His need is supplied (Phil. iv:19).
> His trials are compensations (11 Cor. iv:17).
> And his way is watched (Job xxiii:10).

*   *   *   *

The joy of the Lord comes to those who follow the Lord of the joy. Joy-finders are Lord-followers.

Kept by Christ

"He is able to keep that which I have committed unto Him"

(2 *Tim.* i:12)

On one occasion Dr. Dale was asked by a Roman Catholic priest, whom he greatly respected, when he was going to cease from public work and begin to look after his soul. Dale's reply was not only characteristic of the man, but an index of the difference between the two religious ideals. "I have given my soul to Christ to look after, and He can do it much better than I can."

KEPT FOR CHRIST

Christ's love keeps the soul love-full (II Cor. v:14).
His joy keeps the heart joyful (John xv:11).
His peace keeps the mind restful (Phil. iv:7).
His truth keeps the life healthful (John xvii:17).
His mercies keep the inner being praiseful (Ps. ciii:1, 2).
His grace keeps the spirit powerful (II Cor. xii:9).
And His glory keeps the outlook cheerful (Col. iii:4).

*　　*　　*　　*

Concentrate your faith on Christ by following only Him, and He will *consecrate* you in His grace in making you like to Him.

Kept for Christ

"Preserved (R. V. "Kept for") in Jesus Christ" (*Jude i.*)

"I am just like a packet that is all ready to go by train —packed, corded, labelled, paid for, and on the platform, waiting for the express to come by, and take me to glory," so said the late James Smith, of Cheltenham, as he was lying on his bed of sickness. Can we not see a parable in the simile used?

> Every true child of God is "packed" up in the beautiful covering of the Christ of God (II Cor. v:21).
> "Corded" by the imperishable cords of the love of God (Hosea xi:4).
> "Labelled" with the unmistakable seal of the earnest of the Spirit of God (Eph. i:13).
> "Paid for" by the unparalleled price of the blood of the Son of God (I Cor. vi:20).
> "On the platform" of the unique grace of God (Rom. v:2).
> "Waiting" for the express of the coming of the ·Beloved of God (Phil. iii:20, 21).
> And then to be taken into the splendour of the glory of God (Rev. xxi:10, 11).

*　　*　　*　　*

The Lord finds His portion in the saints, as well as the saints finding their portion in Him.

DEVOTIONAL BIBLE STUDIES

Kept Momentarily

"I the Lord do keep it; I will water it every moment"

(*Is. xxvii*:3)

One of the most interesting things in hymnology is the origin of a hymn. We will refer to the one written by the late Major Whittle, known as "Moment by moment," the first verse of which is:

"Dying with Jesus, by death reckoned mine;
Living with Jesus, a new life Divine;
Looking to Jesus, till glory doth shine—
Moment by moment, O Lord, I am Thine."

Major Whittle was led to write this hymn in the following manner. During the World's Fair at Chicago, in a meeting, the hymn, "I need Thee every hour," was sung. When the meeting was over, as the people were dispersing, Henry Varley put his arm round the shoulders of the Major, and said to him, "I am not satisfied with Christ every hour, I need Him every *moment*." Whereupon the Major went home and sat on into the small hours of the morning, penning the above hymn, which has been an inspiration to many and a blessing to all who have heard it.

The constancy and comfort of the Lord's keeping is beautifully and blessedly emphasized in Ps. cxxi.

(1) The Fact of His Keeping—"The Lord is thy keeper."

(2) The Vigilance of His Keeping—"Shall neither slumber nor sleep."

(3) The Comfort of His Keeping—"The Lord is thy Shade."

(4) The Time of His Keeping—"Day * * * Night."

(5) The Holiness of His Keeping—"Preserve thee from all Evil."

(6) The Inness of His Keeping—"He shall preserve thy soul."

KINDNESS

(7) The Continuance of His Keeping—"The Lord shall preserve thy going out and thy coming in, from this time forth and even for evermore."

* * * *

If we *look up to* the Lord and delight in Him, we shall have no time to *look down* and get into the dumps.

Kindness

"I will surely shew thee kindness' (2 *Sam. ix*:7)

Robert Louis Stevenson wrote in a letter: "It is the history of our kindnesses that alone make the world tolerable. If it were not for that, for the effect of kind words, kind looks, kind letters, multiplying, spreading, making one happy through another, and bringing forth benefits, some thirty, some fifty, some a thousandfold, I should be tempted to think our life a practical jest in the worst possible spirit."

"Kindnesses," says J. R. Miller, "are the small coins of love. We should always be ready to scatter these bright coins wherever we go. Kindnesses are usually little things that we do as we go along the way."

"They are little, simple things to do—
To sweep a room, to bake a loaf of bread,
Kiss a hurt finger, tie a baby's shoe,
To mend a crying schoolboy's broken sled.

"Such little, simple things. But they above,
Who on our little world attendant wait;
And joyful wait, note only if through love
The deed be done, to count the work as great."

We do not know the value of these little acts, or their far-reaching influence. In the parable, we are told how a mustard seed grew into a tree, amid whose branches the birds perched and sang. It is said that the fuchsia was first introduced into England by a sailor boy, who brought a single plant from some foreign country as a present for his mother. She put it in her modest window, and it became an attraction to all who passed by. From that little plant came all the fuchsias in England. The boy did not know when, in loving thought for his mother, he carried home the little plant, what a beautiful thing he was doing, what a ministry of good he was starting, how widely the influence of his simple thought of love would reach. We never know when we do any smallest thing in love for Christ what the end of it will be, what a harvest of good will come from it.

> Kindness is God-like in its action and proves we know His love to us—See Titus iii:4, and Eph. ii:7.
> Kindness is a part in God's chorus of grace, which faith adds to itself (2 Pet. i:7).
> Kindness is obligatory to faith, for we are exhorted to "Be kindly affectioned one to another with brotherly *love*" or kindness (Rom. xii:10; Heb. xiii:1).
> "Unfeigned *love*" or kindness is to be the character of our actions (1 Pet. i:22).
> Kindness is one of the traits of the Holy Spirit's fruit (Gal. v:22), and the garb of the new man (Col. iii:12).

$$* \quad * \quad * \quad *$$

"A word spoken pleasantly is a large spot of sunshine on a sad heart." Therefore, "give others the sunshine, tell Jesus the rest."

Kisses of Love

"Let Him kiss me with the kisses of His mouth" (*Song of Sol. i:2*)

"Nurse," piped a little squeally voice; "Nurse, *why* did you kiss me?" so exclaimed a wee laddie to the nurse in Dr. Barnado's Home. Before the answer could be given, he himself repeated, "It was nice; but why did you, nurse?" And the good woman, who had been trying to keep the tears back, simply stooped down, and whispered to him, "Dear little Ted, you are all alone; you have no mother; you have no one to visit you, and to love you. But I love you, that is why—" and she kissed him again. The child's worn face became irradiated with a light of love to which it had hitherto been a stranger! But presently the boy, looking at his nurse, heaved a deep sigh—a sigh that was heard all over the ward, and that came from a little sad but glad heart, which could not banish memory! And then he exclaimed in a voice, as if he *must* tell nurse that he understood, and was not ungrateful: "But—but" (there *was* a but) "nobody never kissed me afore," explained the little chap; and then his eyes were closed again, and his hands clasped firmly the kind hand of his new-found friend.

The prayer of the child of God, as he is in communion with the Beloved, is, "Let Him kiss me with the kisses of His mouth" (Song of Solomon i:2), and He responds by giving us

The *kiss of reconciliation,* as the father did the prodigal (Luke xv:20).

The *kiss of welcome,* as Laban did Jacob (Gen. xxix:13).

The *kiss of fellowship,* as Joseph did his brethren (Gen. xlv:15).

The *kiss of greeting,* as Aaron did Moses (Ex. iv:27).

The *kiss of love, as* David did Jonathan (1 Sam. xx:41).

The *kiss of friendship,* as David did Barzillai (11 Sam. xix:39).

And the *kiss of approval,* to those who act rightly (Pro. xxiv:26).

* * * *

If we cannot be *apostles* to go to the regions beyond, we can all be *epistles* to live and labor like Christ where we are.

Leaving out the "Not"

"The Lord is my Shepherd, I shall not want" (*Ps. xxiii:*1)

A minister once called on an aged woman to read and pray with her. She commenced to tell him her troubles and poverty, and said she felt sure she should come to want. The good man said nothing in reply, but asked for the Bible as he would like to read to her. He chose the 23rd Psalm, and began reading thus: "The Lord is my Shepherd, I shall want." "Stop, stop," said the old woman, "it isn't put like that in my Bible, read it again." He did so, repeating it as he read it before, whereupon she took the Book from his hand, and looked for herself. She manifested great delight on finding that the word "not," was there. She took the reproof so wisely administered, and never again said that she should want.

To leave out the "not" of some of God's "shall nots" would turn our heaven to hell. Think of the following:

(1) SALVATION—"*Shall not* come into condemnation" (John v:24).
(2) SANCTIFICATION—"Sin *shall not* have dominion over you" (Rom. vi:14).
(3) STABILITY—"*Shall not* be moved" (Ps. xvi:8).
(4) SATISFACTION—"*Shall not* be taken from her" (Luke x:42).
(5) SHINING—"*Shall not* walk in darkness" (John viii:12).
(6) SUCCESS—"He *shall not* fail nor be discouraged" (Is. xlii:4).
And (7) ASSURANCE—"*Shall not* be put to shame" (Rom. x:11).

*   *   *   *

If we *shamble* with God's Word and *prayer*, we shall soon *ramble* where the devil will scare.

Let: Let: Let:

"Let him hear what the Spirit saith" (*Rev. iii*:6)

Archdeacon Madden, of Warrington, was sitting in his study; and heard a succession of noises overhead. Going into the nursery, his little son was hoisting the Venetian blind, and letting it fall, with a bang, to a chant, "Let the sunshine in!" He went back unseen, and drew inspiration from the words, "The time of the singing of birds has come."

LIFE HOOKS

Some of the Holy Spirit's "Lets" are full of meaning, and we shall know they are if we *let* them operate.

CHRIST'S HUMBLE MIND—"*Let* this mind be in you, which was also in Christ Jesus" (Phil. ii:5), by letting Christ be your Mind.

CHRIST'S KEEPING PEACE—"*Let* the peace of Christ rule in your hearts" (Col. iii:15), by allowing Christ to be the Arbitator in all things.

CHRIST'S INSTRUCTING WORD—"*Let* the Word of Christ dwell in you" (Col. iii:16), by letting Christ be the Teacher.

CHRIST'S SEASONING GRACE—"*Let* your speech be always with grace, seasoned with salt" (Col. iv:6), by letting Christ be your Seasoning.

CHRIST PERFECTING LOVE—"*Let* us go on to perfection (Heb. vi:1), by being borne on by His love.

CHRIST'S ATTRACTIVE PERSON—"*Let* us run the race with patience, looking unto Jesus" (Heb. xii:1).

CHRIST'S HALLOWING COMPANY—"*Let* us go forth therefore unto Him" (Heb. xiii:13), for He is hallowed and hallows all who come in contact with Him.

*   *   *   *

When we hearken to the voice of the Spirit in His Word, then we know the vitality of the Spirit in our hearts.

Life Hooks

"Prepared unto every good work" (2 *Tim.* ii:21)

"In the London docks may be seen 'life hooks,' hanging ready for use at a moment's notice, for the rescue of the drowning; they are consecrated to this one service, and hence, have a sacredness attached to them; to tamper with them is to subject yourself to a heavy penalty, and this is right."

135

DEVOTIONAL BIBLE STUDIES

Every believer should be an instrument, ready for the Master's use.

He should be a "sharp threshing instrument" (Isa. xli:15).
A "vessel meet" (II Tim. ii:21).
A "polished shaft" (Isa. xlix:2).
A fruitful branch (John xv:5).
A legible epistle (II Cor. iii:2).
A faithful witness (Acts i:8).
And a true ambassador (II Cor. v:20).

*   *   *   *

Nobility and ability are two good bilities to possess, especially if they are nobility of character and the ability of grace.

Life in Christ

"He that hath the Son hath life" (1 *John v*:12)

Dr. Magee, in speaking of the life of the Christian, says: "The life of the Christian is not a natural, but a supernatural life. Christ established on earth a kingdom, *within which is to be found that which is not to be found beyond its limits.*" In a word, we claim for Christianity, that it is not a code of morals merely, nor a philosophy, nor a creed, nor a system of religious discipline; but that, over and above all these, it is a *life,* a new vital force in the world, and that this vital force is in the Christ we worship.

That Christianity is a "life" may be seen if we take but seven words in the tenth chapter of John.

(1) The *"saved"* of complete deliverance from sin's control and consequences through Christ's merit and mercy.
(2) The *"in and out"* of hallowed fellowship in life's worship and work.
(3) The *"pasture"* which is the outcome and reward of walking with the Lord and in His Word (John x:9).
(4) The *"hear"* of attentive faith to the Saviour's voice, which expresses itself in obedience to His Word.

(5) The *"follow"* of the walk of holiness in treading in the footsteps of Christ's example (John x:27).

(6) The *"know"* of the Shepherd's personal acquaintance with each of His blood-bought sheep, and the *"know"* of the sheep's acquaintance with their Leader (John x: 4, 14, 27).

And (7) the *"My hand"* and *"the Father's hand"* of love's powerful grip to keep the sheep to, and for, Himself (John x:28, 29).

*   *   *   *

The Christian life is not a label to put on, but a life to be lived out. Christ is the Life and the Liver-out.

Life in Death

"Be filled in the Spirit" (*Eph. v:*18, *R. V., mar.*)

The maintenance of spiritual life in an atmosphere poisonous to the spirit, is the practical problem of the Christian in this world of sin. It can be done only through the inbreathing of the Holy Spirit. A most interesting parallel of this is to be found in an account of an invention by Dr. Eugene Erlwein. He has patented a railroad car in which fish may be transported alive though entirely removed from the water, so that "fish alive and kicking" may now be received at any distance from the waters in which they are captured. In other words, the salmon of the Columbia, the trout of the Maine, the bass of Florida, may be shipped to any part of the United States with as great facility as a bale of hay or a crate of oranges. And when the fish reach their destination they are as lively as if they were in their native element, although they have not seen the water since they were taken from the sea or river." This is done by keeping the fish in oxygen, with or without the use of water. In the fish car, the fish are kept in a small amount of water, which is constantly circulated through a machine which extracts the carbonic acid gas and charges it with oxygen.

In like manner the Christian lives a spiritual life in an atmosphere deadly to the unprotected spirit, because the Spirit of God, like oxygen, is breathed into him in the constant exercise of prayer and communion with God.

The following seven Scriptures give some little idea of what is found as we are found in the atmosphere of the Spirit. The Greek preposition *"en"* is found in each sentence, and is given in italics:

(1) *Power*—"Cast out demons *by* the Spirit" (Matt. xii: 28).

(2) *Joy*—"Joy *in* the Holy Ghost" (Rom. xiv:17).

(3) *Holiness*—"Sanctified *by* the Holy Ghost" (Rom. xv: 16).

(4) *Access*—"Access *by* one Spirit" (Eph. ii:18).

(5) *Prayer*—"Praying *in* the Spirit" (Eph. vi:18; Jude 20).

(6) *Love*—"Love *in* the Spirit" (Col. i:8).

And (7) *Ministry*—"*In* the Holy Ghost" (1 Thess. i:5).

* * * *

Respond to the ability of God by prayer, and that will cause you to abound in activity for Him.

Life Which is Worth Living

"Life Indeed" (1 *Tim. vi*:19, *R. V.*)

One has said, *"Life* is short—only four letters in it. Three-quarters of it is a *'lie'* and half of it is an *'if.'"* We may add, by transposing the letters you can make it into a *"file."* The child of God can make something better of the word *life* by making an acrostic on it in association with Christ, and say,

L—"Living in Christ, I am saved" (Rom. viii:1, 2).

I—"Instructed by Christ, I am rested" (Matt. xi:29).

F—"Following after Christ, I have fellowship with Him" (John xii:24-26).

E—"Enduring through Christ, I am victorious" (Phil. iv:- 13).

* * * *

He who possesses eternal life need not advertise the fact; but the life proclaims itself in acts of love.

LIVING NAME, BUT A DEAD LIFE

Living after Death

"Their works do follow them" (*Rev. xiv:13*)

No useful Christian leaves this world without being missed. When Josephine was carried out to her grave, there were a great many women of pride and position who went out after her; but I am most affected by the story that 2,000 of the poor of France followed her coffin, wailing until the air rang again, because they had lost their last earthly friend. "Blessed are the dead who die in the Lord; they rest from their labors, and their works do follow them!"

There are certain individuals who are mentioned in the New Testament, whose works are following them, by the influence they have, and are exerting.

(1)   Abraham the believer (James ii:21).
(2)   Stephen the faithful (Acts vi:5).
(3)   Mary the devoted (Mark xiv:9).
(4)   Dorcas the useful (Acts ix:36-42).
(5)   Epaphras the prayerful (Col. iv:12).
(6)   John the loving (John xiii:23).
(7)   Paul the consecrated (Phil. iii:7-14).

*   *   *   *

The memory of the wicked is like a dead tree, it soon decays and is forgotten; but the savour of a holy life is like radium, it is indestructible in its beneficence and influence.

Living Name, but a Dead Life

"Thou hast a name that thou livest, and art dead" (*Rev. iii:1*)

"Right opinion, except it springs from obedience to the truth, is but so much rubbish on the golden floor of the temple." So says one of our modern writers. Right opinion should be as the rudder to the ship, supposing always the opinion is born of the truth of God, guiding to right action. But to hold the truth, so as to have a correct view of it only, and not be held by it, that it may be lived out, is to be wrong.

> Right opinion, without a corresponding action, is,
> To have companionship with king Saul in his disobedience (I Sam. xv:22, 23).
> To be like the man who built his house on the sand (Matt. vii:26).
> Like the disobedient son, who promised to do, and did not (Matt. xxi:30).
> Like Israel, who observed rites and ceremonies, but who were displeasing to Jehovah (Isa. i:13, 14).
> Like Judas, who, while being in the company of Christ, was acting against Him (John xiii:27).
> Not like those of whom Christ speaks, when He speaks of those who are His near relations (Matt. xii:50); and not like His true disciples (John viii:31).

*　　*　　*　　*

The measure of the power we possess is to be gauged by the weight of our character. What we are, tells; not what we say. To have the voice of prate, and not the virtue of practise, is to be a hypocrite.

Located

"In Christ Jesus" (Eph. i:1)

Having to visit St. Louis during the World's Fair, I was rather amused at being asked by a man, "Have you got your location, sir?" He meant, had I secured apartments. He evidently took me for a visitor to the World's Fair, and thought I was looking for a lodging. A Christian does not need a location, for he is in the

140

LOOK BENEATH THE SURFACE

best of locations, being in "Christ." (2 Cor. v:17) ; and being in Christ, he should be careful to locate himself

In the love of God for inspiration (Jude 21).
In the truth of God for sanctification (11 John 4).
In the Spirit for preservation (Gal. v:16).
In the peace of God for pacification (Phil. iv:7).
In the Lord for exultation (Phil. iii:1).
In the faith for opposition (1 Pet. v:9).
And *in the grace* of God for inudation (11 Tim. ii:1). To be located in Him is to be in the best of locations.

* * * *

It is not the man that makes the Christian, it is the Christ in the man that makes the man a Christian.

Look Beneath the Surface

"Judge not according to the appearance, but judge righteous judgment" (*John vii:24*)

Mr. Roosevelt, when President of the United States, made an inspection of the immigrant station at Ellis Island. He was pointed out to a German woman as the President.

She could not be made to understand the terms, so "Kaiser," or "Chief" of the Americans was suggested to her.

This she understood, and pulling out a dollar-note from her pocket, she made a deep study of the Indian in full war-paint and feathers whose vignette is portrayed thereon.

She then looked at the President, once more gazed at the dollar-note, and, seeing no resemblance between the Indian and Mr. Roosevelt, burst into laughter, and cried out in German: "You can't fool me!"

In her ignorance the woman judged that the man before her should correspond to the figure on the dollar-note. We often make a similar mistake when we judge things from a standpoint of our own, or by what seems to be.

(1)   Lot thought the well-watered plain of Sodom was the best place for occupation, but he found it led to soul vexation and loss (Gen. xiii:10; II Pet. ii:8).

(2)   Ahab summed up Elijah as a troubler and an "enemy," but he was himself what he thought the prophet was (I Kings xviii:17; xxi:20).

(3)   Job was misrepresented by his friends, when they said the reason of God's chastisement upon him was because of sin committed (Job viii:6), whereas God was but testing His servant.

(4)   Peter judged he was doing God's service when he urged Christ to "pity Himself" and keep from the cross, whereas he was the instrument of Satan in seeking to keep Christ from Calvary (Matt. xvi:22, margin).

(5)   The friends of Christ thought He was "beside himself," because of His peculiar and powerful ministry (Mark iii:21) they were ignorant of His Divine personality and work.

(6)   Festus said Paul was "mad," because of his holy enthusiasm and boldness in declaring the gospel—he did not know that he himself was wrong, therefore not capable of judging (Acts xxvi:24. 25).

(7)   Simon Magus judged that the working of the Holy Spirit was some new kind of sorcery, and that he could be initiated into its secret if he paid for the knowledge (Acts viii:18-22).

(8)   And the apostles were judged to be upsetters of the order of things, whereas they who thought they "turned the world upside-down" were wrong-side up themselves (Acts xvii:6).

*   *   *   *

The best way to make all *sure* is to keep all *pure*.

Love's Action and Attitude

"Like as a father pitieth his children, so the Lord pitieth them that fear Him" (*Ps. ciii*:13)

"Why don't you walk straight?" said an angry nurse to a wee mite of a girlie, who had fallen down, through her want of attention; and she accompanied her interrogation with a vigorous shake, which made the poor child cry with intensity.

LOVE'S BANDS

I could not help thinking that our heavenly Father, when He picks us up, through our own fault in falling, never deals with us after the fashion of the rough shake of the nurse.

(1) With every expression of regret, there is a promise of help (Hosea xiii:9).

(2) With every rebuke of love, there is a pledge of restoration (Jer. iii:20-22).

(3) With every question of enquiry, there is an answer of grace (Gen. iv:6, 7).

(4) With every stroke of chastisement, there is a purpose of love (Jer. xxxi:18).

(5) With every cry of disappointment, there is a revelation of mercy (Matt. xxiii:37).

(6) With every call to duty, there is a promise of blessing (Jer. i:7, 8).

(7) And with every move of Satan, there is a countermove by Christ (Luke xxii:31, 32; II Cor. xii:7-9)

*   *   *   *

Love is an *eradicator* and an *indicator,* for it not only expels the evil, but it also compels to obedience.

Love's Bands

"Bands of Love" (*Hosea xi:4*)

"There are four kinds of love," so said a friend in course of conversation.

"The Perfect loving the Perfect,
The Imperfect loving the Imperfect,
The Perfect loving the Imperfect,
The Imperfect loving the Perfect."

The Father loving the Son proves the first (John iii:35).

The Pharisees loving the uppermost seats, and Demas loving the world illustrates the second (Luke xi:43; 2 Tim. iv:10).

God loving the world is evidence of the third (John iii:16). and the believer loving the LORD proclaims the fourth (1 John iv:19).

143

DEVOTIONAL BIBLE STUDIES

The Perfect loving the imperfect is illustrated in the bands of Love's binding.

The two main bands of love which hold the saints to the Lord, are, the fact of it, and its manner. The following seven bands of love bind us to His heart.

(1) *Christ's Life illustrates His Love.* On seven different occasions we read of Christ being "moved with compassion." (1) When He saw the crowd as harassed and tired sheep (Matt. ix:36); (2) when He beheld the people discouraged because of John's death (Matt. xiv:14); (3) when the people were faint with hunger (Matt. xv:32); (4) when He looked upon the sightless eyes of the blind men; (5) when He heard the cry of the beseeching leper (Mark i:41); (6) when He saw the man possessed with demons (Mark v:19); and (7) when He looked upon the tears of the sorrowing mother (Luke vii:13). There is no need too great for Him to meet, no weariness that He cannot rest, no discouragement that He cannot remove, no hunger that He cannot satisfy, no ignorance that He cannot enlighten, no disease that He cannot cleanse, no demon that He cannot expel and no sorrow that He cannot comfort.

(2) *His Cross Displays His Love* (Gal. ii:20; Eph. v:2, 25). As we gaze upon the cross the whole being of Christ speaks with substitutionary love, and the whole environment is replete with vicarious suffering! His heart of love bleeds in death, to cleanse us; His hands of love are wounded, to heal us; His feet of love are nailed, to release us; His side of love is pierced, to assure us; His back of love is lacerated, to endow us; His body of love is stripped, to clothe us; His lips of love are parched, to bless us; His tongue of love is agonized, to calm us; His head of love is cursed with thorns, to crown us; His cross of love is shameful, to enrich us; and His death of love is awful, to quicken us.

The whole surroundings of the cross throb with love. The darkened heavens are bright with love's joy; the rending rocks are opened with love's grace; the cruel tree is blooming with love's fruit; the hate of man is the dark background for love's action; the malice of hell is the opportunity for love's triumph; the mockery of the crowd is the call for love's patience; and the suffering for sin unfolds the provision of love's grace.

(3) *His grace confirms His Love.* Loved, loosed, and lifted are the suggested thoughts as we listen to the

LOVE'S BANDS

music of Love's action: "Unto Him that loved us and washed us from our sins in His own blood and made us kings and priests unto God" (Rev. i:5). Loved with a love which is continuous in blessing (R. V. "Loveth"); "loosed" (R. V.) from all binding influences that are enslaving in their hold; and lifted to the honor and dignity of kingly and priestly service. The colored man said, "grace means, receiving everything for nothing." Love blesses us with its blessing (Eph. i:3), benefits us with its grace (2 Cor. ix:8), beautifies us with its clothing (Eph. vi:10-16), brightens us with its joy (Luke xv:24), bequeathes us with its riches (Phil. iv:18), binds us to its affection (Eph. ii:7), and builds us with its truth (Acts xx:32).

(4) *His Truth affirms His Love.* Christ loves His own to the end (John xiii:1). The word *"telos"* rendered *"end"* in John xiii:1, is translated *"uttermost"* in 1 Thess. ii:16. He loves to the uttermost of our need, and to the uttermost of His grace. The use of *"telos"* where it is rendered *"end"* may illustrate what love has done, is doing, and will yet do. The end of love's work was, that Christ might be *"the end* of the law for righteousness" (Rom. x:4); the end of love's bestowment is that the Lord might lead us through the path of holiness to *"the end"* of everlasting life (Rom. vi:22); Love's service is to confirm us "unto *the end"* of all His requirement (1 Cor. i:8); and Love's name is the assurance that He will accomplish all His plan, for He is "the Beginning and *the End"* (Rev. i:8; 21, 6; 22, 13). Whom Love takes up, Love never gives up. His Love, as He assures us in His Word, is, Divine in its nature (1 John iv:8), eternal in its character (Jer. xxxi:3), constant in its affection (S. S. viii:7), tender in its regard (John xi:36), faithful in its service (John xvii:17), practical in its discipline (Heb. xii:6), and powerful in its keeping (Deut. xxxiii:3).

(5) *Christ's Contemporaries testify to His Love.* John the apostle tells of Christ's particular love for Martha, Mary and Lazarus, and when the Jews saw Christ weeping at the grave of Lazarus, they said, "Behold how He loved him," and Christ commands us "to love each other even as He loves us (John xi:5, 36; xiii:23). He does not lose us in the crowd. He generally uses the personal pronoun "thou" or "thee" and not the plural "you." "I will, be thou clean," He said to the leper (Mark i:41), "To-day, thou shalt be with Me in Paradise" was His promise to the dying thief (Luke

xxiii:43). He recognized what the little girl affirmed, when in reply to her brother's question, what loving one another meant, "why you are *one* and I am the other." Christ is the One who always loves the other.

(6) *Christ's Spirit imparts His Love.* The love of God is shed abroad in our hearts by the Holy Spirit (Rom. v:5). The intensity of love's operation may be better understood when we see the use of the Greek word *"ekchuno."* The word is rendered *"spilled"* in Luke v:37; *"gushed out"* in Acts i:18, *"poured out"* in Acts x:45, and *"ran greedily"* in Jude ii. The Spirit of God is the imparter to infuse and inflame with the love of God. When He burns with Holy intensity, there will be the flame of constant loyalty.

(7) *Christ's Operation through us demonstrates His love.* The watchword of Paul was, "The Love of Christ constraineth us" (2 Cor. ✓:14). Here again we have an expressive word. The word is translated *"throng"* in speaking of a pressing crowd, *"held"* in describing a a detaining force (Luke xxii:63), *"Pressed"* in stating Paul's being held by the Spirit's power (Acts xviii:5), it is used to describe a person in a *"strait"* place (Phil. i:23) and of one *"taken with"* a fever (Luke iv:38). The love of Christ is a power to move us in holiness of life, a pressure to confine in the will of God, as a guard to confine in the truth, a hand to detain us for the service of God, and an enviroment in which the graces of the Spirit thrive.

Love's binding is our blessing, for He, who is Love, binds us to Himself and makes us like Himself. When He loves in us, He always loves to purpose.

Love's Endurance

"Love * * * endureth all things" (1 *Cor. xiii*:7)

The following is related of one Solomon Eccles, who was committed to prison for refusing to swear, and who while in prison was scoffed at by one Evans. Evans pulled off his hat in a scoffing manner to Solomon, who thereupon advised him to be sober. "This put the man in a chafe, and he struck Solomon a violent blow on the cheek, upon which Solomon turned to him the other cheek, and he struck him again on that. Solomon again turned to him the other, and he again struck him the third time. All of which Solomon bore patiently, thus literally performing the precept of Christ, and obtaining a Christian conquest over his opposer."

Endurance is ever an evidence of the work of grace, and the reality of faith. The stony ground hearer endures "for a time" (Mark iv:17), but there is no lastingness. The links in the golden chain of endurance are as follows:

(1) The *Example of Endurance* is Christ, and we are exhorted to "consider Him" who "*endured* the cross" and "*endured* * * * contradiction" (Heb. xii:2, 3).

(2) The *Power of Endurance* is the Lord, for He says, "I make to *endure*" (Psa. lxxxix:29, 36).

(3) The *Secret of Endurance* is faith in God, as Moses found, who "*endured* as seeing Him who is invisible" (Heb. xi:27).

(4) The *Witness of Endurance* is borne as we "*endure* hardness," "*endure* all things," and "*endure* afflictions," (II Tim. ii:3, 10; iv:5).

(5) The *Worship of Endurance* is evidenced as we "*endure* grief, for this is acceptable" (I Pet. ii:19, R. V.).

(6) The *Blessedness of Endurance* is emphasised by the Spirit when He says, "Blessed is the man that *endureth* temptation" (Jas. i:12; v:11).

(7) The *Reward of Endurance* is illustrated in Abraham, who "after he had patiently *endured,* obtained the promise" (Heb. vi:15).

*   *   *   *

Love is never concerned about its ease, it loves to sacrifice itself for others, and is never concerned about its sacrifice.

Love's Example

"Because He laid down His life for us, we ought to lay down our lives for the brethren" (I *John iii*:16)

In George MacDonald's *Mary Marston,* he represents Mary talking to Mr. Redmain, who is conscious of his past wicked life, as he is face to face with death. He asks her the question: "You think God answers prayer, do you?"

"I do."

"Then I wish you would ask Him to let me off—I mean, to let me die right out when I do die. What's the good of making a body miserable?"

"That, I am sure it would be of no use to pray for. He certainly will not throw away a thing He has made because that thing may be foolish enough to prefer the dust-hole to the cabinet."

"Wouldn't you do it now, if I asked you?"

"I would not. I would leave you in God's hands rather than inside the gate of heaven."

"I don't understand you. And you wouldn't say so if you cared for me! Only, why should you care for me!"

"I would give my life for you."

"Come now! I don't believe that."

"Why, I couldn't be a Christian if I wouldn't!"

"You are getting absurd!" he cried. But he did not look exactly as if he thought it.

"Absurd!" repeated Mary. "Isn't it that what makes *Him* our Saviour? How could I be His disciple, if I wouldn't do as He did?"

"You are saying a good deal!"

"Can't you see that I have no choice?"

"*I* wouldn't do that for anybody under the sun!"

"You are not His disciple; you have not been going about with Him."

"And you have?"

"Yes, for many years. Besides, I cannot help thinking there is One for whom you would do it."

"If you mean my wife, you never were more mistaken. I would do nothing of the sort."

"I did not mean your wife. I mean Jesus Christ."

"O, I daresay! Well, perhaps! if I knew Him as you do, and if I were quite sure He wanted it done for Him."

"He does want it done for Him—always and every

day—not for His own sake, though it does make Him very glad. To give up your way for His is to die for Him; and when anyone will do that, then He is able to do anything for him; for then, and not till then, He gets such a hold of him that He can lift him up, and set him down beside Himself."

To act like Christ proves we are Christ's.

Love's Walk—"Walk as He walked" (1 John ii:6).
Love's Place—"Walk in the light as He is in the light" (1 John i:7).
Love's Grace—"Forgiving one another, even as God for Christ's sake hath forgiven you" (Eph. iv:32).
Love's Service—"I * * * washed your feet, ye ought to wash one another's feet" (John xiii:14).
Love's Purity—"Purifieth himself, even as He is pure" (1 John iii:3).
Love's Endurance—"An Example, that ye should follow His steps" (1 Pet. ii:21).
Love's Love—"Love one another, as I have loved you" (John xiii:34).

*　　*　　*　　*

When enthusiasm is kindled by the fire of Calvary's love, it will find an outlet in ministering, as Christ did, to the need of others. The sun shines the sun because it is the sun that shines.

Love's Mantle

"Love covereth a multitude of sins" (1 *Pet. iv:8*, R. V.)

The artist of Alexander the Great was very desirous of producing a faithful portrait of the great general, but he was anxious to hide the ugly scar upon the side of his face, which was the telltale of a wound received in one of his battles. He, therefore, represented the great conqueror in a reflective mood, with his head resting upon his hand, and his fore-finger covering the disfiguring scar. Love ever seeks to cover the scars which are the marks left by the old master sin.

How does love cover sin? Certainly not by aiding others in sin, nor by minimising its evil, nor by excusing its iniquity. How, then?

(1) By acting towards others, as God has acted towards us, in a forgiving spirit (Ps. xxxii:5), as Joseph did to his brethren (Gen. xlv:4-15).

(2) By seeking to heal the effects of sin in the repentant sinner, by pouring into his heart and mind the oil of prayerful sympathy and the joy of encouragement, as the good Samaritan did to the spoiled man (Luke x:34).

(3) By seeking to remove the shame, which another's folly has brought upon him, as Noah's sons did when they discovered their father in a drunken condition, and covered him up (Gen. ix:23).

(4) By restoring a brother who has fallen, in the spirit of Christ, that he may be prevented from being tripped up again, as Paul sought to restore, and to guide the Church at Corinth in their conduct towards the erring brother (1 Cor. v:5; 11 Cor.. ii:7, 8).

(5) By rescuing those who are liable to sin through unholy associations, as the angels did Lot (Gen. xix:10, 11).

(6) By removing temptation out of the way of those who are weak, by our personal example, as the Holy Spirit directs in Rom. xiv.

And (7) By refusing to talk about the past of anyone, who has repented, whether it be saint or sinner, as the Lord Himself, who not only forgives, but forgets too (Heb. x:17).

* * * *

The love of God is a torrent to bear us on in its sweep; love is a channel to hem us in, in its sway; and an ocean to embrace us in its fulness. Love is a power to move us, a sphere to limit us, and a fulness to enrich us.

Love's Recognition

"I know Him, whom I have believed" (2 Tim. i:12, R. V.)

Children are ever helpful in the expression of their faith and the devotion of their love. The following incident is a practical illustration. A little girl, whose Sunday School teacher had died some time before, had a dream that she was in Heaven, and went round being introduced by her friend to several well-known characters. The girl, in relating the dream to her mother, said, "My teacher introduced me to Paul, and Abraham, and David, and a lot of other Bible characters."

"Did she not introduce you to Jesus?" asked the mother."

"Oh, no," was the prompt reply, "I knew Jesus as soon as I saw Him, I did not need an introduction to Him."

Those who have been introduced to Christ by the Holy Spirit, do not need any further introduction to Him, for the moment we see Him we shall know Him

By the *nail-prints* of His atonement (Zech. xiii:6).
By the *glory-face* of His splendor (Rev. xxii:4).
By the *lifting-power* of His attractability (1 Thess. iv:17).
By the *welcome-voice* of His greeting (Cant. ii:10).
By the *corresponding-likeness* to His face (Phil. iii:21).
By the *love-companionship* of His presence (1 Thess. iv:17).
And by the *unsurpassed-following* of His retinue (Rev. xix:11-14).

*   *   *   *

To know Christ is the secret of power; to win Christ is the secret of growth; to love Christ is the secret of joy; to abide in Christ is the secret of victory; to follow Christ is the secret of faith; to listen to Christ is the secret of knowledge; and to walk with Christ is the secret of rest.

Love's Sacrifice

"The Love of Christ * * * One died for all" (2 *Cor. v:*14)

The Favorite Verse of the Welsh Revival in 1859 was—

> "The Man Who was nailed for sinners,
> Who suffered for sinners like me,
> Himself drank the cup of our sorrow
> Alone on Mount Calvary.
> Thou Fount of Love Everlasting,
> Thou Home of the Counsel of Peace,
> Bring one to the Bonds of the Covenant
> That never will cease."

The Favorite Verse of the Revival of 1905, was—

"This is love vast as the ocean;
This is pity like a flood;
Jesus Christ, my life to purchase,
Freely shed His precious blood.
Who will not His death remember?
Who refuse His praise to sing?
Love like this demands our homage—
Who will make Heaven's arches ring?"

The fact of the gospel, the death of the Saviour, is the fulcrum upon which the Spirit of God always rests the lever of His Word to raise a lost sinner. Christ came to the cross to die that there might be a gospel to preach (1 Cor. xv:3), and in that gospel there is

The *panacea* for every ill (Rom. iii:25).
The *placater* for every turmoil (Col. ii:14).
The *pattern* for every grace (2 Cor. v:14).
The *power* for every service (2 Cor. v:14).
The *provider* of every blessing (Heb. ix:12).
The *promoter* for every Christian act (Rom. xiv:15).
And the *procurer* of every glory (1 Thess. iv:14).

* * * *

The Lord's heart is hungry for the love of His people, even as He hungered unto death to prove His affection for them.

Christ in His love is God's expression of His compassion and regard for us. We do well to think with God about His thought of us.

Loving One Another

"A New Commandment I give unto you" (*John xiii:34*)

A little girl, of three or four years old, learned the Bible text, "Love one another." "What does 'love *one another*' mean?" asked her next oldest sister, in honest doubt as to the meaning. "Why, I must love you, and you must love me; and I'm *one* and your're *another*," was the answer. Who can improve on that exegesis?

Some fourteen times we are told to "love one another."

> To "love one another" is obedience to the *"new commandment"* (John xiii:34; xv:12, 17; 1 John iii:23; 2 John 5).
> The *evidence* of discipleship (John xiii:35).
> The *debt* that is to be paid (Rom. xiii:8).
> The *grace* in which we are to abound (1 Thess. iii:12).
> The *proof* of being God-taught (1 Thess. iv:9).
> The *mark* of being born again (1 Pet. i:22).
> The *sign* of sonship (1 John iii:11).
> The *stamp* of heaven's college (1 John iv:7).
> The *fulfilment* of the obligation resting upon us (1 John iv:11).
> And the *witness* of God's indwelling presence (1 John iv:12).

*   *   *   *

The way to obtain the *fulfilment* of God's promises, is to *fill* to the *full* His commands, and the new commandment is to love one another.

Marks of Jesus

"The marks of the Lord Jesus" (*Gal. vi:17*)

Adelina Patti, the great singer, on her recent marriage to Baron de Cederstrom, left an order at her home that her mail should all be forwarded to the Cannes post-office. On her arrival she went to the post-office and asked if there were any letters for the Baroness Adelina de Cederstrom-Patti. "Lots of them." "Then give them to me." "Have you an old letter by which I can identify you?" "No, I have nothing but my visiting card. Here it is." "Oh, that's not enough, madam; any one can get visiting cards of other people. If you want your mail, you will have to give me a better proof of your identity than that." A brilliant idea then struck Mme. Patti. She began to sing. A touching song she chose, the one beginning, "A voice loving and tender"—and never did she put more heart into the melody. And marvellous was the change as the brilliant music broke the intense silence. In a few minutes the quiet post-office was filled with people, and hardly had the singer concluded the first few lines of the ballad when an old clerk came forward and said, trembling with excitement, "It's Patti! There's none but Adelina Patti who could sing like that." "Well, are you satisfied now?" asked the singer of the official who had doubted her identity. The only reply which he made was to go to the drawer and hand her the pile of letters. If we are to convince the world of the divinity of Jesus Christ and His power to transform poor sinful human hearts and lives into His own likeness, then we must prove it by the living testimony of our lives. We must learn to sing the heavenly music.

As Mme. Patti proved her identity by what she could do, so every child of God proves his oneness with Christ by the following seven traits. A believer is one who is

(1) Looking at Christ (John i:29, 36; Heb. xii:2).
(2) Leaning on Christ (Cant. viii:5).
(3) Listening to Christ (Matt. xi:29; John x:27).
(4) Loving like Christ (Eph. v:2).
(5) Living as Christ (1 John ii:6).
(6) Labouring with Christ (2 Cor. vi:1).
(7) Longing for Christ (Phil. iii:20).

*   *   *   *

Love in its correspondence to Christ is not the gush of sentimentality, but the grace of similarity to Him.

Mastering Difficulties

"We laboured in the work * * * none of us put off our clothes * * continued in the work * * the wall was built" (*Neh.* iv:21, 23; v:16; vii:1).

Stevenson would have gloated over the building of Mile Rock Lighthouse. Mile Rock, jagged, ragged, at the entrance of San Francisco Harbor, has long been a danger and terror to sailors. It is but sixteen feet above mean low water. At mean high water its surface area is but 1,000 square feet. Too big at the base to be blown up. Surrounded by a collection of perilous swift eddies and currents. Government engineers made plans for a lighthouse there, but who would build it? A San Francisco man, James A. McMahon, took the contract. He took out a lot of skilled laborers in a schooner. They looked at Mile Rock and respectfully declined. They wanted to live. So McMahon gathered a force of those amphibious dare-devils called "deep-sea" sailors. They went to work last fall. Sometimes they could work an hour a day; sometimes not at all; and always they took their chances, and were copiously banged, bruised, and all but drowned. The first thing to do was to chisel the rock, so as to leave a pinnacle. Round this, steel plates were to be set, forming a cylinder forty-two feet high, to be filled with cement, and so, with the co-operation of the pinnacle, made considerably more solid than the solid rock. The shape of the rock was such that an elliptical base, forty feet by twenty-five at its widest, had to be built. Outside this was the rock's "slippery slope," like Gettysburg's in the poem. The amphibious McMahonites had to come up to the rock in boats, jump ashore as they steadied these on the crest of the wave, tumble into the seething caldron sometimes, be yanked with difficulty out, creep, crawl, cling, climb, swim—man-flies man-fish, man-barnacles. Sometimes the storm raged so that they could not be taken off for hours. In three months the rock was chiselled, and awaited the plates. Think of the difficulty of landing all that heavy stuff: the 1,200 barrels of cement for the foundations; the tons of steel for the base and for the tower, fifty feet high, which was to surmount it, and carry a third-order light and a fog-signal. A plucky, skilful, and memorable work. McMahon and his amphibious deep-sea men are to be commended for the accomplishment of their difficult task.

Nothing is accomplished without perseverance, plod, and hard work.

> Those who are "not weary" will reap (Gal. vi:9);
> The runner with patience will reach the goal (Heb. xii:1);
> The ardent one who presses on will receive the prize (Phil. iii:14);
> The diligent believer enters into the larger rest (Heb. iv:11);
> The persevering pleader is the glad receiver (Eph. vi:18);
> The one who continues in the Word proves his discipleship (John viii:31);
> And the faithful one unto death receives the crown of life (Rev. ii:10).

*　　*　　*　　*

Trials are not always toothsome, but they are always wholesome. Sanctified trials will keep a saint from getting crusty, musty, and rusty.

Medicine of Grace

"A merry heart doeth good like a medicine" (*Prov. xvii:22*)

A Hindoo trader in Kherwara market once asked a Christian convert, "What medicine do you put on your face to make it shine so?"

Penna answered, "I don't put anything on."

"No; but what *do* you put on?"

"*Nothing.* I don't put anything on."

"Yes you *do—all* you Christians do; I've seen it in Agra, and I've seen it in Ahmedabad and Surat, and I've seen it in Bombay."

Penna laughed, and his happy face shone the more as he said: "Yes, I'll tell you the medicine; it is happiness of heart."

The ingredients which compose the medicine called "Happiness of heart," are,

Holiness of life (1 Peter i:15).
Humbleness of mind (Col. iii:12).
Yieldingness of spirit (Rom. vi:13).
Circumspectiveness of walk (Eph. v:15).
Pureness of heart (Matt. v:8).
Rightness of motive (2 Cor. v:14).
And singleness of aim (2 Cor. v:9, R. V.).

When these are mixed together, in equal portions, with the
water of faith, and taken three times a day, then they
soon make the receiver enjoy spiritual health, which
is evidenced in the happiness that follows.

* * * *

If we walk in the *light,* in fellowship with the Lord, we
shall act *right* for Him, in our life before men.

Memories of Calvary

"A place called Calvary" (*Luke xxiii:33*)

"A land without ruins is a land without memories—a
land without memories is a land without history. A land
that wears a laurel crown may be fair to see; but twine
a few sad cypress leaves around the brow of any land,
and be that land barren and bleak, it becomes lovely in its
consecrated coronet of sorrow, and it wins the sympathy
of the heart and of history. Crowns of roses fade—
crowns of thorns endure. Calvaries and crucifixions take
the deepest hold on humanity."

What does Calvary say?

(1) Sin put away (Heb. ix:26);
(2) Satan defeated (Col. ii:14, 15);
(3) God satisfied (1 John iv:10);
(4) Law magnified (Gal. iii:13);
(5) Love manifested (John iii:14-16);
(6) Self crucified (Gal. ii:20);
(7) World transfixed (Gal. vi:14);
(8) Heaven opened (1 Peter iii:18);

157

(9)   Peace made (Col. i:20);
(10)   Forgiveness provided (Luke xxiv:46, 47);
(11)   Holiness secured (Heb. xiii:12);
(12)   Communion assured (Eph. ii:13);
(13)   Cleansing procured (Rev. i:5);
(14)   Glory entered (Rev. vii:14).

*   *   *   *

The Cross of Calvary casts its red hue upon the glory of heaven; yea, its roseate hue is its glory, for the *Lamb* is the light thereof.

Mustard

"Alexander the coppersmith did me much evil" (2 *Tim. iv*:14)

A well-known business man was asked the question, by a reviewer from a certain daily newspaper, "You have been surprised, I dare say, to find how many people know you of whom you have never heard?" "I received a letter from a gentleman who said that nine years ago he was a passenger with me on a P. and O. boat in the East, and he endeavored to recall himself to my memory by the circumstance that he once passed me the mustard."

There are some men mentioned in the Bible, who are conspicuous because of the mustard of ill which they did to others.

Jeroboam injured others by his evil influence (1 Kings xv:30).
Ahab by his wrong doing (1 Kings xxi:20).
Hymeneus and Philetus by their error (2 Tim. ii:17, 18).
Demas by his worldliness (2 Tim. iv:10).
Diotrephes by his pride (3 John 9).
Achan by his covetousness (Josh. vii:20, 21).
Theudas by his audacity (Acts v:36).
And Alexander by his evil (2 Tim. iv:14).

*   *   *   *

Sin is its own hell, and creates its own pangs; and Holiness is its own heaven, and brings untold pleasures.

NEED SUPPLIED

Nail Print Blessings

"The print of the nails" (*John xx:25*)

In Annie Swan's *Maitland of Laurieston,* John Maitland is represented as being torn by doubt, and worried by the speculations of worldly philosophy. He says: "I wish—I wish I could believe; I want to believe, but I can't. The critical questioning mania has got a hold of me, and I know not where it will end."

Whereupon Aunt Leesbeth, a godly woman, replies: "Oh, fecht on; fecht it oot manfully, and dinna lose heart. Efter ye see't, lad, and ken what the Saviour did for ye, ye'll hae a grup o' Him naething on earth will loose. I've never been a doubter myself, but I'm no' ane that blames Thomas a'thegither. He was an honest chiel; an' I believe, laddie, that the Lord has as muckle sympathy wi' the doubters noo as He had then. Haud at Him, John, my man, an' He'll show ye the print o' the nails and syne ye'll cry, as Thomas did, 'My Lord and my God!' "

The death of Christ in the operation of its blessing is
The *peacemaker* for the believer (Col. i:20);
The *world-divider* for the Christian (Gal. i:4);
The *self-annuller* to the child of God (Gal. ii:20);
The *devil-destroyer* to the member of Christ (Heb. ii:14);
The *consecrating-separator* to the saint (Heb. xiii:12);
The *soul-inspirer* to the worker (2 Cor. v:14, 15);
And the *glory-assurer* to the saved (Titus ii:13, 14; 1 Thess. iv:14).

*   *   *   *

The nail prints of Calvary are indelible in their marking, and lasting in their impression. The nails of the cross fasten securely, and fix permanently.

Need Supplied

"My God shall supply all your need according to His riches in glory by Christ Jesus" (*Phil. iv:19*)

Mr. C. H. Spurgeon, in speaking of the Orphanage, related: "I remember being in the Borough Market on one occasion, when a salesman said to me, 'Here are six

159

dozen bunches of turnips; you may have them for the orphans, if you like; and I hope somebody else will send the mutton.' The turnips were sent home, and, shortly after their arrival, a Surrey farmer delivered a sheep, which he had fattened and killed for the orphans. A coincidence? Yes, certainly! But who ordained it? It is clear that there was no human conspiracy, for neither of the donors knew of the other's intention. There may be an affinity between mutton and turnips, but no chemical law brought them together to furnish a meal for a family of orphan children. 'The Father of the fatherless' knows how, by the promptings of His Spirit, to quicken resolve, and thus command the gifts which honor faith, fulfil promise, and answer prayer. Had the factor withheld the turnips, the farmer might have brought the mutton all the same; or had the farmer sent his sheep to market, the factor might have given the turnips; but that the two gifts were coincident, does more than suggest a Divine providence—it proves it! A wise rule in giving thus receives an illustration. Each donor gave what he had, and never knew what crowning awaited his gifts. To refuse turnips because we cannot give mutton, or to withhold mutton because we cannot send turnips, is to allow an unworthy motive to stifle a generous impulse.

The above shows our God is a God of detail.

   (1)   He supplies our cupboard (Matt. vi:33);

   (2)   He clothes our back (Matt. vi:30);

   (3)   He numbers our hairs (Matt. x:30);

   (4)   He orders our steps (Ps. xxxvii:23);

   (5)   He bottles our tears (Ps. lvi;8);

   (6)   He books our thoughts (Mal. iii:16);

And (7) He holds our hand (Isaiah xlii:6).

*   *   *   *

There is no need to supply, when He supplies *all* our need.

Neverslip

"My feet did not slip" (2 *Sam. xxii*:37, R. V.)

"Neverslip," was the announcement about a certain shoe, which was advertised on a hoarding in New Jersey. It is not for me to advertise the advertisement, but it is at least a suggestive one as to what should be true of every Christian. I have heard of a vessel called the Neversink; this we may say is true of the ark of God's salvation and all those who are in it. But the Lord desires that we should know the saving of His grace in the larger sense, for He not only saves us from sinking into the hell of our deserving, but He can save to the holiness of His keeping, so that we never slip. The reason why David was kept, was, as he says, "Thou hast enlarged my steps under me so that my feet did not slip."

The word the Psalmist uses is rendered in another place *"slide"* (Ps. xxvi:1-27-31) and *"shake"* (Ps. lxix: 23). The way not to slip is to keep off the devil's slides, for if we get on them we are sure to slip down to our shaking. There is another word rendered *"slip"* which means not to be moved, and is often translated *"moved."* If we ponder a few places where the words occur we shall find food for meditation.

(1) A Confident Faith—"I have trusted also in the Lord" (R. V. "without wavering"), "therefore I shall not *slide*" (Ps. xxvi:1);

(2) A Good Ballast—"The law of the Lord is in his heart; none of his steps shall *slide*" (Ps. xxxvii:31);

(3) A Gripping Prayer—"When I said, my foot *slippeth;* Thy mercy, O Lord, held me up" (Ps. xciv:18);

(4) A Marred Testimony—"As a troubled fountain and a corrupted spring, so is a righteous man that *giveth way*" (A. V. *"falling down"*) "before the wicked" (Prov. xxv:26, R. V.).

(5) A Keeping Presence—"Because He is at my right hand I shall not be *moved*" (Ps. xvi:8).

(6) An Impregnable Position—"They that trust in the Lord are as Mount Zion, which cannot be *moved* but abideth for ever" (Ps. cxxv:1, R. V.).

DEVOTIONAL BIBLE STUDIES

(7) A Glorious Consequence—"My feet have held fast to Thy paths, my feet have not *slipped*" (Ps. xvii:5 R. V.).

* * * *

The grip of God's hand will keep us from slipping in His ways.

Obscuring the Light

"We wait for light, but behold obscurity" (*Isa. lix:9*)

Worshiping in a Baptist Chapel in the South of England, I noticed the windows on one side of the building were more or less covered with ivy, thus obscuring the light. Many churches and individual Christians are like those windows, they are obscuring the light of the Lord's blessing from others, thus instead of being light-givers they are light-retarders.

(1) The *blindness of unbelief* not only darkens the believer, but it also obscures his testimony and so keeps the light from those in association with him (Matt. xv:14).

(2) The *ophthalmy of self-sufficiency* will keep the soul from beholding the glory of the Lord (Rev. iii:17).

(3) The *bushel of commerce* will hide the light of witness bearing (Matt. v:15).

(4) The *bed of sloth* will stupify the activity of Godliness (Mark iv:21).

(5) The *short-sightedness of neglect* will hinder the full development of the Christian life (2 Peter i:9).

(6) The *mote of misjudgment* will dim the sight of brotherly love (Matt. vii:3),

(7) And the *cataract of pride* will shut out from fellowship with God (1 John ii:16).

* * * *

When we obscure the light of the Gospel, we not only keep the light from ourselves, but from others, also.

OPPORTUNITY

On and of the Rock

"Living stone * * * ye also" (1 *Pet. ii*:4, 5)

A well-known servant of Christ once remarked to a godly deacon, "I am not only *on* the Rock, but I am cemented *to* the Rock, and the cement is as hard as the Rock itself, so there is no fear of my perishing; unless the Rock falls, I cannot fall; unless the Gospel perishes, I cannot perish." This is evident if we believe what the Holy Spirit says, for He says of believers, that they

Partake of Christ's life (1 Peter ii:5),
Share in His position (Eph. ii:6),
Are united in His headship (1 Cor. xii:12),
Are receivers in Him of God's righteousness (2 Cor. v:21),
Are loved in God's love for Christ (John xv:9),
Are recipients of His preciousness (1 Peter ii:7, R. V., margin),
And then they are to be sharers of His glory (John xvii:24).

* * * *

Communion with the Lord, by having everything in common with Him, is the proof of our *union* with Him.

Opportunity

"Now is the accepted time" (2 *Cor. vi*:2)

A great surgeon stood before his class to perform a certain operation which the elaborate mechanisms and minute knowledge of modern science had only recently made possible. With strong and gentle hand he did his work successfully, so far as his part of the terrible business went; and then he turned to his pupils and said: "Two years ago a safe and simple operation might have cured this disease. Six years ago a wise way of life might have prevented it. We have done our best as the case now stands; but nature will have her word to say. She does not always consent to the repeal of her capital sentences." Next day the patient died.

163

DEVOTIONAL BIBLE STUDIES

The right thing done at the right time will secure the right end.

The hour to hear Christ's voice is "*now*" (John v:25);
The time to obey the Spirit's command is "*to-day*" (Heb. iii:15);
The occasion to repent is "*now*" (Acts xvii:30);
The opportunity to secure the blessing of the Gospel is "*now*" (Rom. iii:19);
The time for the Christian to be fully awake is "*now*" (Rom. xiii:11);
The day to serve the Lord is "*now*" (2 Cor. vi:2);
And the times to wait on the Lord are "morning, noon, and night" (Ps. lv:17).

* * * *

To neglect the present opportunity for service, is to miss the service and reward which the opportunity gives.

Our Unseen Leader

"The Captain of their Salvation" (*Heb. ii:10*)

In chapter sixty-eight of *The Scottish Chiefs*, William Wallace disguises himself as a Frenchman, that he may test his men as to valor and patriotism.

The Scots, 8,000 strong, are met by 10,000 English, but by hard fighting put them to flight. Later in the day the enemy is reinforced, by another 10,000, and comes against the Scots, only to meet with another defeat. Near the close of day a third 10,000 is joined to the enemy, and the nearly 30,000 come against the few Scots who are left: the Scots, terror-stricken, in despair, begin to fly. In vain Wallace, as Guy de Longueville, rushed into the thickest of the carnage and called to his men to fight. To them he was a foreigner and untried. Wallace felt the crisis, and spurring his steed up the steep ascent where he could be seen by the whole army, took off his helmet, and waved it in the air with the shout: "Scots, you have this day vanquished the Southrons twice. If you be men, remember Cambus-Kenneth, and follow William Wallace to a third victory."

PERFORMING THE PROMISES

Our Captain and Leader, the Lord Jesus, assures us of victory on the following grounds:

(1) Because of *what He is*—He is "the Captain of our salvation" (Heb. ii:10);

(2) Because of what *He has done*—He has destroyed "him that had the power of death" (Heb. ii:14);

(3) Because of *His victories* (Col. ii:15);

(4) Because of *His assurance* (John xvi:33);

(5) Because of what *He says* (1 Cor. x:13);

(6) Because of *His keeping and presence* (1 John v:18, R. V.; 1 John iv:4);

(7) Because of the stimulus of His promised reward (Rev. iii:21).

*　　*　　*　　*

The unseen are the real things and the seen are the unreal. Faith sees the unseen and makes them real

Performing the Promises

"I will perform that good thing which I have promised" (*Jer. xxxiii:14*)

The Paris newspapers related a story of a hoax which was played on the King of the Belgians. The King is a connoisseur of pictures, and, passing through an exhibition, he was much struck by a pastoral picture of sheep grazing at sundown. He asked the artist what was the price of the painting, and, to his astonishment, was informed that it was fifty francs a head of sheep. Very rapidly the eye of the King passed over the flock, and he decided to buy the picture. "There are about a dozen sheep," he said to the artist, "so that will come to 600 francs." "Fifty francs per sheep," replied the artist bluntly; "but if your majesty agrees we can count them after delivery of the picture." The King agreed, and the picture was sent to the hotel. The next day the artist called, and the King offered him a cheque for the amount he had stated. "One moment, if you please," said the artist. "Those are sheep also," pointing to a number of white dots in the background of the picture. "I thought they were specks of dust," replied the King. On looking at the picture again his majesty had to admit that there was undoubtedly a large flock in the far distance. "How many in all?" he asked the artist. "Exactly a thousand," was the reply. Without another word the King made out a new cheque for the amount, adding that kings always kept to their word.

The words of an earthly king may fail, but the promise of the King of kings will never fail. The promise to Israel, which heads this section, suggests many things.

    (1) A Meanful Contrast—"The crafty * * * cannot *perform* their enterprise" (Job v:12). Of the sinner, it may be said, as God said of King Saul, he "hath not *performed* My commandments" (1 Sam. xv:11); and of man, in his endeavour to do right of himself, the cry ever goes up, "To will is present with me, but how to *perform* that which is good I find not" (Rom. vii:18).

    (2) A Clear Testimony—"The Lord hath *performed* His Word" (1 Kings viii:20; 2 Chron. vi:10). "The Lord * * * hath raised up * * * to *perform*," &c. (Luke i:68-72).

    (3) A Sure Promise—"I will watch over My word to *perform* it" (Jer. i:12, R. V.; Ezek. xii:25; Isa. ix:7).

    (4) An Inspired Confidence—"Thou wilt *perform*" (Micah vii:20). "He will *perform*" (Phil. i:6). "God that *performeth* all things for me" (Ps. lvii:2).

    (5) A Good Resolve—"I will *perform*" (R. V., "confirmed"); "I will keep Thy righteous judgments" (Ps. cxix:106).

    (6) A Needful Spur—"Now therefore *perform* the doing of it" (2 Cor. viii:11).

    *   *   *   *

"Whosoever wills whatsoever God wills, is pleased whatever happens.

Pilgrimage

"Strangers and pilgrims" (1 *Peter* ii:11)

"A poor Irish laborer, who had spent forty years of his life amid the bricks and mortar of a great city, went out to the country for a few days on a special job. One morning, as he stood in the field, he heard a sudden whirr of wings, and saw a little bird shooting up into the air, and immediately there came a burst of music that filled his eyes with tears, and sent him to sit down on one of his rough building stones, until the floods of memories had surged through his simple heart. An American, who had never noticed the song of the lark, asked him what was the matter.

" 'Oh,' said the poor Irishman, 'that bird made me think of the ould counthry, and the days long gone by.' Poor fellow, he had not heard the lark since his childhood, and it made him feel he was a stranger in a strange land."

The Children of Israel, sheltered by the blood of the paschal lamb, are an interesting type of the Christian pilgrim. They, and we start from the blood-sprinkled houses of redemption,

(1) They fed on the roast lamb, we feed on Christ (Exod. xii:8; John vi:54).
(2) They had their loins girded, ours are strengthened with the girdle of truth (Exod. xii:11; Eph. vi:14).
(3) They were shod for their journey, our feet are protected with the "preparation of the gospel of peace" (Exodus xii:11; Eph. vi:15).
(4) They had a staff to support them, we have the staff of the Lord's care (Exod. xii:11; Ps. xxiii:4).
(5) They came out of Egypt, we come out from the world (Exod. xii:51; 2 Cor. vi:17).
(6) They were sanctified at the Lord's command; we are sanctified in Christ (Exod. xiii:12; 1 Cor. i:2).
(7) They were led by the cloud and fire, we are led by the Holy Spirit (Exod. xiii:21; Rom. viii:14)).

* * * *

He who lives in the power of the world to come, lives to purpose in the world that is.

Power of God's Word

"Blessed are they that keep His testimonies" (*Ps. cxix:2*)

A colporteur, in Hainault, relates the following incident:—"At Montigny, a Roman Catholic village, I asked a woman if she would buy the Holy Scriptures.

DEVOTIONAL BIBLE STUDIES

" 'No,' she answered, 'I am not going to be caught again. Seven months ago a man like you came here and he talked so much that to get rid of him I bought this book, a New Testament. I had begun to read it, for one has nothing to do on Sunday, when a woman came in, and, seeing what I was doing, said: "What! you read such bad books! Don't you know that it is a Protestant book?" I told her that I did not, and I promised myself never to open it again.'

" 'When you read it did you find any Protestantism in it, or anything else that you disapproved of?'

" 'Oh, no.'

" 'It is just as though, after churning your butter, which you know to be excellent, someone came in and asked you if you were not afraid to eat that butter, which you ought to know is bad and even dangerous. You would know how to answer her, knowing the contrary to be true.' "

The Bible proves itself, just as the missionary said of the butter. The assertion that a good thing is bad does not prove it is so, it only demonstrates the dark prejudice which is in the mind of the objector. Remember what is said of the word of God.

(1) It is *enlivening in contact,* for it is "quick and powerful" (Heb. iv:12).

(2) It is *enlightening in operation,* for it maketh "wise the simple" (Ps. xix:7, 8).

(3) It is *enduring in substance,* for it "abideth for ever" (1 Pet. i:23).

(4) It is *emancipating in ministry,* for Christ says the truth makes free" (John viii:32).

(5) It is *ennobling in effect,* for it communicates its nature to those who receive it, hence, Christ prays that we may be sanctified by means of it (John xvii:17).

(6) It is *enforcing in authority,* as the people confessed when they listened to Christ; and what is true of the Living Word is also true of the Written Word (Luke iv:32-36; Jer. xxiii:29).

POWER OF PRAYER

(7) It is *encouraging in promise,* for His "precious promises" ever make us "partakers of the Divine nature"
(2 Peter i:4).

*   *   *   *

As the shining of the sun proves the sun which shines,
so the Word of God proclaims the God of the Word.

Power of Prayer

"Much availeth the supplication of a righteous man when it is
energised" (*Jas. v:16, Rotherdam*)

A missionary from India on board an Atlantic liner
related the following striking answer to prayer which
he witnessed when a boy at his native place: On that occasion he was rather late at the meeting for prayer. He
noticed a number of ungodly men, who were standing
outside the meeting-house, and he asked why they were
there. They replied, "The Pastor is inside praying for
rain" (there had been no rain for sometime, and everything was parched up), "and we are waiting outside to
see the clouds come." "There is one," exclaimed one of
the young men all of a sudden, and, sure enough, the
rain began to come, and it rained for a week. Thus,
there was a practical demonstration of the power of
prayer.

> Prayer is a *heaven-opener,* as is seen at Christ's baptism
> (Matt. iii:16).
> Prayer is a *glory-revealer,* as is demonstrated at Christ's
> transfiguration (Mark ix:3, 4).
> Prayer is a *prison-opener,* as is made known in Peter's de-
> liverance from prison (Acts xii:7-12).
> Prayer is a *work-qualifier,* as is manifest in the early dis-
> ciples (Acts iv:31).
> Prayer is an *efficient-server,* as is exemplified in the service
> of Epaphras (Col. iv:12).
> Prayer is a *strength-minister,* as Christ found in Gethsem-
> ane (Luke xxii:41-43).
> Prayer is a *rain-bringer,* as Elijah's experience illustrates
> (James v:18).

*   *   *   *

Prayer in its effectiveness is bottomed on God's prom-

169

ises, and then when God has performed His promises, it is pinnacled by our praises.

* * * *

Prayer is the wire that puts us in communication with the Lord, and answered prayer is the transmission of His power to us.

Power of the Holy Spirit

"Ye shall receive power, after that the Holy Ghost has come upon you" (*Acts i:8*)

Rev. F. B. Meyer says: "When I was a boy I used to go to the Polytechnic, in London, where my favorite diversion was a diving-bell. which had seats round the rim, and which, at a given time, was filled with people, and lowered into a tank. We used to go down deeper, deeper into the water, but not a drop of water ever came into that diving-bell, though it had no bottom, and the water was quite within reach, because the bell was so full of air that, though the water lusted against the air, and the air lusted against the water, because air was being pumped in all the time from the top, the water could not do what it otherwise would. If you are full of the Holy Ghost, the flesh life is underneath you; and though it would surge up, it is kept out."

There is the *power of His grace* to keep steady in the storm of trial, even as the ballast in the vessel keeps it from "turning turtle" (Acts iv:31).

There is the *power of His life* to move us in the will and word of God, even as the bird can wing its way through the air by the strength of its inherent life (Rom. viii:2).

There is the *power of His holiness,* which can make the character beautiful with likeness to Christ, even as the flowers are beautiful with the sun's rays (Eph. iii:16).

There is the *power of His truth,* which imparts its nature to those who receive, even as the food received and digested gives strength and fibre to the body (John xv: 26).

PRAYER

There is the *power of His compassion* to inspire us to care for others, even as the light of the lighthouse warns the mariner of the dangerous reefs, and speaks of the harbour of refuge (Phil. ii:1-4).

There is the *power of His unparalleled supply*, which attracts every noble heart, even as the oasis in the desert attracts the weary traveller (Phil. iv:19).

And there is the *power of Christ Himself*, to which the Spirit ever leads (Acts vii:56).

*   *   *   *

When the dew of God's Spirit saturates our spiritual nature, it makes the doing of God's will an easy matter.

Prayer

"Lord help me" (*Matt. xv:25*)

A notice hung against one of the pillars in the parish church of an English village. It was to the following effect, that he who entered the building would offer up three requests, viz., for himself, for those who minister in this place, and for those who attend this place. All true prayer strikes out in these three directions: First for oneself, then for the Lord's servants, and then for the unsaved. We emphasise the first, for it is important to be personal in our pleadings, as the following seven "me's" indicate and illustrate:

(1) The *penitent sinner's* cry is, "Lord, be merciful to *me* a sinner" (Luke xviii:13);

(2) The *feeble saint's* petition is, "Keep *me* as the apple of the eye" (Ps. xvii:8);

(3) The *ignorant scholar's* request is, "Teach *me* Thy paths" (Ps. xxv:4);

(4) The *tempted warrior's* supplication is, "Let not mine enemies triumph over *me*" (Ps. xxv:2);

(5) The *troubled disciple's* cry is, "Lord, save *me*" (Matt. xiv:30);

DEVOTIONAL BIBLE STUDIES

(6) The *searched one's* petition is, "Lead *me* in the way everlasting" (Ps. cxxxix:24);
And the *believing suppliant's* prayer is, "Lord, remember *me*" (Luke xxiii:42).

*   *   *   *

To *strive* in earnest and believing prayer is to *thrive* in the Christian life.

The holy prayer of the *stammering* saint is music in God's ears, but the *clamoring* of self-interest is a discordant note to Him.

Prayer's Comprehensiveness

"In everything * * * let your requests be made known unto God"
(*Philippians iv:6*)

Annie Anderson, a character in *Alex Forbes of Howglen*, by George MacDonald, is represented as being sent to bed by her unkind guardian—"Groping her way up the steep ascent, she found her room without difficulty. As it was a clear, starlight night, there was light enough for her to find everything she wanted; and the trouble at her heart kept her imagination from being as active as it would otherwise have been, in recalling the stories of ghosts. She got into bed, and began saying her prayers, when she was startled by hearing a scratching noise, which she knew came from rats. What followed is here related:

" 'I tried to cry oot, for I kent' at it was rottans; but my tongue booed i' my mou' for fear, and I cudna speak ae word.'

"The child's fear of rats amounted to a frenzied horror. She dared not move a finger. To get out of bed with those creatures running about the room was as impossible as to cry out * * * her heart cried—

" 'O God, tak care o' me frae the rottans.'

172

PRAYERS HINDERED

"There was no need to send an angel from heaven in answer to this little one's prayer; the cat would do. Annie heard a scratch and a mew at the door. The rats made one frantic scramble, and were still."

Too often we miss the privilege we have in making known our requests in *"everything."* We quite believe the "everything" has to do with the big things of life, but we do not think so regarding the small things.

The main thing suggested by the above is, the Lord uses secondary things in answering our petitions.

Moses cried to the Lord when the Israelites were bitten by fiery serpents, and the Lord's healing came through the looked-to brazen serpent (Num. xxi:9).
The ravens feeding the prophet Elijah (1 Kings xvii:4-6).
The king healed of his carbuncle (Isaiah xxxviii:21).
The cleansing of Naaman from his leprosy (2 Kings v:6-14).
The woman being made whole through touching the hem of Christ's garment (Mark v:27, 28).
The stretching of Elisha on the young child (2 Kings iv:33-35).
And the saturating of Gideon's fleece with the dew (Judges vi:36-40), are a few of the many instances of how God uses means in answering prayers.

*   *   *   *

Prayer is made up of petition, plea, and intercession. Petition for personal blessing, such as "Lord help me;" plea for the fulfilment of promise; and intercession or supplication for others.

*   *   *   *

Prayer is the environment which kills the microbes of spiritual disease, and brings spiritual health and vim.

Prayers Hindered

"That your prayers be not hindered" (1 *Peter iii:7*)

" 'I should die 'fore I wake.' said Donny, kneeling at grandmother's knee, 'if I should die 'fore I wake—'
" 'I pray,' " prompted the gentle voice, 'go on, Donny.' "

"Wait a minute," interposed the small boy, scrambling to his feet, and hurrying away downstairs. In a brief space he was back again, and, dropping down in his place, took up his petition where he had left it. But when the little white-gowned form was safely tucked in bed, the grandmother questioned, with loving rebuke, concerning the interruption.

"But I did think what I was sayin', grandmother; that's why I had to stop. You see, I'd upset Ted's menagerie, and stood all his wooden soldiers on their heads, just to see how he'd tear round in the mornin'. But, if I should die 'fore I wake,' why—I didn't want him to find 'em that way, so I had to go down and fix 'em right. There's lots of things that seem funny if you're going to keep on livin', but you don't want 'em that way if you should die 'fore you wake."

"That was right, dear; it was right," commended the voice with its tender quaver. "A good many of our prayers wouldn't be hurt by stopping in the middle of them to undo a wrong."

There are many things which will hinder our prayers.

> Sin in the camp hindered the prayer of Joshua (Josh. vii:6-10).
> Iniquity, or idols, in the heart will hinder the answer to prayer, as the Psalmist says (Ps. lxvi:18).
> Disobedience to the Lord's word will hinder prayer, as the wise man declared (Prov. xxviii:9).
> A condemning heart will hinder the requisite confidence to answered prayer (1 John iii:21, 22).
> Unbelief will hinder prayer, for faith is a condition attached to the fulfilment of promise (Heb. xi:6).
> Non-dependence upon the Holy Spirit will hinder effectual prayer (Rom. viii:26; Jude 20).

*   *   *   *

Sometimes God's children place themselves in positions where God's power cannot touch them.

174

Prayer: The Vent of Need

"Men ought always to pray" (*Luke xviii:1*)

A Scotch laborer, who was a Christian man, went to work for a farmer who was not a believer. The latter was a liberal paymaster, but the former only stayed with him a few days. He was asked by a neighbor why he had left. *"There was no roof on the house,"* was his reply. The Scotchman's meaning may be found in the saying of an old writer, who affirms that a dwelling in which prayer is not offered up to God daily, is like a house without a roof, in which there can neither be peace, comfort, nor safety.

The man knew the benefit and blessing of prayer, and felt he could not do without it. They who value prayer, look after their best interests. They who neglect prayer, open the door for evil intruders; for prayer is not only a protection from the rain of Satan's malice, but it is also a preventative of sin's intrusion. To neglect prayer is to burden ourselves with care, to shut ourselves out of blessing, to enfeeble our faith, to dim the eyes of our hope, to damp the fire of our zeal, to relax the grip of our tenacity, to weaken the heart of our love, and to rob our service of its strength, as Trench well says:—

"Why should we do ourselves this wrong.
Or others—that we are not always strong:
That we are ever overborne with care:
That we should ever weak or heartless be,
Anxious or troubled, when with us is prayer;
And joy, and strength, and courage are with Thee?"

Why, indeed! To do so, is to demonstrate our folly. Let us ponder the privilege of prayer, that we may the better appreciate its worth.

Prayer is the *Vent of Need.* The needy man is ever the pleading one.

(1) *Prayer is a sin-killer,* as the Psalmist infers when he states iniquity in the heart will keep his prayers from being answered (Ps. lxvi:18). When we pray that sin may be killed, prayer is kept alive.

175

DEVOTIONAL BIBLE STUDIES

(2) *Prayer is a power-bringer,* as the disciples at Pentecost illustrate. While they prayed, the Spirit in His power came (Acts i:14; ii:1).

(3) *Prayer is a victory-gainer,* as Nehemiah demonstrates, for he accomplished his task in the face of his enemies because he made his "prayer unto God" (Neh. iv:9).

(4) *Prayer is an obstacle-remover,* as Peter's deliverance evidences, for he was brought out of prison in answer to prayer (Acts xii:5).

(5) *Prayer is a holiness-promoter,* for prayer takes us to God in our need, and brings God with His supply, hence, we are charged to pray always and in everything (Eph. vi:18; Phil. iv:6).

(6) *Prayer is a blessing-bringer,* as Elijah found when he prayed in his praying for rain (Jas. v:17, 18 margin).

(7) *Prayer is a body-healer,* for we are assured "the prayer of faith shall save the sick" (Jas. v:15).

* * * *

To be a suppliant to the Lord in telling our need is good; but to be an intercessor for the needs of others is better. "Lord, help me," cried the woman who prayed for her daughter. We always get help when we get help for others.

Praying and Paddling

"Joined together" (*Ex. xxviii:7*)

A colored preacher on a visit to this country, told a provincial audience the other day, how he escaped from slavery. He said: "When I was escaping from slavery, and found myself out on the ocean, I prayed to God to help me, and He did help me. I found some boards, and got on them. Well, what did I do then? Did I stop praying, and think because I had got a few boards I could get along alone, and didn't need the Lord's help any more? No. I took a stick for a paddle, and went to paddling and praying; and by paddling and praying I got through."

PRAYING WITH A RESERVATION

There is sound philosophy in the old preacher's talk: "Faith without works is dead."

We show our love by our *obedience* (John xiv:21);

We evidence our sanctity by our *separation from evil* (1 John iii:10);

We proclaim our brotherhood by our *actions* (1 John iii:17);

We prove the spirituality of our worship by our *loyalty* (Matt. vii:21);

We tell out our discipleship by our *continuance* (John viii:31);

We manifest the reality of our conversion by our *fruit-bearing* (John xv:4, 5);

And we declare our faith by our *works* (James ii:17, 18).

    *   *   *   *

To work effectually for God we need to continually wait upon Him. The wheels of work only run smoothly when they are oiled by the oil of prayer.

Praying with a Reservation

"Ye ask amiss" (*Jas. iv:3*)

Some time ago I told a very simple story, says Theodore Monod. It was about a child I know, the son of one of my relatives. He had a bad habit that children often have—he was a little bit of a boy—that of sucking his thumb. Well, he was told he must give it up, and one evening in his prayer he was heard to say: "O God, bless Edward, and make him give up sucking his thumb." That was a very good prayer. But, after a pause, he went on: "O God! don't bless him, because he is going to suck his thumb all the same." I think there is a world of practical teaching in that. The little fellow was more candid than we often are, and he understood that it was no use asking God to do a thing for him when he was determined it should not be done. I fear that in more important matters a great many of us are just like that little boy. We ask God to deliver us from this or that, when all the time there is a voice (although it does not

177

DEVOTIONAL BIBLE STUDIES

express itself in the prayer) saying: "I shall go on all the same."

>We ask amiss when we ourselves are amiss, like the children of Israel, who out of their self-desire asked for flesh (Ps. lxxviii:18).
>We pray amiss when we are amiss with our brethren, for we cannot expect the Lord to bless us if we have an unforgiving spirit (Mark xi:25).
>We pray amiss when we want something for our own gratification, and not for God's glory (Jas. iv:3, R. V.).
>We pray amiss when we have no definite petition. The whatsoever of the Lord's *promise* supposes a "*what* do you want" (John xiv:13).
>We pray amiss when we should be acting instead of asking, as the Lord told Joshua in referring to Achan (Josh. vii:10).
>We ask amiss when we do not depend upon the Holy Spirit. We need to pray in the Spirit (Jude 20) and to let the Spirit pray in us (Rom. viii:26).
>We pray amiss when we ask in a dictatorial spirit, instead of keeping in the line of God's will (I John iii:20-22; v:14, 15).

* * * *

The *flame* of prayer is fed by the *fuel* of meditation. Think how Christ prayed, and you will soon pray like Christ.

Prepared

>"To make ready" (prepared, same word as in *Luke ii*:31) "a people prepared for the Lord" (*Luke i*:17)

All day long the snow had fallen, as if with quiet, steady purpose. As the light faded, the wind rose, and rose till the night was of the wildest. In each little house on the country-side the inmates knew that they were cut off from their neighbors, and that that night there could be neither coming nor going. Light after light in the little village went out, and all was dark. ' Yet, though it was now near midnight. there was one window—had there been any one but God to see it—in which still shone a light. It was in the farmhouse high on the hillside. For within an old man lay dying. Late in the evening

178

PREPARED

he had taken a turn for the worse, and his daughter began to be afraid, knowing that on such a night she could send for no one, either doctor or minister, and fearing she might have to face the Angel alone. Hour after hour she watched and waited. She looked on the grey locks that had once been black as the raven, on the pale cheeks once red as berries, on the strong, straight nose that still spoke to her of all his strength and uprightness. Never again, she murmured to herself, would she see him in the little church bearing the vessels of the Lord—the tallest, dearest figure among all.

"Father," she said at length, "wull I read a chapter to ye?"

But the old man was in sore pain, and only moaned. She rose, however, and got the Book, and opened it.

"Father," she said again, "what chapter wull I read to ye?"

"Na, na, lassie," he said; "the storm's up noo: I theeket (thatched) my hoosie in the calm weather."

And thereafter she waited without fear. So those who are in the confidence of faith are without fear, for

They have responded to the prepared feast of the Gospel (Matt. xxii:4).

They are ready or prepared for an answer for the reason of their hope (1 Pet. iii:15).

As sanctified ones they are "prepared unto every good work" (2 Tim. ii:21).

Being panoplied in God's armour, their feet are shod "with the preparation of the Gospel of peace" (Eph. vi:15).

As exhorted ones to "be perfect" (same word as *"perfect"* is rendered *"prepared"* in Heb. x:5), they are prepared or adjusted to God's will (1 Cor. xii:11).

As taught ones the Holy Spirit reveals the things which He has "prepared for those who love Him" (1 Cor. ii:9).

And Christ assures them He has gone to "prepare a place" for them (John xiv:2, 3).

* * * *

The best way to *prove* God's will is to *approve* what He says in His word by our obedience.

179

DEVOTIONAL BIBLE STUDIES

Preserved

"Preserved in Jesus Christ" (*Jude* 1)

An old man once said, "I am preserved: not like pickles, sour, but like jam, sweet." Christians should be like jam. which is guaranteed to keep sweet at all times, under all circumstances, and in all climes.

If we are in the realm of Christ's kingdom (Col. i:13);
Living in Christ's love (John xv:9);
Sanctified in Christ's truth (John xvii:17);
Indwelt by Christ's Spirit (Rom. viii:9);
Strengthened in Christ's grace (2 Cor. xii:9);
Calmed in Christ's peace (Col. iii:15, R. V.);
And keeping in Christ's company (Luke xxiv:29, 32), then we shall be sweetened by what He is, and be sweet in His sweetness.

*   *   *   *

To be *concentric* in love to Christ, often means we are *eccentric* in the eyes of the world.

Preserved by Love

"Preserved in" (R. V., "kept for") "Christ Jesus" (*Jude* i.)

Mr. Spurgeon, on one occasion, went to visit the late James Smith, of Cheltenham, when the latter was stricken with paralysis. Mr. Spurgeon had heard that he was troubled with many conflicts, and said to him, "Friend Smith, I hear you have many doubts and fears."

"Who told you that?" he enquired; "for I have none."

"Do you never have any? Why, I understood you had many conflicts."

"Yes, I have many conflicts, but I have no doubts. I have many wars within, but I have no fears."

We cannot doubt our Father's love, nor can we fear as to our eternal safety if we trust the Lord Jesus, for in His Word of grace we are assured.

PRESENCE OF THE LORD

We shall "never perish" (John x:28);
That we possess "eternal life" (1 John v:13);
That we are "sealed with the Holy Spirit unto the day of redemption" (Eph. iv:30);
That our "life is hid with Christ in God" (Col. iii:3);
That we are "loved unto the end" (John xiii:1);
That we are "kept by the power of God" (1 Pet. i:5);
And that none is "able to pluck us out of His hand" (John x:28).

*   *   *   *

Love put Christ on the cross to take our place, and will not be satisfied till it has placed us with Him on the throne.

Presence of the Lord

"The Lord is with them" (*Zechariah x*:5)

Rev. F. B. Meyer relates a beautiful story of a little girl staying at a summer hotel in Norway. "She was of that trying age when small fingers are beginning to find their way about the piano, striking as many wrong notes as right ones; and young nerves do not seem particularly sensitive to the anguish which such attempts are capable of inflicting on others. She knew one or two tunes sufficiently well to be able to make them out with one finger; and with these she made the guests familiar to their despair.

"But one day a brilliant musician came to the hotel, took in the situation, and sat down beside the small musician, accompanying her with the most exquisite improvisation. Each note of hers only gave him a new *motif* for chords of surpassing beauty, whilst the drawing-room, now crowded with people, breathlessly listened.

"When the performance was over, the illustrious accompanist took the little maiden by the hand, and led her blushing round the company, saying, 'Let me introduce to you, ladies and gentlemen, the young lady to whom you are indebted for the music to which you have been listening.'

DEVOTIONAL BIBLE STUDIES

"It was true. They were indebted to her for the music, because her efforts had led to his magnificent accompaniment; but his part in the joint performance had led to a deep impression, and it was *he* whom they were destined to remember."

The Lord's Presence makes all the difference. He fills every need, and is the Worker to achieve. The words *"with them,"* as associated with the Lord's Presence, suggest much. He is with us as

(1) *The sinner's Entertainer* for fellowship—"This man receiveth sinners, and eateth *with* them" (Luke xv:2).
(2) As the *enemies' Exterminator*—"The Lord was *with them*" (Judges i:22);
(3) As *the sanctifying Lord*—"They shall know that I the Lord their God am *with them*" (Ezekiel xxxiv:30);
(4) *The manifest Worker*—"The Lord working *with them*" (Mark xvi:20);
(5) *The gracious Recognizer*—"The Lord taketh my part *with them* that help me" (Ps. cxviii:7);
(6) *The efficient Multiplier*—"The hand of the Lord was *with them*" (Acts xi:21);
(7) And as *the loving Encourager*—"God hath done *with them*" (Acts xiv:27; xv:4).

* * * *

The pavilion of God's presence is the Saint's place of rest, and the panoply of God's armour is his coat of mail for Victory.

Presence and Prayer

"Abide with us" (*Luke xxiv:29*)

The author of the well-known hymn, "Abide with me," wrote the immortal verse after he had been compelled, through ill-health, to relinquish preaching. Thus on his couch he did more lasting work than he did in the pulpit.

His daughter has related the circumstances as follows: "The summer was passing away, and the month of September had arrived, each day seemed to have a special value as being one day nearer his departure. His family were surprised and almost alarmed at his announcing his intention of preaching once more to his people. His weakness, and the possible danger attending the effort, were urged to prevent it, but in vain. 'It was better,' he said, 'to *wear* out than to rust out.' He did preach, and afterwards assisted at the Communion. He was much exhausted, yet his friends had no reason to believe it had been hurtful to him. In the evening of the same day he placed in the hands of a dear and near relative the little hymn, 'Abide with me.'"

In the earliest manuscript the hymn had eight verses, and there were words and sentences which have been altered since. The following was the original:

"Abide with me! fast falls the even-tide;
  The darkness thickens; LORD, with me abide!
  When other helpers fail, and comforts flee,
  Help of the helpless, O abide with me!

"Swift to its close ebbs out life's little day;
  Earth's joys grow dim, its glories pass away;
  Change and decay in all around I see;
  O Thou, Who changest not, abide with me!

"Not a brief glance I beg, a passing word,
  But as Thou dwelt with Thy disciples, Lord,
  Familiar, condescending, patient, free,
  Come not to sojourn but abide with me.

"Come not in terrors, as the King of kings;
  But kind and good, with healing in Thy wings;
  Tears for all woes, a heart for every plea;
  Come Friend of sinners, and abide with me.

"Thou on my head in early youth didst smile;
  And, though rebellious and preverse meanwhile,
  Thou hast not left me, oft as I left Thee;
  On to the close, O LORD, abide with me!

"I need Thy presence every passing hour;
What but Thy grace can foil the tempter's power?
Who like Thyself my guide and stay can be?
Through cloud and sunshine, O abide with me!

"I fear no foe, with Thee at hand to bless,
Ills have no weight, and tears no bitterness:
Where is death's sting? where, grave, thy victory?
I triumph still, if Thou abide with me!

"Hold then Thy cross before my closing eyes!
Shine through the gloom, and point me to the skies!
Heaven's morning breaks, and earth's vain shadows flee;
In life, in death, O LORD, abide with me!"

These words "abide with us" are:

(1) The believer's prayer in life (Luke xxiv:29);
(2) The soldier's stay in conflict (Ex. xxxiii:14, 15);
(3) The pilgrim's plea in pilgrimage (Gen. xxviii:15);
(4) The mourner's joy in sorrow (Isa. xli:10);
(5) The worker's courage in testimony (Matt. xxviii:10);
(6) The servant's cry in trial (Neh. iv;4; vi:9);
(7) And the disciple's comfort in death (Ps. xxiii:4).

*   *   *   *

To abide in Christ is obedience to Him (1 John iii:24,
R. V.); for Christ to abide in us is to be possessed by
Him (Eph. iii:17); and to abide with Christ and for
Him to abide with us is communion with Him.

Prevailingness of God's Word

"So mightily grew the Word of God and prevailed"
(*Acts xix:20*)

"Do you see this Bible?" said the chief man of a
village to a missionary. "I was a rough blasphemer a few
months ago; men trembled before me; boys ran to hide

when they saw me; no man dared to stand before me. To-day, my arm is broken, my heart is wax; I am a little lamb; the children look upon me with wonder. That Book has done it all."

Another said: "Until a few weeks ago I used false weights and measures. I got a Bible from the hand of a boy in the street, and took it to my shop. Immediately there commenced a din which nearly drove me crazy; the controversy between the Bible and my false measures made my head ring. I seized the Bible, and would have flung it out of the door, but with a loud voice it spoke, saying, 'With me you drive God from you.' I could not do that. I destroyed my false measures and immediately the uproar ceased, and now I sleep like a child, and my neighbors always see me happy."

As we read the records of the early Church, we find that wherever the gospel of Christ was received some definite result was achieved.

(1) It is a *power-giver,* as illustrated in the healing of the lame man (Acts iii:7, 8).

(2) It is a *demon-expeller,* as demonstrated under Philip's preaching at Samaria (Acts viii:5-8).

(3) It is a *joy-bestower,* as manifested in the gladness of the Ethiopian eunuch (Acts viii:39).

(4) It is a *soul-amazer,* as seen in the conversion of the deputy at Paphos (Acts xiii:12).

(5) It is a *caste-dissipator,* as appears in the blessing of the Gentiles at Antioch (Acts xiii:46-48).

(6) It is a *heart-opener,* as stated in the Lord's dealings with Lydia (Acts xvi:14).

And (7) It is a *sin-expeller,* as we see in the burning of the books of superstition at Ephesus (Acts xix:18-20).

*　　*　　*　　*

A holy life is the best commentary on the Holy Bible. Not to be a walking Bible is to be wasting libel.

DEVOTIONAL BIBLE STUDIES

Profoundness of the Simple Gospel

"The Gospel of Christ" (*Rom. i:16*)

J. H. La Trobe, in *The Methodist Times,* referring to the *"breadth* of the gospel of the kingdom," says, "we are ofter urged to preach the simple gospel, but the gospel preached by many is so simple as to disappoint or disgust any intelligent man who has a love for his fellows and a noble conception of life. This simple gospel makes Christ a mere fire-escape from a hell conceived on the lines of the Pagan Tartarus, into a heaven which is far away in points of distance and of time."

Why skit at those who preach the simple gospel? The simple gospel has for its basis the death and resurrection of Christ, according to the Apostle Paul, who says, "I declare unto you the gospel * * * by which also ye are saved * * * how that Christ died for our sins according to the Scriptures; and that He was buried, and that He rose again the third day according to the Scriptures" (1 Corinthians xv:1-4). The facts of the gospel, Christ's death and resurrection, are the mightiest factors which can be put into Society.

> They are a *means of escape* from the wrath to come (1 Thess. i:10).
> They are the *motive powers* of spiritual and self-sacrificing service (II Cor. v:14-16).
> They are the *makers of character,* for no one can know them without being made like to them (Phil. iii:10).
> They are the *movers of heart* to influence us to act in a God-like manner (1 John iii:16).
> They are the *music of heaven* to give gladness and peace, for the living Christ with the pierced hands always gives these benedictions (John xx:20, 21).
> And they are the *medium of blessing,* for the reason why earth has no sorrow which heaven cannot cure, is because Christ has procured every blessing by His sorrow on the cross (Isa. liii:5). These are simple factors, but they produce profound results. Let mankind know these things in their livingness, and they will be lifted into such a plain of morality and spirituality, that there shall be no want to want.
> "Wanting is what?"

186

PROHIBITION PROVOKES OPPOSITION

The gospel of the death and resurrection of Christ is a panacea for every ill, and the power to all and every good.

*   *   *   *

Taking the Water of Life means salvation (Revelation xxii:17), letting it be within, as a well springing up, is satisfaction (John iv:14), and allowing it to flow out in blessing to others is service (John vii:38).

Prohibition Provokes Opposition

"When the commandment came, sin revived" (*Rom. vii:9*).

A recent writer on Anarchism says:—

"The paradox is certainly true of the Anarchists, that repression does not repress. The French Government published in 1894 an "Anarchist Album," containing about 500 photographs of Anarchists, which is used by the police of every country.

"Within two months afterward President Carnot was assassinated. That same year saw Anarchism rampant in nearly every country in Europe. According to Detective-Inspector Sweeney a more stormy year than 1894 has not been known to the police since the forces of Anarchy were first put through any sort of organization. In his published reminiscences, Mr. Sweeney, who was in the Criminal Investigation Department of Scotland Yard, runs over the Anarchist crimes of that 'very black twelvemonth.' " Verily, prohibition provokes opposition.

Eve was warned not to eat of the tree, but she did it, and was cast out of Eden (Gen. iii:24);

Achan was told not to touch the accursed thing of Jericho, but he coveted and took, and was accursed (Josh. vii:20-25);

Naomi knew it was not in the mind of God for her to go to Moab, but she went, and came back empty (Ruth i:21);

David went right in the teeth of God's command in sin-
ning with Bathsheba, and was punished (2 Sam.
xii:9-11);

And Paul felt that law stirred up the sin in him, which he
was prohibited from doing (Rom. vii:15-21).

*   *   *   *

The evil of man's nature is provoked by the righteousness of God's law. When law says "Thou shalt not:"
man in his self will says: "I will."

Proofs of Conversion

"Be Converted" (*Matt. xiii*:15; *xviii*:3)

A Chinaman applied for the position of cook in an
American family, which belonged to a fashionable church.
The lady asked him: "Do you drink whisky?"
"No; I Clistian man."
"Do you play cards?"
"No; I Clistian man."
He was engaged, and was found honest and capable.
By-and-bye the lady gave a party, during which the wine
flowed in abundance, and cards were played for high
stakes. John did his part acceptably, but the next morning
he appeared before his mistress.
"I want to go."
"Why, what is the matter?"
"I Clistian man—I told you so before. No heathen. No
workee for heathen!"
The one thing which is evidenced by the Chinaman's
reply is, that wherever the work of God is real in the
heart, it shows itself in a thoroughness in putting away
all that is evil.

The Thessalonians gave up their idols (1 Thess. i:9).

The Ephesians burnt their books of magic (Acts xix:19).

The Corinthians gave up their evil course of living (1 Cor.
vi:11).

PROSPERITY OF ADVERSITY

Zacchæus gave up his cheating (Luke xix:8).
Saul of Tarsus gave up his persecution (1 Tim. i:13).
The Christians at Rome gave up the service of sin (Rom. vi:17).
And the Colossians gave up their enmity to God (Col. i:21).

*　　*　　*　　*

When the Christian is in evidence, he is the best evidence of Christianity.

Prosperity of Adversity

"Sorrowful, yet alway rejoicing" (2 *Cor. vi*:10)

A popular writer describes a young girl who had to sleep in a garret infested with rats, who had prayed to the Lord to send them away, and recognized an answer to her petition when the cat, appeared upon the scene, he aptly puts the cat in juxtaposition to the rats, by saying, "There was a place where prayer was heard as certainly as at the mercy-seat of old—namely a little garret room, with holes in the floor, out of which came rats; but with a door as well, in at which came the prayed-for cat."

Where there are rats in our lives, there are sure to be cats. In other words, there are compensations in life. There are joys in our sorrows, crowns in our crosses, mercies in our miseries, love in our losses, His appointments in our disappointments, and compensations in our contradictions.

Jacob found a Bethel in his stony pillow (Gen. xxviii:18, 19).
Moses got a commission in the back side of the desert (Ex. iii:1-4).
Joseph discovered the way to the palace was by means of the pit (Ps. cv:17-22).
David turned the taunt of Goliath into a triumph (1 Sam. xvii:43-50).
Paul touched the Throne of Grace by means of the thorn in the flesh (11 Cor. xii:8, 9).
John beheld the Paradise of God when banished to the Isle of Patmos (Rev. i:9).
And Christ Himself knew that the valley of suffering led to the mount of glory (Luke xxiv:26).

"He was better to me than all my hopes,
  He was better than all my fears;
He made a bridge of my broken works,
  And a rainbow of my tears.
The billows that guarded my sea-girt path,
  But carried my Lord on their crest;
When I dwell on the days of my wilderness march,
  I can lean on His love for the rest.

"There is light for me on the trackless wild,
  As the wonders of old I trace,
When the God of the whole earth went before
  To search me a resting place.
Never a watch on the dreariest halt
  But some promise of love endears;
I read from the past that my future shall be
  Far better than all my fears."

*   *   *   *

The way to kill *despair* is to give yourself to *prayer*, for prayer is the great killer of every ill.

Purchased by Blood

"Bought with a price" (1 *Cor. vii*:23)

Sir George Douglas, Bart., in the *Life of Major-General Wauchope, C.B., C.M.G., LL.D.*, who fell at the head of the Highland Brigade at Magersfontein, calls attention to the fact that in the war he donned the "red heckle" of the Black Watch, of which he had written to his second wife, what he rightly calls one of the most beautiful soldiers' letters in our language:

"I've been looking for this enclosed everywhere, and at last I have found it. It is my red heckle, as worn in my helmet in the years 1885 and 1886. It was also at Suakim in 1884. The red heckle is what the old 42nd love—it is our distinguishing mark. I have been shot with that red heckle. Keep it as long as you are my wife. It really is what I love best of that kind of thing; it has so much in it—or, rather, it represents so much to me of old tradition, of the noble men who gave their all for this old land. It isn't beautiful, and it is faded; but I do love it so dearly * * * And I think those in the Service who knew me would say, if I were gone, that this heckle would bring me more to mind to them than anything else, because I have loved our red plume so much."

The red heckle of Christ's atoning death is ever present to the believer, and he loves to wear it by remembering he is dead to sin in His death for sin.

Something of what the death of Christ meant to Him and what it means to us may be gathered from the four following Scriptures:

(1) A GREAT PURCHASER—"Denying the Lord that *bought* them" (II Pet. ii:1).
(2) A GREAT PRICE—"*Bought* with a price" (1 Cor. vi:20).
(3) A GREAT END—"*Redeemed* us to God by Thy blood" (Rev. v:9).
(4) A GREAT SEPARATION—"*Redeemed* from among men" (Rev. xiv:3, 4).

The word *agorazo* is rendered *"bought,"* and *"redeemed"* in the above Scriptures.

*   *   *   *

If we *ignore* the blood of Christ's atonement, we shall *deplore* the want of His peace.

Queer Places

"In a Strait place, Thou hast made room for me" (*Ps. iv*:1, *Rotherham's translation*)

Sauntering into the old-fashioned Episcopal Church building at Biggleswade, we saw a swallow flying from rafter to rafter. It did not seem to be at home. The bird had evidently flown into the building, and could not find its way out. Many of God's children have got into queer places by their folly; but they have not found it so easy to get out of them.

DEVOTIONAL BIBLE STUDIES

David in the court of Achish (1 Sam. xxi:10).
Jonah in the sea-monster's belly (Jonah i:17).
Abram in Egypt (Gen. xii:10).
Lot in Sodom (Gen. xiii:12).
Elijah under the juniper tree (1 Kings xix:4).
The man of God out of Judah in the old prophet's house
(1 Kings xiii:19).
And Peter in the judgment hall of the world (Luke xxii:55-
62), are a few examples.

*   *   *   *

The Lord often extricates His saints from their difficulties, but He none the less reminds them of their dis-
graces.

Redeeming the Time

"Redeeming the time" (*Eph.* v:16)

Lord Rosebery relates that when Mr. Gladstone was
staying at Dalmeny in 1879, he kindly consented to sit
for his bust. The only difficulty was that there was no
time for sittings. So the sculptor, with his clay model,
was placed opposite Mr. Gladstone as he worked, and
they spent the mornings together, Mr. Gladstone writing
away, and the clay figure of himself less than a yard off
gradually assuming shape and form. Anything more
distracting I cannot conceive, but it had no effect on the
busy model.

The Lord's people should be equally diligent in business
(Rom. xii:11).
Quick in obeying the Lord's commands, for He bids us
"make haste" (Luke xix:5).
The King's business requires haste, therefore there must
be no tardiness in performing it (1 Kings xxi:8).
The rest of faith can only be enjoyed as we are alive to its
privilege (Heb. iv:11, R. V.).
The workman who is approved of God is he who dili-
gently applies himself to his task (11 Tim. ii:15, R. V.).

REMEMBER

The lawful runner in the race is he who obtains the victor's
crown (1 Cor. ix:25).
And he who is "zealou: in good works" is the one who is
commendable to the Lord (Titus ii:14).

*   *   *   *

There are those who covet to possess the gifts of others
who do not use the ones they have got.

Remember

"Thou shalt remember all the way which the Lord thy God led
thee" (*Deut. viii:2*)

Looking out of the window as the express train thun-'
dered on its way, as I sat with my back to the engine,
the curve round which we had come and the distant way
over a viaduct were plainly visible. It is not without its
benefit to look back on the track one has come in the experiences of the Christian life, for one is able to see

The deliverances the Lord hath wrought (Deut. v:15).
The way He hath led (Deut. viii:2).
The blessings He has bestowed (Deut. xxxii:7-12).
The victories He has won (Deut. xi:2-7).
The darknesses He has brightened (Neh. ix:12, 13).
The service He has rendered (Deut. viii:14-18).
And the encouragements He has given (Joshua xxiii:14).

*   *   *   *

Look in! Look up! Look out! Look back! *Look in,*
and see your vileness (Job xl:4). *Look up,* and behold
your Saviour's loveliness (Heb. xii:2). *Look out* and
ponder the need of man's helplessness (Matt. ix:36-38;
John iv:35) ; and *look back* and remember what the Lord
has done.

DEVOTIONAL BIBLE STUDIES

Repentance

"Repentance toward God" (*Acts* xx:21)

Augustine has well said, "He hath ill repented whose sins are repeated." Repentance is a change of mind wrought by the Holy Spirit and shown in the action. The word repent means to think differently, to change one's views after consideration, hence to change one's purpose or course of action. Remorse is sorrow for the consequence of sin, but repentance condemns the sin which brought the consequence. Tears are in the eyes of repentance, confession is on its lips, God's mind about sin is in the thought, walking from sin are its feet, brokenness is in its heart, taking hold of Christ are its hands, and humbleness of manner is its mien.

(1) The imperativeness of repentance is heard in God's command to repent (Mark i:15; Acts xvii:30).

(2) Christ emphasizes the necessity of repentance (Luke xiii:3, 5).

(3) The goodness of God is the promoter of repentance (Rom. ii:4).

(4) The companions of repentance are godly sorrow (2 Cor. vii:10), faith (Mark i:15), and good works (Acts xxvi:20).

(5) The cause of repentance is God Himself, for He gives it, and its end is "unto life" (Acts xi:18).

(6) The reason of repentance is found in the Christ of Calvary's atonement and resurrection, and the blessing of repentance is made known in the sins being forgiven, and the seasons of refreshing assured (Acts iii:18, 19).

(7) The preaching of repentance is based upon the authoritative command of Christ (Luke xxiv, 46, 47), and is illustrated in the testimonies of the early Christians (Mark vi:12; Acts ii:38, R. V.).

(8) God's appreciation of repentance is manifest in the joy He is said to experience when one sinner repents (Luke xv:7, 10).

* * * *

Repentance thinks God's thought about sin and hates it; takes God's side against self and dies to it; and turns to God Himself and serves Him.

194

Rewards

"Praise, honour, and glory at the appearing of Jesus Christ"
(1 *Pet. i:7*)

Queen Victoria, when visiting the military hospital at Netley, to see the wounded men who had returned from an Indian Frontier Campaign, had the pleasing duty of pinning the coveted Victoria Cross upon the breasts of two of the soldiers, one of whom was Piper Findlater, who, although wounded severely, continued to play his pipes when the British were engaged with the enemy. When her Majesty was about to put the V. C. on the breast of Findlater he said: "I can stand up, your Majesty." "Oh, no," replied her Majesty; "I will rise." And suiting the action to the word, she rose from her chair, and attached the cross to the breast of his jacket.

The Queen honored the man who had honored his country by his bravery. Thus shall it be with the faithful ones and the overcomers, when our Lord Jesus returns.

(1) Reward of the watchful Servant—Christ's personal service (Luke xii:37).

(2) Reward of the Enduring Believer—"A crown of life" (Jas. i:12).

(3) Reward of the Diligent Saint—An abundant entrance into Christ's Kingdom (2 Pet. i:11).

(4) Reward of the Talent User—The Lord's gracious approval (Matt. xxv:21-23).

(5) Reward of the Pound-Employer. Rule over many cities (Luke xix:17).

(6) Reward of the Overcomer—A place on Christ's throne (Rev. iii:21).

(7) Reward of the Faithful Attender—"A full reward" (2 John 8).

* * * *

To remember that the Lord remembers what we do for Him, is a recompense in itself, in addition to the promised reward.

DEVOTIONAL BIBLE STUDIES

Right in His Own Eyes

"The way of a fool is right in his own eyes" (*Prov. xii*:15)

Thomas B. Reed once visited friends in Watch Hill, R. I., and he enjoyed himself so much that he missed a train which he expected to take at Westerly. It was imperative that he should reach Boston to keep an important engagement, and the train that had gone was the last one eastbound stopping at Westerly that night. There was, however, an express passing through at nine o'clock. Mr. Reed telegraphed to the superintendent in Boston:

"Will you stop express at Westerly at nine p. m. for a large party?"

The answer came: "Yes, will stop train."

Mr. Reed waited, and when the express came to a standstill he started to board a car.

"Where is the large party we stopped for?" inquired the conductor.

"I am the large party," returned Mr. Reed, with dignity.

There are many who think it quite right to take others in, when the action is their own, but they would be quick to condemn a similar action in others. What does the Lord say about things right in our own eyes?

(1) A Fenced Life—"Go not about after your own heart and your *own eyes*" (Numbers xv:39, R. V.).

(2) A Distinct Command—"Ye shall not do * * * whatsoever is right in his *own eyes*" (Deut. xii:8).

(3) A Lawless Condition—"Every man did that which was right in his *own eyes*" (Judges xvii:6; xxi:25).

(4) A Self Estimate—"Righteous in his *own eyes*" (Job xxxii:1).

(5) A Needful Injunction—"Be not wise in thine *own eyes*" (Prov. iii:7).

(6) A Sorry Case—"A generation that are pure in their *own eyes*, and yet are not washed from their filthiness" (Prov. xxx:12).

ROOTAGE FOR FOLIAGE

(7) A Terrible Woe—"Woe unto them that are wise in their *own eyes*" (Isa. v:21).

* * * *

The inflation of self-righteousness is an abomination to God. They who justify themselves condemn God, but they who condemn themselves justify God.

Rootage for Foliage

"Grow up into Him" (*Eph. iv*:15)

"What beautiful laurels! How fresh and green they are!" remarked one friend to the other, as he called attention to some beautiful laurels, which were growing at the side of a garden, as they were walking down an avenue of fir trees in the west of Bournemouth.

"Yes," was the reply, "that beautiful foliage means good rootage. Where there is not a proper trench dug, and good soil put into it for the trees, the tops of the laurels die off, which is an indication at once there has been no fresh root growth owing to the rock-sand and gravel beneath."

"Ah, that is also true in regard to Christian growth. There must be rootage in the things of God, if there is to be a correspondence in the life," was the responsive exclamation.

Rootage in the grace of God gives the strong and healthy foliage of graciousness in the life (2 Tim. ii:1).

Rootage in the love of God makes the conduct bright with the beautiful foliage of helpful acts of kindness (Eph. iii:17; 1 John iii:14-17).

Rootage in the truth of God forms the bright foliage of correspondence to it, and makes the soul healthy and wealthy in the World of His grace (III John 1-4).

Rootage in the holiness of God produces the evergreen foliage of holy living (1 Pet. i:15).

Rootage in the righteousness of God will cause the trees of righteousness to bring forth the fruits of righteousness, which means consistent and commendable action in our dealings with others (Phil. i:11).

Rootage in the gentleness of Christ must generate in the conduct a similar trait in the foliage of character (Ps. xviii :35).

And Rootage in the gladness of the Lord will cause the perfect foliage of His unspeakable joy, and the blossom of His unsurpassed glory to be fragrant in the soul to His praise (1 Pet. i :8).

* * * *

When the roots of our faith take hold of the soil of God's Word, the foliage of our character will be bright and beautiful.

Sacrifice

"The sacrifice of Himself" (*Heb. ix* :26)

A well-known Christian worker was once asked how a certain Christian enterprise was to be successfully carried out. *"Somebody's life blood"* was the terse and trenchant reply. Success in the true sense of the word, is always obtained at the expense of sarcifice.

Adam had an opened side before he got his beautiful bride (Gen. ii :21).

Isaac was laid on the altar before he met with Rebekah (Gen. xxii :2, 9; xxiv :67).

Jacob served fourteen years for Rachel before he got her (Gen. xxix :18-28).

Job lost his possessions before he got the double portion (Job xlii :10).

David's three mighty men risked their lives before they obtained for the king the desired water from the well at Bethlehem (1 Chron. xi :17-19).

The apostles hazarded their lives to propagate the gospel (Acts xv :26).

Christ gave Himself up to death before He could see of the travail of His soul (Matt. xxviii :20; Isa. liii :10, 11). Calvary's cross not only proclaims the substitutionary benefits of Christ's death, but also the Divine principle that sacrifice is essential to every blessing and benefit of the Christian life.

* * * *

We must burn out before we can give out. We cease to bless when we cease to bleed.

Sacrifice

"The sacrifice and service of your faith" (*Phil. ii*:17)

"In the Galerie des Beaux Arts in Paris there stands a famous statue. It was the last work of a great genius, who, like many a genius, was very poor and lived in a garret, which served as studio and sleeping room alike. When the statue was all but finished, one night a sudden frost fell on Paris. The sculptor lay awake in the fireless room and thought of the still moist clay, thought how the water would freeze in the pores and destroy in an hour the dream of his life. So the old man rose from his couch and heaped the bed-clothes reverently round his work. In the morning when the neighbors entered the room the sculptor was dead." He sacrificed his life to preserve his work. All work means sacrifice.

(1) *Christ's sacrifice is the inspiration to sacrifice.* Of Christ it is said, "He gave Himself up for us, an offering and a sacrifice to God" (Eph. v:2, R. V.). Unless the fire of our sacrifice is lighted at the altar of Christ's sacrifice there will be some trait of selfishness about it.

(2) *Love is the incentive to sacrifice.* Christ loved me and "gave Himself up for me" (Gal. ii:20, R. V.). Love never thinks of cost, nor consequences, its concern is to meet the need of the object of its affection, like David's mighty men when they risked their lives in getting the drink of water for their beloved king (1 Chron. xi:18).

(3) *Surrender is the law of sacrifice.* "This is you reasonable service" (Rom. xii:1), says the Holy Spirit, as He urges us to present "our bodies a living sacrifice." The yielded life of obedience is neither hard nor irksome to the one who is captivated by the love of Christ. He who yields to the Spirit of Power finds the power of the Spirit yielded to him.

(4) *Service is the occupation of sacrifice.* Paul was willing to be poured out "as a drink offering" (Phil. ii:17, R. V. margin), in order to serve the saints, herein he showed his relationship to Him who came not to be

ministered to, but to minister, and to give His life a ransom. The highest place in Heaven's order is to take the lowest position in humble service. Love to Christ shows itself in labor for others.

*   *   *   *

Willingness is the soul of sacrifice. The lash of authority might move the slave to sacrifice his ease, but the love of attraction by Christ is the motive which constrains us to follow in the steps of Him, who said "I delight to do Thy will, O My God!"

Saint's Dependence

"Without Me, ye can do nothing" (*John xv*:5)

"To render Great Britain and Ireland self-supporting, they need 13,000 square miles at the present yield of 29.07 bushels per acre—an area about one-fourth the size of England. But this is not available, for much of the land, now under barley and oats, would not be suitable for wheat.

"For the present, then, the annual deficit of 180,000,000 bushels must be imported and under these circumstances a permanently higher price for wheat is a calamity that must ere long be faced."

The above facts, given by Sir W. Crookes, proclaim the dependence of Britain upon other countries for food supplies.

But how much greater is the believer's dependence upon the Lord for spiritual supplies. Britain is only partially dependent upon other countries; we are *absolutely* dependent on the Lord.

As *sinners,* we need the atoning Saviour to justify us (Rom. iv:25).

As *saints,* we need the holy Saviour to sanctify us (John xvii:19).

As *soldiers,* we need the equipping Lord to arm us (Eph. vi:10, 11).

As *servants*, we need the Living Christ to send us (John xx:21).

As *stewards*, we need the keeping Master to preserve us (II Tim. i:12, R. V., margin).

As *suppliants*, we need the Holy Spirit to inspire us (Rom. viii:26).

And as *seekers*, we need His teaching to instruct us in the knowledge of Divine things (I Cor. ii:9-14).

* * * *

The supply of God's grace is suitable for our need, sufficient in its bestowment, sustaining in its blessing, and adapted to our requirements.

Salt

"Ye are the salt of the earth" (*Matt. v:13*)

Every ton of Atlantic water, when evaporated, yields 81 lbs. of salt; a ton of Pacific water, 79 lbs.; Arctic and Antarctic waters yield 85 lbs. to the ton; and the water of the Dead Sea, 187 lbs.

I wonder how much Salt of Grace some professing Christians would yield, if they were analyzed? (Col. iv: 6). The Lord says of His people, "Ye are the salt of the earth" (Matt. v:13). Salt as used in the Scriptures is indicative of many things.

It is binding in its import (Lev. ii:13; II Chron. xiii:5).
Healthful in its application (II Kings ii:20, 21).
Savory in its taste (Job vi:6).
Suggestive of soundness (Mark ix:50).
Good in its service (Luke xiv:34).
Illustrative of witness-bearing (Matt. v:13).
And typical of grace (Col. iv:6).

* * * *

The Lord does not expect more from us than what He gives us, but He does expect us to use what He imparts.

DEVOTIONAL BIBLE STUDIES

Sanctification Which Needs Sanctifying

"I cannot endure iniquity and sacred festival" (*Rotherham's translation Is. i:13*)

Ben was the 5-year-old son of good Methodist parents. One Sunday, while his mother was getting a meal ready, he ran into the kitchen. Sniffing delightedly at the savory odors, he exclaimed:

"Thank the Lord, we are going to have chicken for dinner."

"Ben, Ben!" cried the horrified mother, "don't you know you ought not to say such things?"

"Why, not?" replied Master Ben. "I'd like to have you know I've been sanctified, and I can say what I please."

Many professedly sanctified are as self-assertive and self-expressing as the above boy. "I have found out my sanctification needs to be sanctified," said one who had come into the pure light of God's holiness, and found out her sinfulness. There is no self so abhorrent to the Lord as the religious self of self-righteousness. Humility is the essence of holiness, the qualification for service, and the delight of heaven. When humility exists it is unconscious of its virtue, and loves to bloom out of sight.

Mixtures are an abomination to Jehovah, and compromise is hateful in His sight. The clean cut, and clear out and out life, is expressed in the following ascending scale of true sanctification.

The *"Come out"* of whole-hearted separation (2 Cor. vi:17).
The *"purge out"* of all sin's leaven (1 Cor. v:7).
The *"walk in the light"* of fellowship with the Lord (1 John i:7).
The *"yield your members"* of a consecrated body (Rom. vi:13; xii:1).
The *"filled with the Spirit"* of the Spirit's entire possession (Eph. v:18).

202

SATAN: A DEVOURER

The *"walk as Christ walked"* in obedience (1 John ii:6).
The *"do all to the glory of God"* in all things (1 Cor.
x:31).

*   *   *   *

To use the things of God for our own ends, is to abuse
the blessings He bestows. His glory is the goal of all
good.

Satan: A Devourer

"Seeking whom he may devour" (1 *Pet. v*:8)

A well-known barrister at an assize in South Wales,
was cross-examining a hostile witness, who had been particularly shrewd in his replies. "They sometimes call
you a Devonshire dumpling, don't they?" asked the barrister, with a mischievous twinkle in his eye. "I believe
they do," replied the witness. "But you are not a Devonshire dumpling?" quoth the barrister. The witness waited
till the laughter in court had subsided. "Hey, but if I
had been a doompling," he drawled out at length, "you
laryers 'ud a' gobbled I up before now!"

The Bible speaks of one who is ready to gobble up,
or to use the exact word, "to devour" (1 Pet. v:8).

Satan seeks to devour the good seed of God's Word when
it is sown (Matt. xiii:4).
He seeks to get men to devour the powers God has given,
like the prodigal (Luke xv:30).
He endeavors to get unprincipled men to devour widows'
houses (Matt. xxiii:14).
He incites believers to act unkindly to each other, and this
is spoken of as devouring each other (Gal. v:15).
He moves the ungodly to devour believers by persecuting
them (II Cor. xi:20).
And he would devour Christ and His own, if he could
(Rev. xii:4).

*   *   *   *

Be not food for Satan's feeding, but be a faithful
friend for the Spirit's leading.

Secret of Endurance

"He endured, as seeing Him" (*Heb. xi:27*)

We reverse the sentence and make it read: "Seeing Him, he endured." Which at once gives us the thought, that seeing the Lord is the secret of endurance. Not seeing Him is to miss our way in life and find ourselves in the bog of despair. Seeing Him is to find the clue to every maze, and the secret to every mystery.

It is one of the conceits of ancient poetry that the oarsman, Charon, was permitted on one occasion to visit the earth. From a lofty mountain-top he looked down upon the palaces and works of man. As he went away he said: "All these people are spending their time in just building birds'-nests. Building birds'-nests to be swept away in the floods, when they might be erecting palaces of immortal beauty to dwell in for ever—thus indeed must much of the best of our life and work in this world appear to the angels who look down upon us from heaven and see things as they are."

The best way to look at things is to do as Moses did, not to be looking at things at all, but at Him,

> Looking at Him we shall be able to *"endure hardness"* as good soldiers (II Tim. ii:3), for we shall see Him as the Captain leading us to victory.
>
> Looking at Him we shall be able to *"endure afflictions"* (II Tim. iv:5), for we shall see Him as the Strengthener by His grace (II Cor. xii:9).
>
> Looking at Him we shall be able to *"endure chastening"* (Heb. xii:7), for we shall see Him as our loving Father training us by His discipline (Heb. xii:6).
>
> Looking at Him we shall be able to *"endure persecutions"* (Heb. xii:2, 3), for we shall see Christ as our Great Exemplar.
>
> Looking at Him we shall be able to *"endure grief"* (I Pet. ii:19), for we shall see we are following in the steps of the Saviour (I Pet. ii:21).
>
> Looking at Him we shall be able to *"endure temptation"* (Jas. i:12), for we shall see Him with us in the fire (Dan. iii:25).

SEEINGNESS OF THE SPIRITUAL

And looking at Him we shall be able to *"endure trial"* (Heb. vi:15), for we shall see Him as the Tester of our faith (1 Pet. i:7).

*   *   *   *

We magnify earth's trifles when we look at them, but we glorify God when we see Jesus in all things and see all things in the light of Him.

Seeing His Face

"We shall see Him as He is" (1 *John iii*:2).

An American visitor having heard George Müller preach, at the close of the address went up to him and taking him by the hand, said, "I so enjoyed your sermon. I may never see you again here, but I shall meet you up yonder." The old man lifted up his face aglow with light from heaven and said, "I shall see His face, I shall kiss His feet."

To see the Lord is the fulfilment of Christ's promise (John xvi:10, 16, 17, 19, 22).
The realisation of our hope (Job. xix:26, 27).
The reward of our suffering (Acts vii:56).
The manifestation of His glory (Isa. lxvi:18).
The sight which shall enrapture (Isa. xxxiii:17).
The climax of our bliss (1 John iii:2).
The heaven of our heaven (Rev. xxii:4).
And the outcome of purity (Matt. v:8).

*   *   *   *

The light of heaven is the face of Jesus, and we correspond to it by having His likeness.

Seeingness of the Spiritual

"To be spiritually minded is life and peace" (*Rom. viii*:6)

There is a legend of a wonderful bell which rings in heaven, and whose sweet notes only those can hear whose hearts are pure and gentle.

"It is said, somewhere, at twilight
 A great bell softly swings,
And a man may listen and hearken
 To the wondrous music that rings.
If he puts from his heart's inner chamber
 All the passion, pain, and strife,
Heartache and weary longing,
 That throb in the pulses of life;
If he thrusts from his soul all hatred,
 All thoughts of wicked things,
He can hear in the holy twilight
 How the bell of the angels rings."

Mark it is only the spiritually minded that hear the music of the heavenly bell. The same truth is emphasised again and again in the pages of Holy Writ.

The *"pure in heart"* are "blessed," and "see God" (Matt. v:8).

The *"meek* shall inherit the earth" (Psa. xxxvii:11).

The *"obedient"* eat the good of the land (Isa. i:19).

Moses, the man of God got to know the ways of God (Ps. ciii:7).

Abraham, the man of prayer, was told God's purpose in relation to the wicked (Gen. xviii:17, &c.).

Paul, the sufferer with Christ, heard the unspeakable words of Paradise (II Cor. xii:2-4).

Levi, the faithful for God, entered into the blessings of the covenant of peace (Mal. ii:4-6).

Elijah, the man who stood before God, brought down the fire from heaven (I Kings xvii:1; xviii:36, &c.).

Elisha, the man of faith, saw the compassing army of the Lord's protection (II Kings vi:17, &c.).

And John, the leaner on Jesus' breast saw the door opened in heaven (Rev. iv:1).

*   *   *   *

To have the spiritual mind of the Spirit, we need to mind the Spirit in the mind of His Word.

206

Self-Abasement

"Stood and confessed their sins" (*Neh.* ix:2, 3)

No man in Scotland has a more saintly memory than Robert Murray McCheyne, and yet he said, "No one but God knows the abyss of sin in my heart."

To another saintly man, some one said, when he was on his death-bed, "How happy you must be; the gates of heaven will be crowded with your converts waiting to greet you." But he replied, "Take the man away; if I can but crawl into heaven on my hands and knees before the gate shuts, I'll be the most blessed man in heaven."

An aged father, when he was complimented on his work for Christ, said, "Call me not a saint; I am a devil."

The following Biblical confessions of some of God's holy ones will go further to illustrate, that those who have lived nearest the Lord, ever had a bad opinion of themselves:

Job said, *"I am vile"* (Job xl:4).
Isaiah cried, *"I am undone"* (Isa. vi:5).
The Bride asserts, *"I am black"* (Cant. i:5).
David exclaims, *"I am poor and needy"* (Ps. xl:17).
Peter declared, *"I am a sinful man"* (Luke v:8).
Paul confessed, *"I am carnal"* (Rom. vii:14).
And Christ Himself says, *"I am a worm"* (Ps. xxii:6).

* * * *

When good self is on the top of bad self, keeping it down, good self is very proud of its achievement.

The only way to get rid of self is to die to it in the death of Christ. Christ's death is the death of self, as well as the deliverer from sin.

If the letters which make up the word "self" are reversed with the addition of an "h," the "flesh" is revealed. Self is always the flesh in some form.

DEVOTIONAL BIBLE STUDIES

Self-Forgetfulness

"Let him deny himself" (*Luke ix:23*)

A friend, visiting a lighthouse, lately, said to the keeper, "Are you not afraid to live here? It is a dreadful place to be constantly in." "No," replied the man; "I am not afraid. We never think of ourselves here." "Never think of yourselves! How is that?" The reply was a good one. "We know that we are perfectly safe, and only think of having our lamps burning brightly, and keeping the reflectors clear, so that those in danger may be saved." That is what Christians ought to do. They are safe in a house built on a rock which cannot be moved by the wildest storm, and in a spirit of holy unselfishness, they should let their light gleam across the dark waves of sin, that they who are in peril may be led into the harbor of eternal safety.

Those who forget themselves, in living for others, live for God.

> Jonathan forgot himself when he gave his kingdom to David (1 Sam. xxiii:17).
>
> Mephibosheth forgot his possession in thinking of David (2 Sam. xix:30).
>
> Isaac forgot himself in doing his father's will (Gen. xxii:7, 8).
>
> Naomi forgot herself in seeking to regain the lost inheritance for Ruth (Ruth iii:1-5).
>
> The little captive maid forgot her captivity in thinking of the need of her master (2 Kings v:2, 3).
>
> David's mighty men forgot their danger in breaking through the ranks of the Philistines to gratify the wish of their master (1 Chron. xi:18).
>
> The Apostles Paul and Barnabas were men who forgot themselves, out of love for the Lord Jesus (Acts xv:26).

*   *   *   *

To exercise self denial is one thing and to deny self is another. In the first, certain things are denied to self; but in the second, self itself is denied.

208

Self-Holiness

"Great swelling words" (*Jude* 16)

Dr. J. Parker said, "Suspect every man who declares himself to be holy in a perfect degree. He may be able to produce credentials substantiating his claim, but above all things first examine the credentials. A friend said to me that he heard a man make this observation, namely, that 'he was so full of the Holy Ghost that he did not believe the Holy Ghost Himself could find any more room in his soul for occupation.'

"I knew nothing about the man who made that declaration, but I instantly said, 'That man is a bad man whoever he is.'

"Said my friend, 'Do you know the man?'

" 'Not at all,' I replied; 'but he is a bad man.'

" 'Well,' said he, 'it is curious that you did not know of the case, for not long after that, he created a most painful scandal in the Church.' "

Again and again in the pages of Holy Writ, the men who give out their own worthiness soon evidence their utter worthlessness. The white-wash of self-assertion generally hides the corruption which is in the sepulchre of their own carnal nature.

Gehazi declared faithfulness when he had by his covetousness proved his unfaithfulness (2 Kings v:20-27).

Hazael professed that he was unable to perform a treacherous act, but straightway went and murdered his master (2 Kings viii:8-15).

Ananias and Sapphira made a great profession of whole-hearted consecration, when all the time they were keeping back part of the price (Acts v:1-10).

The Pharisees professed righteousness, but Christ said that they were whited-sepulchres filled with the corruption of their own unrighteousness.

Diotrephes gave out he was somebody, but he was only a wind-bag (3 John 9, 10).

DEVOTIONAL BIBLE STUDIES

Nebuchadnezzar swelled out with the great pride of his "*I*," but he soon came to the dust (Dan. iv:30-36).

Theudas gave out he was somebody and soon ended in nothing (Acts v:36).

* * * *

Those who *adore* themselves, will find that God *abhors* them. Self-righteousness is a coin not current with heaven.

Separation Means Safety

"Enter not into the path of the wicked" (*Prov. iv:*14)

Dr. Casagrandi, of Rome, employed a number of women wearing long skirts, to walk for one hour through the streets of the city, and after their promenade was over he had taken their skirts and submitted them to a careful bacteriological examination. He found on each skirt large colonies of noxious germs, including those of influenza, tuberculosis, typhoid fever, tetanus, and numerous other bacilli, which also were represented on each skirt. That women should willingly submit themselves to the filth, to say nothing of the possible danger, of trailing skirts has long been a wonder to sensible people. The ordinary sticky mud which prevails in the streets of any city adheres closely the moment a garment touches the ground. It dries in the course of a few hours, and is then shaken off when the skirt is cleansed at home. Thus the vilest germs of the street invade the privacy of the best-kept houses.

The Christian who wishes the garments of his spiritual life to be kept clean, must obey the following negative commands of the Lord:

(1) The "*Be not*" of the unequal yoke (2 Cor. vi:14).

(2) The "*Touch not*" of separation (2 Cor. vi:17).

(3) The *"Love not"* of desire (1 John ii:15).
(4) The *"Set * * * not"* of affection (Col. iii:2).
(5) The *"Walketh not"* of unholy association (Ps. i:1).
(6) The *"Give not"* of exclusiveness (Matt. vii:6).
(7) And the *"Enter not"* of temptation (Matt. xxvi:41).

*   *   *   *

The place of separation to the Lord is the place of power, as well as of purity.

Shewing Forth His Excellencies

"Return to thine own house, and shew how great things God hath done unto thee" (*Luke viii:39*).
"Shew forth the excellencies of Him" (1 *Pet. ii:9*, R. V.)

There was a chief in Natal, South Africa, who did not object to his people becoming Christians, but he decidedly objected to their becoming *bad* Christians. He put it this way: "If you become better men and women by being Christians, you may remain so; if not, I won't let you be Christians at all." We cannot be Christian without being better, for He has called us out of darkness into His marvellous light, that we should show forth His excellencies, and the first place in which this is to be done is in our own home.

How can we "shew how great things the Lord hath done?"

(1) By shewing our faith is real by our works—*"Shew Me thy faith by thy works"* (James ii:18, margin).
(2) By a "good life," evidencing our knowledge is valid—"Let him *shew* by his good life his works," &c. (James iii:13, R. V.).
(3) By obedience, demonstrating our love for others—*"Shew* ye to them * * the proof of your love" (2 Cor. viii:24).
(4) By fruit-bearing, testifying the reality of conversion—"They *shew* * * * how ye turned to God from idols" (1 Thes. i:9).

(5) By long-suffering, thus shewing our relationship to Christ—"I obtained mercy, that in me first Jesus Christ might *shew* forth all longsuffering" (1 Tim. i:16).

(6) By careful attention to study in Divine things, thus proving we seek God's approval—"Study to *shew* thyself approved unto God" (2 Tim. ii:15).

(7) And by earnest diligence in continuing in the ways of God—"*Shew* the same diligence" (Heb. vi:11).

* * * *

His excellencies make us excellent. Let us remember they are His, and not ours.

Shining

"Let your light shine" (*Matt. v:16*)

When the late Earl of Beaconsfield, as Mr. Disraeli, was leader of the House of Commons, after a long sitting of the House, in the early hours of the morning he was making for Downing Street, deep in thought. He was accosted by a shoeblack, who asked him if he would have his boots blacked. The statesman, in an automatic way, put his foot on the box, and the boy commenced operations. Suddenly Disraeli was conscious of the situation, and looking down on the boy said, "What is the best word in the English language?" "Shine, sir," was the boy's prompt reply. To shine for Christ is the best possible shine. To shine for Christ is

(1) To bear *witness of Him* as John did (John v:35).
(2) To be *consistent in Him* (Phil. ii:15).
(3) To be an *influence for Him* (Matt. v:16).
(4) To be *obedient to Him* (Matt. v:16).
(5) And to be *transfigured with Him* (Matt. xvii:2).

* * * *

We may sing "O for the wings of a dove!" but it is better to shine in the ways of God. Shining is the best kind of singing, and makes the singer sing to purpose.

Shining Saints

"Let your light so shine" (*Matt. v:16*)

"About 400 years ago there lived a man. in Italy, who wanted to do something for the world. He painted a picture for a little obscure chapel near his home—a picture of the Christ Child and the Mother. In the face of the Child he painted a soft light, which has been a wonder and a delight ever since. It was a warm and hallowed light, which brightened the face of the mother as she bent over her child, and filled all the scene with a gentle radiance. The picture was a benediction to the peasants who lived about the village. They had their sorrows, their cares, their struggles, and that soft light cheered and heartened them, and made their hard, narrow life mean more to them. They called the painter Ariel, the light bringer, because he had brought that holy shining into their lives. We may all serve Christ in this way— not by painting pictures like Correggio's, but by carrying heavenly light on our faces in the love that shines there, and does not fade out in the darkest night."

What the light is, Christians should be.

As the light is *illuminating* in its ministry (Luke ii:32).
Gladdening in its coming (Ecc. xi:7).
Beautifying in its touch (Isa. lviii:8).
Healing in its service (Mal. iii:2).
White in its nature (Matt. xvii:2).
Warming in its glow (John v:35).
And *quick* in its movements (2 Cor. iv:4).

So believers should be illuminating in their testimony, gladdening in their life, beautifying in their character, healing in their service, holy in their conduct, warm in their love, and quick in their obedience.

*   *   *   *

Meekness of spirit is the best *meetness* for service. *Be,* before you *do,* and then you will have *power* in your *performance.*

213

DEVOTIONAL BIBLE STUDIES

Shut Up and Shut In

"I am *shut up* and cannot come forth" (*Ps. lxxxviii*:8). *"Shut* the door upon thee" (2 *Kings iv:*4)

The first Scripture speaks of the Psalmist's utter helplessness. When we get to the point of utter extremity, God steps in with His bountiful plenty. The widow in Elisha's day was shut up to God, which was a gracious preparation for being shut in with Him, and then when she came out she was able to pay all her debts by God. We should have more to give out to others, if we were oftener found in the throne room of prayer with God. The lamp of testimony must be fed with the oil that is got from the Great High Priest in the sanctuary.

"Down in the depths of Draper Colliery, several hundred feet under the surface and almost directly under his own home, Michael McCabe, thirty years old, of Gilberton, is entombed. He is behind thousands of tons of slush and dirt, alive, but doomed to death, beyond all hope of rescue." So read one of the newspapers in describing an accident which occurred on November 11, 1907, in Mahanoy City, in the State of Pennsylvania. And the paper in continuing the recountal of the sad incident, said, "He has been imprisoned since 1 p. m. Saturday, when he fired a blast which caused a cave-in extending to the surface, where the slush banks were situated. He fled in the wrong direction and got into a blind shaft. A fellow workman managed to get out of that wing of the colliery before the roof caved in. The mine breach extends to the surface, where it yawns sixty feet wide, right in front of McCabe's home, where his wife and six children vainly hope for his rescue. Mine officials say it may be a year before it will be possible to reach the place where the man is shut up."

Happily after the above was written, the man was rescued.

"Shut up!" How the words sound like a death-knell, and what a voice of reminder they have as we look at the

214

SHUT UP AND SHUT IN

words as they occur in the Holy Writ, reminding us of what sin does.

(1) ISOLATION. "The priest shall *shut* him *up* that hath the plague" (Lev. xiii:4, 5, 21, 26, 31, 33). This was the Lord's direction when there was any sign of leprosy in the individual. The same rule applied to a garment (Lev. xiii:50, 54), or to a house (Lev. xiv:38), and even the one who entered the leprous house was "shut up" and was unclean (Lev. xiv:46). Sin, like leprosy, always separates from God and His service, whether it be in the inner life of the individual, in the outer garment of the life, in the assembly of God's house, or those who have fellowship with those who are in sin.

(2) SEPARATION. "Jericho was straitly *shut up*" (Josh. vi:1). The inhabitants shut themselves up, but they did not know they were separated to doom, as the margin indicates, "Jericho did *shut up*, and was *shut up*." If the words "accursed" and "utterly destroyed" are pondered in Joshua vi. and vii., remembering the Hebrew word means "devoted," as in the margin of vi:17, it will be seen the city was separated to destruction, devoted, or consecrated to judgment. This made Achan's sin the more sinful. He took of the "accursed" (devoted) thing, and became an accursed man. If men will not be consecrated by grace to their blessing, they will be devoted by judgment to their condemnation.

(3) SALVATION. "*Shut up* unto the faith" (Gal. iii:23). The word rendered "*shut up*" means to be inclosed so that there is no escape. It is given "*inclosed*" in Luke v:6 in speaking of fish being inclosed in a net, and it is translated "*concluded*" in calling attention to Israel being "*concluded* * * * in unbelief," and the sinner being "*concluded* under sin" (Rom. xi:32; Gal. iii:22). Unbelief shuts the unbeliever up in the Prison of Doubting Castle; sin shuts the sinner up under the bane of condemnation, Scripture confirms the sentence, and the law shuts the unsaved up to the faith of the Gospel, for it is only in that faith, that salvation is found in Christ, and deliverance is possible.

(4) PERSECUTION. "Herod *shut* John *up* in prison" (Luke iii:20); and Saul confessed. "The saints did I *shut up* in prison" (Acts xxvi:10). The Enemy's stick of persecution is often a staff to help the saint along. Bedford Jail, Aberdeen prison, the Tower of London, the French Bastile, are immortalized, not because of the

evil men who persecuted the saints, but because of
saintly John Bunyan, the seraphic Samuel Rutherford,
Madame Guyon, and others, who consecrated them and
found them wells in the desert and fountains of blessing to others. If it were lawful we might pass a vote
of thanks to his Satanic Majesty for bringing so much
meat out of the eater, honey out of the rock, and water
of blessing out of the flinty rock.

(5) COMMUNION. "When thou hast *shut* thy door" (Matt.
vi:6). The word might be rendered "shut up thy door,"
for it is so given in Matt. xxiii:13, in speaking of those
who *"shut up"* the kingdom of heaven. There are some
things we can only tell in secret to our Father: and
before this is done, there must be the shut door, keeping out all disturbing elements. Yea, even more, the
shut door is emblematic of the separated heart to the
Lord, for there can be no communion with Him unless
there is separation to Him and concentrated waiting
upon Him.

(6) CONCLUSION. The conclusion of the Holy Spirit is
simple and direct in the case of one who professes to
love God and *"shutteth up* his bowels of compassion"
against the need of a brother (1 John iii:17). Love
to God is expressed in love to our fellows. The very
evidence of knowing God in His grace, is letting that
grace flow out to others' help. The fire of love is
fanned into a flame of warm help by the breath of the
Spirit of God.

(7) UNION. "The doors were *shut*" (John xx:19-26), or
"shut up," for so the word is given in speaking of
Satan being *"shut up"* in the bottomless pit (Rev. xx:3).
The fearful disciples were driven together by a common fear and bolted themselves in the upper room,
but there the uncommon Saviour met them, and drove
away their fears, imparted His peace, assured their
hearts, breathed new life into them, gladdened their
spirits, and commissioned them anew for service.

* * * *

The union of God's saints is essential for Christ's new
visitations. There are things which can only come to
God's people as they are of one accord, and the world is
shut out. Lookers-on scare away the gentle Dove of
God's Spirit.

SINNER'S CHARACTER

Siding with God

"Who is on the Lord's side" (*Ex. xxxii:26*).

In the war of 1861, a timid supporter said to Lincoln, that he hoped the Lord would be on the side of the North. Lincoln replied, "About that I am not at all concerned; but only that we should be on the side of the Lord." That is the one thing needful, and that once assured, we may go forward bearing our witness and doing our duty, whether losing, whether winning, undismayed by the foes of truth and righteousness, and certain that the cause of God will finally be triumphant!

To be on the Lord's side

Means obedience to Him (Ex. xxxii:26-28).
Approval from Him (Luke ix:50).
Help to Him (Judges v:23).
Separation in Him (Dan. iii:1-25).
Fellowship with Him (Josh. v:13, 14).
Supply through Him (John xv:5).
And reward from Him (Matt. xix:28).

*   *   *   *

He always wins who sides with God. God is on our side, when we are on the side of God.

Sinner's Character

"The whole head is sick," &c. (*Isa. i:5*)

The Rev. James McQueen, one of the ministers of Syke, used to relate that a man by the name of McPherson, from the braes of Lochabar, came to him for the christening of one of his children. As he was a stranger, the minister enquired his name, connections, and what parish he had come from; and, in particular, if he had brought a testimonial of his character?

"Huich? A testimonial? Fat pe she?"

"Why, it is just a written account of the character you have borne, and testified by the minister and elders of the parish."

"Oach, no, Mr. McQueen, she didna brought her."

"But you ought to have done so. What was the reason you did not bring it with you?"

"Because herself was thoughting she would be as petter without it."

Practically the Scot admitted he had no character but a bad one. This is true of the sinner, for God says:

His heart is bad (Jer. xvii:9).
His mind is carnal (Rom. viii:7).
His reason is gone (Ecc. ix:3).
His way is corrupt (Gen. vi:12).
His understanding is darkened (Eph. iv:18).
His tongue is poisonous (Rom. iii:13).
His hands are violent (Isa. lix:6).
His eyes are blind to spiritual things (2 Cor. iv:4).
His ears are deaf to the voice of God (2 Tim. iv:4), and that
His whole nature, from the crown of the head to the soles of his feet, is diseased with iniquity (Isa. i:5, 6).

*　　*　　*　　*

Sin has blinded the eyes of man's understanding, hence, he cannot see himself as he is, nor the evil of sin, nor iniquity in its blackness. The sin of the sinner, has blurred the eyes of the sinner to his sin.

Sleeping Sickness

"Awake thou that sleepest, and arise from the dead" (*Eph. v*:14)

Who has not read about that strange "sleeping sickness" which finds so many victims in Central Africa? They sink into a fatal lethargy. Between 1901 and 1904 more than 100,000 persons died of it in Uganda. Where it appears, the majority of the population may be regarded as dead men. The British Government has discovered that the sleeping sickness is caused by a blood parasite

SLEEPING SICKNESS

which enters the body by means of a fly bite. Little or
no pain is felt at the time. The parasite, sucked up by
the fly from the blood of the animal it bites, multiplies in
the man. For even as long as three years he may not
know that anything is the matter with him. At last the
protozoan reaches the cerebro-spinal canal. The lym-
phatic glands of the neck are affected. The blood-vessels
of the brain are obstructed. The brain is no longer
nourished. Death is unavoidable. Of course the natives
see no connection between the fly bite and the death so
long removed. They let the flies bite, and will not even
take the trouble to brush them off. The white man cuts
down the jungle about the house, and makes that fly-
proof and mosquito-proof. Though they know the cause
of the disease, the doctors are powerless to save the
natives.

How many there are suffering from a worse disease
than sleeping sickness, namely, spiritual slumber.
Spiritual sleep means:

(1) To be in a *state of ignorance,* as the three disciples
on the mount of transfiguration (Luke ix:32).

(2) To be in a *state of unwatchfulness,* as Christ indicates in the parable of the tares and wheat (Matt.
xiii:25).

(3) To be *out of fellowship* with Christ, as is seen when
the disciples slept in the garden instead of watching
with Him (Matt. xxvi:40, 43, 45).

(4) To be in a *state of prayerlessness,* as may be gathered
by Christ's rebuke to His disciples (Luke xxii:46).

(5) To be in a *state of unreadiness* for Christ's return
(1 Thess. v:6, 7).

(6) To be in a *state of disobedience,* as Jonah was when
asleep in the boat going to Tarshish, when he ought to
have been in Nineveh (Jonah i:6).

And (7) To be in a *state of idleness* as the ten virgins
were (Matt. xxv:5).

The injunction is to awake for the Lord is near (Rom.
xiii:11); and the Lord promises to give light as we
obey Him (Eph. v:14).

*   *   *   *

The sickness of the soul generally arises from the sleep-
iness of the saint. To be alive is a sign of health, and the
means of keeping health.

DEVOTIONAL BIBLE STUDIES

Slippery Places

"Slippery places" (*Ps. lxxiii:*18)

A deacon was walking home with his minister one frosty night, when the minister slipped and fell back on the pavement. "Ah," said the deacon, looking at him; "Sinners stand on slippery places." The minister looked up at him as if to assure himself of the fact, and said, "I see they do, but I can't!"

The best way to save ourselves from slipping is to keep away from the slippery places.

> Blind-man's Alley (11 Peter i:9).
> Self-confidence Street (Luke xxii:33).
> Pridewell Square (1 Tim. iii:6).
> Love-of-Money Court (1 Tim. vi:10).
> Selfishness Terrace (2 Tim. iii:2).
> Worldly Conformity Row (Rom. xii:2).
> And Fleshly Place (Rom. xiii:14), are very slippery places, and need to be carefully avoided.

*　　*　　*　　*

The grit of God's truth will give us grip in the slippery places of life. The Lord can make our feet like hind's feet when we have the hearkening ears of obedience.

Sowing and Reaping

"Every man shall bear his own burden" (*Gal. vi:*5)

A woman in affluent circumstances dreamed she was in heaven. The angel who was showing her round, showed her a beautiful mansion. She asked who it was for.

"Your coachman," was the reply.

"That cannot be," she rejoined, "for he only lived in a lodge on my estate."

She was then shown a cottage, and she again enquired for whom it was constructed.

"That is for you," was the answer.

"There must be some error here," she again objected.

"No, there is no mistake; it is true you lived in a much larger building down on the earth, but this is all we could make out of the material you sent up. Your coachman sent up more material, and we were able to make the mansion you see."

There is a principle illustrated in the dream, which is enunciated again and again.

> The servant who traded with the pound and got ten received rule over ten cities (Luke xix:16, 17).
> The man who used his talents got a corresponding reward to the use he made of them (Matt. xxv:20-23).
> The material built on the foundation is the gauge to determine what reward the workman shall receive (1 Cor. iii:12-15).
> The one who adds to his faith the fulness of the Christian graces, has added to him an abundant entrance into the kingdom (2 Pet. i:11).
> The Christian reaps what he sows (Gal. vi:7); and "every man shall bear his own burden," or load; as the farmer in the harvest reaps what he has previously sown. The illustration embodied in the words is that of a harvest home scene as the last load is brought in, and the whole harvest is surveyed. He who would have praise from God, must have something He can praise.

*　　*　　*　　*

The measure of our glory in heaven will be according to the use of our talents on earth.

Sphere of the Saint

"In Christ Jesus" (1 Cor. i:2)

Allen Gardiner's heroic efforts among the Fuegians are well known, and the noble man's death in his endeavor to carry the gospel to them. When his dead body was found beside his boat, it was noticed that a hand was rudely drawn on the rocks pointing to these verses of the 62nd Psalm:—

DEVOTIONAL BIBLE STUDIES

"My soul, wait thou only upon God!
For my expectation is from Him.
He only is my Rock and my Salvation;
He is my Defense, I shall not be moved.
In God is my salvation and my glory;
The rock of my strength, and my refuge is in God."

Mark the words *"In God."* The sphere in which he moved, the element in which he delighted, the atmosphere in which he breathed, and the circle which separated him from all else, was the Lord Himself. Gardiner's environment was above the world, he lived and moved in the heavenly places, and was, therefore, beyond the touch of sin, the discouragement of circumstances, the worry of care, the blandishments of the world, the seductions of the flesh, the blast of suffering, and the folly of pride.

The sphere of the child of God is aptly described as "in Christ Jesus." With this one thought, let us ponder Paul's seven references, in which this sentence occurs, in his second letter to Timothy, and as we do so, we shall discover seven distinct things which are found in Christ and which we find as we live and move, and have our being in Him.

> (1) *"Life* in Christ Jesus" (2 Tim. i:1). The life to which reference is made is greater than physical life, mental life, moral life, social life, etc., it is *"the* life" (R. V.), "the eternal life" (1 Tim. vi:12, R. V.), the "life indeed" (1 Tim. vi:19). *God* is the *giver* of this life (Rom. vi:23), *Christ* is its *Embodiment* (John xiv:6), the *gospel* is its *instrument* (2 Tim. i:10), the *knowledge* of God and Christ is its *meaning* (John xvii:3), *"eternal"* is its *character* (John x:28), *faith* is its *acceptor* (John iii:36), the *Holy Spirit* is its *power* (Rom. viii:2), and *glory* is its *consummation* (Col. iii:4).

> (2) *"Called* * * * in Christ Jesus" (2 Tim. i:9). The calling is a "holy" one. The call comes wholly *from* God, therefore, is all of grace, and it claims wholly *for* God, therefore, it is holy. He who calls is holy, and that to which we are called is holy too. *Light* is the *sphere* into which He called us (1 Pet. ii:9); *holiness* is the *path* in which we are called to walk (1 Pet. i:15); *Christ's Example* is the *model* for our imitation, when

we *suffer* wrongfully (1 Pet. ii:21); we are called to *exhibit* the *graces* of the Spirit (Eph. iv:1-4); *virtue* is the one thing which leads to *glory*, to both of which we are called (2 Pet. i:3); life, liberty, and peace are a *trinity of blessings* we are called to *enjoy* (1 Tim. vi:12; Gal. v:13; 1 Cor. vii:15); and *fellowship with Christ* is the *apex* of the believer's calling (1 Cor. i:9).

(3) *"Hold fast * * * in Christ Jesus"* (2 Tim. i:13). The thing which we are to hold is "the form of sound words." The manner in which the truth is to be held is "in faith and love." The sphere in which the "sound words" are to be held is, "in Christ Jesus;" and the way in which the truth is to be held is aptly described as "hold fast." The word *"echo"* rendered "hold fast," means "to have and to hold," that is, a continuous possession. The apostle may have had in his mind those who had "erred concerning the faith" (1 Tim. vi:21; 2 Tim. ii:18), hence, he exhorts Timothy to "hold fast," and there was only one way to do this, *he must be held to hold*, therefore, his "faith and love" must be "in Christ Jesus."

(4) *"Grace * * * in Christ Jesus"* (2 Tim. ii:1). The grace "in Christ" has many traits, and various are the many things to which it may be compared. This grace is *beauty to charm*, for He is "full of grace" (John i:14); a *well to supply*, for "all grace" is promised (2 Cor. ix:8); a *bar to fix*, for we are exhorted to be "established in grace" (Heb. xiii:9); *clothing to envelop*, as Paul says when he bears testimony to the sufficiency of grace (2 Cor. xii:9); *salt to preserve*, hence, we are to be "seasoned" with it (Col. iv:6); an *atmosphere to stimulate*, hence, we are to "grow in grace" (2 Pet. iii:18); and a *hope to cheer*, for we are looking for the grace to be revealed at the coming of Christ (1 Pet. i:13).

(5) *"Salvation * * * in Christ Jesus with eternal glory"* (2 Tim. ii:10). The salvation mentioned is the future salvation of the body. Salvation has three main aspects. (1) The salvation *wrought out for us* by the death and resurrection of Christ, by which we are delivered from condemnation (Tit. ii:11; Eph. ii:8); the salvation *wrought within us* by the Spirit's effective grace (Phil. ii:12, 13); and the salvation *wrought upon us*, when Christ returns (Phil. iii:20, 21; Heb. ix:28; 1 Pet. i:5).

DEVOTIONAL BIBLE STUDIES

(6) *Godliness* "in Christ Jesus" (2 Tim. iii:12). The God-like One can only make like God. God manifest in the flesh is the One who can manifest God in our flesh. The Brightness of God's glory can make us bright with His glory. The Express Image of the Father can stamp us with the Father's image. The Lord in His beauty can reproduce in us the beauty of Himself.

(7) *"Faith* in Christ Jesus" (2 Tim. iii:15). Faith in Christ is *soul-lifting* in its exercise (Acts xxvi:18), *love-producing* in its outcome (Eph. i:15), *work-enabling* in its grace (1 Thess. i:3), *strength-ministering* in its endurance (2 Cor. i:24), *heart-encouraging* in its trust (Matt. xv:28), *Christ-honouring* in its rest (Gal. ii:20), and *victory-gaining* in its conflict (1 John v:4).

* * * *

"The believer is *sitting* in heavenly places in Christ Jesus (Eph. ii:4-6), while the world *lieth* in the wicked one (1. John v:19)."

Spirit's Diversified Operation

"There are diversities of operations, but it is the same Spirit"
(1 *Cor. xii:*6)

"We have heard of a little child, who so simply trusted Christ for salvation, that she could give no account of any 'law work.' And as one of the old examiners, who thought there could be no genuine conversion without a period of deep conviction, asked her: 'But, my dear, how about the Slough of Despond.' She dropped a curtsey, and said: *'Please, sir, I didn't come that way!' "*

A great mistake is made, when we think the Holy Spirit confines Himself to one mould in His working.

The heart of Lydia was opened gently, like the flower which opens to the kiss of the morning's sun (Acts xvi:14).

The Philippian jailer was shaken to the foundations of his being, like the jail over which he watched (Acts xvi:29, 30).

SPIRIT'S INTERPRETATION

Saul of Tarsus was smitten to the ground, and made to cry out in extreme anguish, like an animal which had kicked violently against an ox goad (Acts ix:5).

The woman of Samaria had her curiosity aroused, as Christ spake to her of the Living Water, till, like a thirsty traveller in an arid plain who sees a spring, she longed for a draught from its satisfying well (John iv:15).

Nicodemus was confronted with a difficulty, like a pedestrian who finds a high wall built across his path, as Christ told him of the necessity of being born again (John iii:4).

The palsied man was surprised into the salvation of God, as Christ told him of the forgiveness of his sins, when he was only looking for healing to his body, like one who finds himself suddenly in possession of a fortune (Matt. ix:2, 6).

And the woman, who was a sinner, with her burden of sinful debt, was relieved of her load by Christ's delivering grace, like one who was sinking beneath a heavy load, and found it lifted from off his shoulders (Luke vii:48).

*　　*　　*　　*

It is one thing to be a channel of the Spirit's communications, and it is another thing to be the subject of His operation. Balaam was the former: Stephen was the latter.

Spirit's Interpretation

"To one is given by the Spirit   * * interpretation" (1 *Cor.* xii:8-10)

At a public meeting a speaker, whose bearing and clothes indicated he was a person of importance, began to speak, but no one was interested. The reason was plain, the people did not understand him. He was a Chinese Prince, and spoke in his own language. Suddenly a young man got upon his feet, and began to interpret the words of the Prince. No longer were the eyes of the people dull, or their countenances unenlightened, but smiles and tears played upon their faces as the interpreted message came to them.

DEVOTIONAL BIBLE STUDIES

When the Spirit works He always interprets. The words, *"being interpreted,"* or *"by interpretation,"* are frequently given by way of explanation.

(1) A Present God—"Emmanuel, being interpreted, God with us" (Matt. i:23).

(2) A Significant Place—"Golgotha * * * being interpreted, the * * place of a skull" (Mark xv:22).

(3) A Meanful Cry—"Eloi, Eloi, lama sabachthani? which is, being interpreted, My God, My God, why hast Thou forsaken Me?" (Mark xv:34).

(4) A Glorious Teacher—"Rabbi, being interpreted, Master" (John i:38).

(5) The Anointed Saviour—"Messias, being interpreted, the Christ" (John i:41).

(6) A Changed Sinner—"Thou shalt be called Cephas, which is by interpretation, a stone" (John i:42).

(7) A Devoted Saint—"Barnabas, which is being interpreted, the son of consolation" (Acts iv:36).

(8) A Royal Priest—"Melchizedek, King of Salem * * * being first, by interpretation, King of Righteousness, and then King of Salem, which is King of Peace' (Heb. vii:1, 2).

Other examples might be given, such as are found in John ix:7; Mark v:41; and Acts xiii:9. All this goes to show, the Spirit is a God of order, and that He makes things clear to those who are taught of God (1 Cor. xiv:33).

* * * *

The interpretations of the Spirit are always illuminating, and inspiring. They educate the mind and enliven the heart.

Spiritual Radium

"Filled with all the Fulness of God" (*Eph. iii:19*)

It is said, "The radium compounds fling emanations into the air without any sensible diminution of bulk, arresting and healing malignant growths, and penetrating the stoutest armor or sheath. So the man, who is full of this Divine quality, is able to heal, penetrate and save, and to do this perpetually without losing aught of his power, which is fed from an unseen source. It is said that there are invisible rays in the shafts of sunlight, not included in the bands of color, which have healing power. So I am persuaded some natures fed from the atmosphere of the unseen radiate a kind of actinic ray, which heals people, and which you cannot account for by their genius, eloquence, imagination, or any other gift, which can be weighed, analyzed, or placed under the microscope."

> The meaning of the word "fulness" in Eph. iii:19 is completeness, perfection, sufficiency. The root word is rendered *"perfect"* (Rev. iii:2), *"complete"* (Col. ii:10) and *"full"* (Phil. iv:18). The use of the Greek word will illustrate its richness.
>
> A CLAIM FULFILLED. Christ's word to John, "Thus it becometh us to *fulfill* all righteousness" (Matt. iii:15).
>
> A WORK ACCOMPLISHED. Christ's conversation on the Mount, "Spake of His decease which He should *accomplish*" (Luke ix:31).
>
> A WITNESS BORNE. The Spirit's coming *"Filled* all the house" (Acts ii:2).
>
> AN OBEDIENCE RENDERED. "When your obedience is *fulfilled"* (2 Cor. x:6).
>
> A NEED SUPPLIED. "My God shall *supply* all your needs" (Phil. iv:19).
>
> AN ATTITUDE MAINTAINED. Stand * * * *complete* in all the will of God (Col. iv:12).
>
> AN ASSURED JOY. "Your joy may be *full"* (1 John i:4).

*   *   *   *

To know the fulness of God experimentally is to receive to the full all the above blessings.

Staying Power

> "Patient continuance in well doing" (*Rom. ii:7*)

"Examples of staying-power. Turn to the realm of science. I read some time ago of an entomologist, Mr. Frank Enoch, watching the movements of a tiger-beetle

DEVOTIONAL BIBLE STUDIES

continuously for a day and night. G. J. Romanes spoke of a whole year's work on one particular branch of scientific enquiry as only counting for apprenticeship. Charles Darwin spent thirty years observing the habits of the common earth-worm. All these are examples of staying-power. Turn to the realm of discovery. Think how Stanley persisted until he penetrated into the heart of Darkest Africa, and how Nansen held on his way until he came nearer the North Pole than any explorer who had preceded him. Among the noblest examples of this order are those which meet us on the foreign mission field. Think of Robert Morrison toiling in China seven years before he gained a single convert, and then toiling for three years more ere he gained a second. Think of Robert Moffat, laboring among the Bechwanas for ten years before seeing any signs of ingathering. Look around; everywhere are evidences of what has been wrought by those who had the power to endure. Near the river Wear, is the national memorial of that saintly and learned Englishman, the Venerable Bede. Talk of staying-power! His life was a splendid illustration and pattern of it. His work, we are told, was done with small aid from others. 'I am my own secretary,' he wrote; 'I make my own notes. I am my own librarian.' But no less than forty-five works remained after his death to attest to his quiet plodding industry. Our abbeys and cathedrals are monuments, not only to the piety and devotion, but also to the staying-power of the men of the Middle Ages. We are in too great a hurry to build now as they built then; we are not patient and painstaking enough."

The following Scriptures where the same Greek word, is rendered *"Patient continuance,"* tell out what the Holy Spirit says about staying-power.

(1) EVIDENCE OF REAL CONVERSION. "Bring forth fruit with *patience*" (Luke viii:15).

(2) TEST OF FAITH. "Tribulation worked *patience*" (Rom. v:3; James i:3, 4).

228

(3) REVEALS SOUNDNESS IN THE SPIRITUAL LIFE. "Sound in faith, love, and *patience*" (Tit. ii:2).

(4) SHOWS WE ARE KEEPING ON IN THE RACE. "Run with *patience*" (Heb. xii:1).

(5) PROVES WE ARE OBEDIENT TO ADD TO OUR FAITH, *"Patience"* (2 Pet. i:6).

(6) NEEDS THE EMPOWERMENT OF THE SPIRIT. "Strengthened unto all *patience*" (Col. i:11).

(7) SUCH ENDURANCE WILL BE REWARDED BY FRUIT. (Rev. ii:2, 3, 19; iii:10).

*   *   *   *

To endure is the way to be sure.

Steps in the Deeper Life

"Still upward" (*Ezc. xli:7*)

"Expressions by an Expert" was the suggestive advertisement in a car. There were given five pictures, under which were the words, "Contemplation," "Expectation," "Realization," "Admiration," "Exultation."

Happy are those believers who have the *contemplation of faith,* in beholding the Lord in a lively trust, like Moses (Heb. xi:27).

The *expectation of prayer,* in waiting upon the Lord in earnest supplication, like the psalmist (Ps. v:3).

The *realization of holiness,* in obeying the Lord fully, like Joshua and Caleb (Josh. xiv:14).

The *admiration of love,* in whole-hearted affection for the Lord, like Mary Magdalene (John xx:1).

And the *exultation of joy,* in glorying in the Lord, like the Apostle Paul (Rom. v:11).

*   *   *   *

Involution, evolution, and revolution are three words which indicate three steps in the Spirit life. The *involution* of His life, the *evolution* of that implanted life in practical godliness, and the *revolution* which is manifested in the different life of the believer.

Stooping to See

"Mary * * * sat at the Lord's feet, and heard His word" (*Luke
x: 39, R. V.*)

Pastor W. Y. Fullerton, in speaking of one of the
temples at Baalbek, in Syria, says: "There is a series of
steps, up which it is still possible to reach the top of the
wall; but the entrance to the stairs was then blocked, so
that the only way to get into the tower was to lie on the
ground on one's face, and wriggle the body through the
tiny aperture. It was a difficult and somewhat humbling
task, yet even several of the ladies accomplished it. This
suggested the strait gate by which entrance is gained to
life eternal, and the eternal truth that it is only when we
humble ourselves that we can be exalted."

In order to reach the top of the wall, the humble position had to be taken. It is the same with spiritual
blessing.

> Zaccheus *"came down"* and found salvation (Luke xix:6).
> Mary Magdalene *"stooped down"* and saw the angels (John
> xx:11, 12).
> The leper *"kneeled down"* and received cleansing (Luke
> i:40).
> The palsied man was *"let down"* and got forgiveness (Luke
> ii:4).
> Peter *"fell down"* before Christ and was humbled (Luke
> v:8).
> Christ *"lay down"* His life and got the sheep (John x:15).
> Mary *sat down* at the feet of Christ and learned the Lord's
> secrets (Luke x:39).

*   *   *   *

The lowly place is always the holy place.

Sufficiency of Christ's Atonement

"It sufficeth us" (*John xiv:8*)

"The Lord is my Righteousness. I am resting in the
finished work of Christ alone for my soul's salvation." So
said an aged saint of eighty-seven, after a long, consistent

230

life in the Lord's service. But she felt that Christ, and Christ alone, could meet the necessity of her soul.

I said: "Christ and His finished work are enough."

Whereupon she exclaimed: "We don't want any more, that is enough; yea, more than enough. Plenty!"

She did not rest in her consistent life, nor her service for the Lord. Christ and His finished work were the Alpha and Omega of her salvation.

The hungry wolves of sin, hell, and death may rage and prowl in search of our life, they cannot touch us if we are sheltered in Christ, for His precious blood is not only the plea that prevails with God for our acceptance, but it is also the power that puts to flight every wolf of hell.

Christ's finished work is the *panacea* for the ill of sin (1 John i:7).

The *peace-maker* for our reconciliation with God (Col. i:20).

The *price* of our redemption from sin's slavery (Tit. ii:14).

The *power* which enables us to overcome Satan's malice (Rev. xii:11).

The *potentiality* which constrains us to live for God (2 Cor. v:15).

The *pattern* for our imitation in dying to self (John xii:24, 25).

And the *propeller* in Christian service (2 Cor. v:14). Those who trust Christ, find Him and His precious blood "more than enough." Trust Him, and you will find Him the same.

*   *   *   *

The finished work of Christ is a work which is finished. This goes without the saying to those who accept what God says, but to those who want to add their say to what He says, it is necessary to say it.

Talkative and Company

"The talk of the lips tendeth only to penury" (*Prov. xiv:23*).

A thoughtful mathematician has just been calculating how far the male human jaw moves in a lifetime of 70 years, and he makes it out to be 6,835,470 inches, which, divided by 63,360, the number of inches in a mile, gives 107 miles and a fraction. But they cornered this mathematician at last. "If your figures are right," they asked, "how far does the female jaw travel in the same time?" He is still at the problem.

We are not prepared to endorse the above quotation *re* the feminine part of it, for the other sex are about equal sinners. There is one thing believers in Christ should ever avoid, namely,

> To be classed with "busy-bodies" (2 Thess. iii:11).
> "Praters" (3 John 10).
> "Boasters" (2 Tim. iii:2).
> "Vain talkers" (Tit. i:10).
> "Tattlers" (1 Tim. v:13).
> "Meddlers" (1 Pet. iv:15, R. V.).
> And unruly speakers (Jude 10).

*   *   *   *

When there is a sting in the tongue there is gall in the heart. A sanctified heart shows itself in a sweet tongue.

Testing of Trial

"The trial of your faith * * * precious" (1 *Pet. i:7*)

A man with a heart almost overwhelmed with trial and temptation, had recourse to a good Bishop of France. He told his case, and added: "I pray for faith, and ask for light, but am overwhelmed with doubts. Surely, if I were not despised of God, He would not leave me to struggle thus with the great adversary of souls." The Bishop thus consoled him: "The King of France has two castles in different situations, and sends a commander to each of them. The Castle of Montleberry stands in a place remote from danger and far inland; but the Castle of La Rochelle is on the coast, where it is liable to continual sieges. Now, which of the two commanders, think you, stands the highest in the estimation of the King—the commander of La Rochelle, or he of Montleberry?" "Doubtless," said the man, "the King values him the most who has the hardest task, and braves the greatest dangers." "Thou art right," replied the Bishop. "Now apply this matter to thy case and mine; for my heart is like the Castle of Montleberry, and thine like that of La Rochelle."

> Trial proves the genuineness of our faith, as illustrated in the children of Ephraim who "turned back" (Ps. lxxviii:9), and Abraham who did not "withhold" what the Lord asked (Gen. xxii:12).
>
> Trial evidences the degree of our faith, as illustrated in the "little faith" of the disciples (Matt. xvi:8), and the "great faith" of the woman (Matt. xv:28).
>
> Trial is sent to wean us from earthly resources as is seen in the Lord's dealing with Gideon (Judges vi:11-14; vii:17).
>
> Trial is a means to greater fruitfulness, hence, the pruning of the Heavenly Husbandman (John xv:2).
>
> Trial is a preventative grace, for the Lord often allows a "thorn" to keep down the flesh and to cast us upon Him in prayer, as He did in the case of Paul (2 Cor. xii:7-9).
>
> Trial is a qualifying grace, for the Lord often sharpens His children on the grindstone of discipline that He may temper us for effective use (Heb. xii:6).
>
> Trial is a fore-runner of reward (1 Pet. i:7).

*   *   *   *

To be tested by the Lord is necessary that we may triumph in Him. Trials make triumphs possible, and triumphs through trial make the Lord precious.

DEVOTIONAL BIBLE STUDIES

The Beautiful Christ

"Chiefest among ten thousand" (*S. S. v*:10)

In the vicinity of the Duomo, in Florence, are the bronze gates that Michael Angelo said were fit to be the gates of Paradise. Once they were covered with exquisite enamel work. The decorators gilded the bronze with gold leaf. But the veneer was very thin; soon the damp, the cold, the heat cracked the delicate frosting, and now it is all gone. To-day the gates stand forth clothed only in their simple splendor. And yet, behold the rich bronze is more beautiful in its simplicity than with its gilded veneer. The storms were kind to the gates, and removed what was meretricious and gaudy, and restored them to their native beauty.

So men have painted portraits of Jesus; they have tried to paint the lily and gild refined gold, but we go back to the portraits of the gospels, and we find there a beauty of the Christ unsurpassed. What can we say of Him?

(1) *His character* was beautiful with holiness in every detail (Heb. vii:26).

(2) *His love* was pure and faithful in all its affection (John xiii:1).

(3) *His service* was true and beneficent in all its workings (Acts x:38).

(4) *His words* were tender and true in all their utterances (John vii:46).

(5) *His life* was consistent in every department (Matt. xxvii:24; Acts ii:22).

(6) *His aim* was single and concentrated in glorifying God (John xvii:4).

(7) *His mission* was to benefit all who would have Him in dying a death which they deserved (2 Cor. viii:9).

*   *   *   *

Christ is Christianity, and the best evidence of Christianity is Christ.

234

"THE BEST"

"The Best"

"Out of all your gifts ye shall offer * * * the best" (*Numbers xviii*:29)

Christ wants the best. He in the far-off ages
Once claimed the firstling of the flock, the finest of the
wheat,
And still He asks His own with gentlest pleading
To lay their highest hopes and brightest talents at His
feet.

He'll not forget the feeblest service, humblest love;
He only asks that of our store we give to Him
The best we have.
Christ gives the best. He takes the hearts we offer
And fills them with His glorious beauty, joy and peace.
And in His service, as we're growing stronger,
The calls to grand achievements still increase.

The richest gifts for us on earth or in the heaven above,
Are hid in Christ. In Jesus we receive
The best we have.
And is our best too much? O friends, let us remember
How once our Lord poured out His soul for us,
And in the prime of His mysterious manhood
Gave up His precious life upon the cross!

The Lord of Lords, by Whom the worlds were made,
Through bitter grief and tears gave us
The best He had.

Here are some Scriptural examples of those who gave
their best to the Lord:

(1) The Centurion honored Christ with His *best confidence* (Matt. viii:10).
(2) Mary of Bethany gave Him her *best love* (John xii:3).
(3) Peter gave Him his *best confession* (Matt. xvi:16, 17).
(4) Martha gave Him her *best service* (Luke x:38, 40).

235

(5) John gave Him his *best attention* (John xix:26).
(6) The women gave Him their *best ministry* (Luke viii:-3).
And the soldiers gave Him the *best compliment* (John vii:46).

*   *   *   *

Our appreciation of Christ is guaged by what we give to Him. When He is the Best in our estimation, we estimate the best is what we can only give to Him.

The Best Robe

"Bring forth the Best Robe" (*Luke xv:22*)

Princess Czartoryski had a wonderful dress made in Paris, on which her coat of arms was produced in jewels on a white satin ground. For this purpose the stones had to be pierced, and, though their value was thus deteriorated, the costume when finished was reputed to be worth $75,000.

The costliness and beauty of the above dress is nothing in comparison with the one of which the poet sings—

"Jesu, Thy blood and righteousness
My beauty are, my glorious dress."

For this "Best Robe" of heaven is

Provided by the God of Grace (Luke xv:22).
Purchased by the blood of Christ (Rev. vii:14).
Personified in Christ Himself (1 Cor. i:30).
And it imparts its nature to those who wear it (Rom. xiii:14).

*   *   *   *

The Best Robe of God's grace was made in the loom of Calvary's dark suffering.

THE FACT OF FACTS

The Darkness

"He made darkness His secret place" (*Ps. xviii:*11)

"Challenge the darkness, whatso'er it be—
Sorrow's thick darkness, or strange mystery
Of prayer or providence! Persist, intent,
And thou shalt find Love's veiled sacrament:
Some secret revelation, sweetness, light,
Waits to waylay the wrestler of the night.
In the thick darkness, at its very heart,
Christ meets, transfigured, souls He calls apart."

(1) In the *darkness of sorrow* may be found the brightness of hope (1 Thess. iv:13-18).

(2) In the *darkness of trial* may be found the approbation of Love (1 Pet. i:7).

(3) In the *darkness of persecution* may be found the stay of the Divine Presence (2 Tim. iv:16).

(4) In the *darkness of suffering* may be found the sufficiency of grace (2 Cor. xii:9).

(5) In the *darkness of a sense of His withdrawal* may be found the largeness of faith (Isa. l:10).

(6) In the *darkness of Gethsemane* is found angelic ministry (Luke xxii:43).

And in the *darkness of Calvary* is a precursor of coming glory (Luke xxiv:26).

*   *   *   *

Use your cross as a crutch to help you on, and not as a stumbling-block to cast you down.

The Fact of Facts

"The Lord is * * * " (*Ps. xcv:*3)

In an Episcopal Church, in Peoria, it is an Easter morning custom for the ushers to greet incoming members of the congregation with "The Lord is risen." An old lady who was deaf, and who had but recently united with the Church, was met by Dr. Tyng with the salutation.

237

"What is it?" she asked, pausing, and placing her hand to her ear.

"The Lord is risen," repeated the doctor.

"Oh, yes!" said the lady absently, as she moved on down the aisle. She was met by another usher, who gave her the same greeting.

"What did you say?" she demanded.

"The Lord is risen," returned the usher.

"Oh, yes, so Dr. Tyng tells me!" she remarked complacently, as she entered a pew.

The Lord has to continually remind His people that He is—

(1) THE READY HELPER—"*The Lord is* my Helper" (Heb. xiii :6).

(2) THE GRACIOUS PROVIDER—"*The Lord is* gracious" (1 Pet. ii :3).

(3) THE FAITHFUL KEEPER—"*The Lord is* faithful, who shall keep," &c. (2 Thess. iii :3).

(4) THE LIBERATING FRIEND—"*The Lord is* that Spirit, and where the Spirit of the Lord is, there is liberty" (2 Cor. iii :17).

(5) THE CERTAIN PROMISER—"*The Lord is* not slack concerning His promises" (2 Pet. iii :9).

(6) THE UNFAILING UPHOLDER—"*The Lord is* at hand" (Present—Phil. iv :5).

(7) THE RISEN REDEEMER—"*The Lord is* risen," &c. (Luke xxiv :34).

* * * *

What the Lord is, makes the saints what they are.

The Gospel, a "Sea of Crystal"

"The Gospel * * * the power of God" (*Rom. i*:16)

George Fox, in writing of one of his experiences said, "I saw a sea of ink and a sea of crystal, and the sea of crystal swept away the sea of ink."

THE HANDS OF CHRIST

The above quotation suggests what the Gospel of God's grace does in the lives of those who believe in Christ, for, as in the millennium, there will be an effective living water current which will wash out the Dead Sea, and make it a living stream (Ezk. xlvii); so the Gospel in the cleansing of the precious blood of Christ, removes the foulness of sin (1 John i:7).

The water of life quenches the fire of unholy passion (John iv:14).

The love of God supplants the desire to sin (2 Cor. v:14-17).

The power of Christ conquers the dominance of evil (Rom. vi:14).

The holiness of the Lord electrifies to whole-hearted devotion to Him (Phil. iv:12, 13), and thus annuls the failure of self-effort.

The presence of Christ destroys all fear of man or devil, For His grace is sufficient (2 Cor. xii:9).

And the coming of Christ drives all impurity away, for it is the soul's ambition, when looking for Him, to be ripe and ready, and thus to have His approval (1 John iii:2, 3).

*   *   *   *

"Mercy is 'from everlasting' to contrive thy salvation, and 'to everlasting' to perfect it."

The Hands of Christ

"His hands" (*Cant. v*:14)

"I do love this beautiful, white, and perfect hand; but I dislike the other, ugly one," said a little girl as she took hold of the left hand of her mother, and pushed the right one, which was marred, crooked, and scarred and twisted. A look of pain was seen in the mother's face for a moment, then she said, "Shall I tell my little girl a story?" "Yes, mamma, please." "One night when you were a baby I smelt fire, and as I hurried to where you were lying in your cot, I found your clothes alight. I tore them from you with my hand, but that hand was burnt as a result. The marred hand is an evidence of what I suffered for you." When the child had heard the story, she exclaimed, "Oh, forgive me, mamma, for calling the scarred hand ugly, I now think it is the more beautiful of the two." The hands of Christ are beautiful because they bear the marks of the nails of Calvary's tree.

The hands of Christ are studded with the jewels of blessing, and they are so, because they were once nailed to the cross (Ps. xxii:16). They were once gory with the blood of suffering, but they are now glorious with the blessings of salvation. He shows His hands to us (John xx:20), let us view them and see what they can do.

The hands of Christ are symbolical of His power; hence, in speaking of the power of the Lord with John the Baptist, it says, "The hand of the Lord was with him" (Luke i:66).

They are—

(1) *Strong to Save.*—Peter found the hand of Christ strong to save, in response to his "Lord, save me" (Matt. xiv:30, 31). He can pluck out of hell's mouth, sin's power, Satan's grip, iniquity's pit, the flesh's influence, self's pursuit, and the world's glamour.

(2) *Potent to Heal.*—The touch of Christ's hand meant cleansing to the leper (Matt. viii:3). Christ can heal, by His touch of power, palsy's sloth, pride's fever, temper's fits, the heart's impurity, the mind's blindness, the knees' feebleness, and the ears' dulness.

(3) *Skilled to Open.*—Christ's hands upon the eyes of the blind man meant sight to him (Mark viii:23). Christ alone can give the inner illumination which shall cause us to see the sinfulness f sin, the sufficiency of Christ's Atonement, the secrets of God's Word, and the splendor of His Person.

(4) *Sufficient to Supply.*—"Thou openest Thy hand, they are filled with good" (Ps. civ:28). The statement is true, providentially, spiritually, and eternally. The good God saves by His good grace, to a good life, and for a good end. There is always more left after we have done taking—as is illustrated in the feeding of the five thousand—than there was before. Taking from God, enriches Him.

THE LIFTING POWER

(5) *Tender to Bless.*—"Put His hands upon them" (Mark x:16) are the words which describe Christ's action in relation to the children. Christ has the touch of the sympathetic friend, the loving mother, the kind father, the gracious brother, the thoughtful sister, the good Samaritan, and the gentle Jesus.

(6) *Strong to Uplift.*—"He laid His hands on her, and immediately she was made straight" (Luke xiii:13). The poor woman was bowed earthwards, and could not lift herself up—like many a believer in Christ, who has life from Christ, but who has not liberty through Him.

(7) *Mighty to Keep* (John x:28).—None can snatch from the hand of Christ, because His hand is encircled by the hand of the Father.

*   *   *   *

The ability and agility of Christ proclaim His power and willingness to bless. He meets the need of the times, and is always timely in His aid.

The Lifting Power

"The gospel is the power of God" (*Rom.* i:16)

It is said that once a skilled artisan in the employ of an Oriental king, had become almost useless at his daily tasks, his hand had lost its cunning, and the work was marred by constant failure. The king sent for him and asked him what had caused the surprising change.

"Ah," he said, "it is my heart that makes my hand unsteady. I am under an awful cloud of calamity and discouragement. I am hopelessly in debt, and my family are to be sold as slaves. I can think of nothing else from morning to night, and as I try to polish the jewels, and cut the facets in the diamonds, my hand trembles, and my fingers forget their wonted skill."

The king smiled and said: "Is that all? Your debt

shall be paid, your family saved, and your cares dispelled. You may take the word of your king and go to work again with a free and fearless heart." That was done, and never was work so skillfully done, never were such carvings and cunning devices in precious gems as the hand of this happy artisan devised when set at liberty from his fears and burdens.

The king's grace made a new man of the artisan.

(1)   The power of *Christ's love* will lift us above hate, and cause us to love Him (1 John iv:19).

(2)   The power of *Christ's joy* will banish the bane of misery, and gladden us with its song (John xv:11).

(3)   The power of *Christ's peace* will turn out carking care, and fill us with its own tranquillity (John xiv:27).

(4)   The power of *Christ's grace* will stiffen the muscles of our spiritual nature, and make us of sterling worth (2 Tim. ii:1).

(5)   The power of *Christ's presence* will keep away all fear, and sustain us in every emergency (Isa. xli:10).

(6)   The power of *Christ's armor* will shield us in every assault of the enemy, as we are strong in Him (Eph. vi:10).

(7)   The power of *Christ's beauty* will entrance and satisfy that we shall not be attracted from Him (Song of Solomon v:16).

*   *   *   *

To deny self we need a greater power than self. Christ Himself is the only one who can dethrone and deny self.

The Power of the Gospel

"The gospel of Christ * * * is the power of God unto salvation"
(*Rom. i:16*)

Griffith John says "The great need of China to-day is vital religion, not a religion which *men can make great but a religion which can make men great*. The Chinese

THE POWER OF THE GOSPEL

need a heavenly principle that shall infuse a new moral and spiritual life into the nation, a mighty power that shall transform them in their inmost being, a Divine inspiration that shall create within their breasts aspirations after holiness and immortality. In other words, what they need is the gospel of Jesus Christ. Apart from Christianity, I can see no hope for China. There is no power in the religious systems of China to develop a holy character, a true manhood. China cannot advance in the path of true progress without a complete change in the religious life of the nation. It is Christ alone who can lead in the glorious dawn of the Chinese Rennaissance, the new birth of a mighty nation to liberty, and righteousness, and ever-expanding civilization. Feeling this to be true in our heart of hearts, we, the missionaries, have come to China to preach Christ, unto some a stumbling block, unto others foolishness; but, unto them that are called Christ the power of God, and the wisdom of God.

The gospel has

Power to quicken those dead in sins (I Cor. iv:15).

Power to enlighten the mind darkened by unbelief (II Cor. iv:4).

Power to save from the thraldom of iniquity (Eph. i:13).

Power to protect against the assaults of the enemy (Eph. vi:15).

Power to brighten the future, so that the horizon is lit up with coming glory (Col. i:23).

Power to bless the saint in the necessity of his experience (Rom. xv:29).

Power to unite believers in fellowship with Christ (Eph. iii:6).

*   *   *   *

There is no need of man, the nature of God cannot meet.

DEVOTIONAL BIBLE STUDIES

The Spread Table

"Thou preparest a table before me" (*Ps. xxiii*:5)

Two poor boys, who had never been in the country, and knew nothing of the sweetness of its air, were sent into the most country of country places. There was plenty of food. They found there was meat for breakfast. They were surprised, as they had not been accustomed to such a luxury. They did their duty, and went out to play. At dinner time there was hot meat, and, what was more astonishing, when they went to supper there was meat again. Meat three times a day was something they had never dreamt of. When they went to bed that night the little one said to his brother, "Jim, if they set that table again in the middle of the night, don't you forget to call me."

The Lord always meets the need of His people in a most ample and satisfying manner. He gives us

(1) The fatted calf of His provision to satisfy us (Luke xv:23).

(2) The whole lamb of His love to bless us (Exodus xii:8; 1 Cor. v:7).

(3) The manna of His grace to strengthen us (Deut. viii:3; John vi:51).

(4) The milk of His Word to nourish us (1 Pet. ii:2).

(5) The wine of His joy to gladden us (Ps. civ:15).

(6) The honey of His promises to nerve us (Ps. xix:10; Isa. vii:15).

And (7) With the fruit of His blessings He assures us (Numbers xiii:23, 24; Eph. i:13, 14).

*   *   *   *

There are two main feeders to the sustenance of the spiritual life, and these are, meditation in the truth, in order to understand it, and application of the truth, so that we may practice it.

Threefold Nature of Man

"Spirit, soul, and body" (1 *Thess. v*:23)

Every man lives in a three-story house. The lower story is the part underground. There he eats and drinks. This is his *physical nature.* Many men never leave the basement. There they live, and there they die, never entering the stories that lie above. The second rises above the first. From its windows the outlook is wider, the light in it is more abundant, and the air purer. This is man's *intellectual department.* Some go up into the second story often, and, though they do not abandon the basement, they use it mostly only for eating. Then there is the third story. This is the highest. Here the air, the sunlight, the outlook are at their best. This is the *spiritual realm.* Few rise into it. In too many cases dust and cobwebs are the sole occupants of what should be the choicest part of the house. The wise man, while he does not abandon the basement or the second story, loves the third story best of all, and there spends much of his time. The contrast between the three parts of man's nature is seen in the following:

Spirit	Soul	Body
Created and made. Job xxxiii:4	"Breathed" Gen. ii:7.	"Formed" Gen. ii:7.
Image and Likeness of God. Gen. i:27.	Distinct from Animal. Gen. ii:7.	Moulded after the form of the spirit. Isa. lxiv:8.
Links man with God. Num. xvi:22.	Indentifies man with Beast. Gen. ix:15, 16.	Associates man with the earth. Gen. iii:19.
Indestructible. Heb. xii:9.	Destructible. Rev. xii:11.	Returns to original dust. Eccle. xii:7.
Consciousness of being. 1 Cor. ii:11.	Life as lived. Matt. xvi:25, 26.	Medium of action. 2 Cor. v:10.
Intellectual 1 Cor. ii:11.	Emotional Col. iii:23.	Instrumental. Rom. vi:12, 13.

DEVOTIONAL BIBLE STUDIES

Spirit	Soul	Body
Exists apart from the body. Eccle. xii :7.	Exists with the blood and unites spirit and body. Lev. xvii :11 R. V.	Dead without the soul and spirit. Jas. ii :26.
Sin has deathized. Eph. ii :1.	Sin has selfized. Jude 19.	Sin has possessed. Rom. vi :6.

*   *   *   *

God the Father speaks of His soul delighting in Christ for us (Matt. xii:18); the Holy Spirit is the Lord within us (Rom. viii:9); and Christ assumed a body as one with us (Heb. x:5).

Thoroughness

"Observe to do * * * all" (*Joshua i:7, 8*)

"The secret of his career," says one, in writing about Lord Curzon, "apart from his brilliant abilities, is that he devoted himself wholly and entirely to politics from his earliest youth. When he was but a stripling, he was making journeys all over Asia; sometimes risking his life—always risking his somewhat poor health—penetrating to remote and perilous spots where mighty empires approach each other's frontiers, and look across the boundary with suspicion, and fright, and defiance. He was writing big books on Persia, Corea, the problems of the East, when most young men of his age were falling in and out of love, or playing polo or cricket, or taking what Carlyle calls 'mud-baths of vice.' And the result is that his career has been glorious; and may end in being still more illustrious."

The soul of success in anything is thoroughness.

(1)   Paul *expresses* it when he says: "This one thing I do" (Phil. iii:13).

(2)   The Psalmist *emphasizes* it, in his "my soul followeth hard after Thee" (Ps. lxiii:8).

246

(3)   God *typifies* it in the whole burnt-offering (Lev. i:1-9; Rom. xii:1).

(4)   The Holy Spirit *demands* it, in His "come out, and be ye separate" (2 Cor. vi:17).

(5)   Christ *enforces* it in His three-fold condition of discipleship (Luke xiv:26, 27, 33).

(6)   The apostle *declares* it in proclaiming what the Lord desires and promises (1 Thess. v:23, 24).

(7)   And the *end* Christ had in dying for us was that we should be thorough, namely, dead to sin, and alive to righteousness (1 Pet. ii:24) ; yea, to God Himself (Rom. vi:11).

*   *   *   *

If we would *talk correctly* in the Christian life, then we must *walk circumspectly* in Christ-like behavior.

Traits of the Word

"Let the Word of Christ dwell in you" (*Col. iii*:16)

"It is told of the widow of Schumann, the musical composer, that whenever she was going to play any of her husband's music in public, she would read over some of his old letters to her, written in the lover days. Thus, she said, his very life seemed to fill and possess her, and she was better able then to interpret his work. If we will read over Christ's Words of love to us until His life enters into us, and His Spirit breathes into our lives, then we can be brave and strong in resisting evil and doing His will." The following seven traits of God's Word are illustrated by seven incidents in Christ's life:

(1)   It is a *Forgiving Word* (1 John ii:12), as seen in Christ's "Thy sins be forgiven" to the woman (Luke vii:48).

(2)   It is a *Joy-giving Word* (Jer. xv:16), as heard in Christ's "Be of good cheer" to the woman with the issue of blood (Matt. ix:22, R. V.).

(3)   It is a *Feeding Word* (1 Pet. ii:2), as illustrated in Christ's direction regard' the Ruler's daughter. He "commanded that something should be given her to eat" (Mark v:43).

(4) It is a *Living Word* (Heb. iv:12), as evidenced in Christ's "Lazarus come forth" (John xi:43).

(5) It is a *Powerful Word* (Heb. iv:12), as shown in Christ commanding the demons to "come out" from the possessed man (Luke viii:29).

(6) It is a *Peaceful Word* (Ps. cxix:165), as demonstrated in His "Peace be still" to the sea (Mark iv:39).

(7) It is a *Reviewing Word* (Ps. cxix:25), as brought out in Christ's dealings with Peter (John xxi:15-19).

*   *   *   *

To judge God's Word is to evidence our folly, but to let God's Word judge us is to demonstrate our wisdom.

Transferred

"Passed from death to life" (*John v:24*)

Two soldiers, remarking upon the death of a comrade, said: "There's another poor fellow got his discharge." "Not that." "Well, if not discharged, I'd like to know what he is?" "Only transferred." "Transferred where?" "To another department." "What for?" "For duty." "What duty?" "Don't know; that depends on what he is fit for."

There is a threefold transference which every believer undergoes.

He is transferred from Satan's realm by being *translated* into the kingdom of God's dear Son (Col. i:13).

He is transferred from selfishness to Christlikeness by being *transfigured* into His image (2 Cor. iii:18, R. V.).

And he is transferred into the Lord's presence by being *transformed* to be like Him and with Him (Heb. xi:5; Phil. iii:21).

*   *   *   *

It is not the elevation of *place,* nor the pride of *race,* nor the beauty of *face,* but the calling of *grace* which makes the man.

Turned and Met

"Turn again to the Lord." "He will turn again" (*Lam. iii*:40;
Micah vii:19)

A writer on gardening says: "A garden I saw recently had a few striking flowers in it, with a hellebore-
like leaf and a lily-like head of large buds that nodded
across the path at one another from bare stems about
three feet higher than the foliage. On inquiring what
they were called, I was informed, with an apologetic
smile, that the only name the cottager knew them by was
"turn-again-gentleman." Immediately, up came the fancy
that this was a true cottage plant evolved by the gardener who really loves his work, because it is so small
and so near to him, and that it had proved so great a
success that even the passing gentleman turned to look
again at it. I do not know whether the flower may not
be common in some districts, but I strongly enjoined the
old woman not to let it die out in her own garden. In
spite of appearances, I daresay she is proud of it, and
will see to its welfare."

The name of the flower suggested a number of passages of Scripture, where the words *"turn again"* occur:
The following thoughts are found therewith:

(1) THE INTERCESSOR'S PLEA—"When Thy people * * *
turn again to Thee * * * then hear" (1 Kings viii:33,
34).

(2) THE SERVANT'S ORDERS—"Charged * * * by the word
of the Lord * * * not to *turn again*" (1 Kings xiii:9).

(3) THE KING'S DECREE—*"Turn again* unto the Lord God"
(2 Chron. xxx:6).

(4) THE LORD'S BLESSING—"If ye *turn again* * * * the
Lord * * * will not turn His face from you" (11
Chron. xxx:9).

(5) THE BACKSLIDER'S PRAYER—*"Turn* us *again*, O God"
(Ps. lxxx:3, 7, 19).

DEVOTIONAL BIBLE STUDIES

(6) THE PROPHET'S REVELATION—*"Turn* ye yet *again,* and thou shalt see" (Ezk. viii:6).

(7) THE LORD'S COMPASSION—"He will *turn again,"* &c. (Micah vii:19).

* * * *

The frequent coming to the throne of grace is the way to *becoming* like Him Who sits on it.

"Twinkler, Tinkler, Tattler"

"Walk in the light" (1 *John* i:7); "Be vigilant" (1 *Pet.* v:8); "Pray without ceasing" (1 *Thess.* v:17)

"There are three things the prudent householder should keep as a protection against burglars—a 'twinkler,' or a light, burning not always at the same window; a 'tinkler,' or bell attached to the window; and a 'tattler,' or a small dog."

The above reminds the believer of the fact there are three things which he should have, to prevent the great enemy (2 Cor. ii:11) getting an advantage, and these are,

> The light of a consistent life, as fed by the oil of the Holy Spirit's indwelling presence and operation (Gal. v:25, R. V.).
>
> The bell of a vigilant watch, so as to be apprized of the thief's approach (1 Pet. v:8).
>
> And the voice of believing prayer, so that the Lord's intervention may be had, to the routing of the enemy (Neh. iv:9).

* * * *

If we walk worthily, pray fervently and watch diligently, Satan will not break into the house of our being.

UNITY

Unanimous

"Stand fast in one spirit" (Phil. i:27)

George MacDonald, in one of his books, tells of two children who prayed the following prayer: "O Lord, tell Sandy and me what to ask for. We're unanimous." They got up from their knees. They had said what they had to say; why say more?

Would that all Christians could be unanimous. If only the following unanimity could be manifested, what power there would be, namely:

Agreement in prayer (Matt. xviii:19).
Oneness in love for each other (John xiii:35).
One accordness in waiting for the Spirit's power (Acts i:14).
Mutual interest in caring for each other (Acts iv:32).
Helping each other in service (Luke v:7).
Bearing each other's burdens (Gal. vi:2).
And thinking of others as better than ourselves (Phil. ii:3).

      *   *   *   *

When we symphonize with God's will, we shall agree with all who are in sympathy with Him.

Unity

"Look * * * on the things of others" (*Phil. ii*:4)

A well-known Ohio judge was noted for his defense of slavery. He was converted from the error of his ways by the following conversation with a runaway slave, who had crossed the Ohio River from Kentucky:

Judge: "What did you run away for?"
Fugitive: "Well, judge, wanted to be free."
"Oh! Wanted to be free, did you? Bad master, I suppose?"
"Oh, no; berry good man, massa."
"You had to work too hard, then?"
"Oh, no; fair day's work."
"Well, you hadn't a good home?"

"Hadn't I, though! You should see my pretty cabin in Kentucky!"

"Well, you didn't get enough to eat?"

"Oh, golly! Not get enough to eat in Kentucky! Plenty to eat."

"You had a good master, plenty to eat, were not overworked, a good home—I don't see what you wanted to run away for."

"Well, judge, *I left de situation down dar open. You can just go down and git it.*"

Christians will find it a healthy exercise to place themselves in the position of others before they pass judgment on them. The *"one anothers"* of the Epistle to the Romans will help to this end among Christians—to keep from wrong-doing on the one hand (Rom. xiv:13), and help to the right on the other hand (Rom. xv:5).

> *Unity of place*—"Members one of another" (Rom. xii:5).
> *Unity in affection*—"Kindly affectioned one to another" (xii:10).
> *Unity of thought*—"Same mind one to another" (xii:16).
> *Unity of love*—"Love one another" (xiii:8).
> *Unity in edifying*—"Edify one another" (xiv:19).
> *Unity in courtesy*—"Receive one another" (xv:7).
> *Unity in concern*—"Admonish one another" (xv:14).

* * * *

Christ is not ashamed to call us brethren, therefore we should not be ashamed to own all whom He owns as Lord.

Unmovable Things

"We receiving a kingdom which cannot be moved" (*Heb. xii:28*)

Humboldt's description of the first earthquake he saw, is significant, because of the question he was led to ask. When he beheld the rivers overflowing, the earth shaking, the houses tumbling, the mountains rocking, and heard the animals howling, and the birds wailing, he said: "Is there nothing solid?" As he asked the question, he looked up to heaven, and there he got his answer, as he himself said: "I looked up to heaven, and all was still there."

V.D.

Those who are in the immovable kingdom of God's grace find there is a solidity, and stability, beyond human ken. What are the reasons of our immovability?

(1) Because we are *in the Immovable One*—"He is my Defense. I shall not be *moved*" (Ps. lxii:6).

(2) Because the *Lord is beside us*—"He is at my right hand, I shall not be *moved*" (Ps. xvi:8).

(3) Because we deal graciously with others—"Well is it with the man that dealeth graciously * * * he shall never be *moved*" (Ps. cxii:6, R. v.).

(4) Because of the Lord's keeping—"He will not suffer thy foot to be *moved*" (Ps. cxxi:3).

(5) Because of the Lord's promise—"I will ordain a place for My people Israel * * * and they * * * shall be *moved* no more" (1 Chron. xvii:9).

(6) Because of the character of the believer—"The root of the righteous shall not be *moved*" (Prov. xii:3).

(7) Because of our dependence upon the Lord in trustful prayer and "obedience"—"Hold up my goings in Thy paths, that my footsteps be not *moved*" (margin, Ps. xvii:5); or, as the Revised Version—"My steps have held fast to Thy paths, my feet have not slipped."

*   *   *   *

If there were more "Amens" in our lives, there would be more "Hallelujahs."

V. D.

"**Very** attentive to hear Him" (*Luke xix*:48)

The Publishers' Circular says, "We wonder if second-hand booksellers are aware that many people construe the letters V. D. after the price of a book to mean very dear as well as very dry. There is often considerable excuse for the error." We shall never find the Book of books "very dry" if we ponder it carefully and prayerfully, but we shall find as we listen to the Lord as He speaks to us therein, that

(1) His "thoughts are *very deep*," for they are a deep which cannot be fathomed (Ps. xcii:5).

(2) His "testimonies are *very sure*," for they are an impregnable rock (Ps. xciii:5).

(3) His testimonies are "*very faithful*," for they speak of the faithful God (Ps. cxix:138).

(4) His "Word is *very pure*," even as refined gold (Ps. cxix:140).

(5) His "Word runneth *very swiftly*," for the Lord is never behind in His messages (Ps. cxlvii:15).

(6) His Word is "*very nigh*," therefore there is no need to seek for it (Deut. xxx:14);

(7) And we are responsible because the Word is what it is, to write it in our testimony "*very plainly*" (Deut. xxvii:8).

*　*　*　*

The Word of God's grace conveys to those who receive it in faith, the grace of God's Word. What the wire is to the power-house and the lamp, the Word is to the believer. It puts us in touch with the supply of the power.

Waiting and Watching for Christ's Return

"We wait for the Saviour" (*Phil. iii:20*)

It was the soul-saving and soul-satisfying truth of Christ's death, which made the friends put upon the tombstone of Matthew and Ann Gibbons, in Bakewell Churchyard, Derbyshire, England, as an expression of their faith and hope in Christ, and made each say as for himself and herself—

> "When from the dust of death I rise,
> To take my mansion in the skies,
> E'en then—shall this be all my plea,
> Jesus hath liv'd and died for me."

WAKEFULNESS OF JEHOVAH

Something similar may be found upon a stone in a churchyard in Matlock, at the head of the graves of John and Ann Cotherill:

"Life is uncertain,
Death is sure,
Sin is the wound,
Christ is the Cure."

There is no doubt of the sureness of sin's wound, for all have sinned, nor can we dispute the fact that life is uncertain, nor do we desire to minimize the truth that "Christ is the Cure" for sin's wound, but we do contradict the statement that "Death is sure." Death is never set before the believer in Christ as something which is certain. The certain thing is the coming of the Lord Jesus Christ for His own (John xiv:3), for this we should

"Look" (Heb. ix:28).
"Wait" (1 Thess. i:10).
"Watch" (Mark xiii:37).
Desire (Cant. viii:14).
Pray (Rev. xxii:20).
Work (2 Pet. iii:12), and
"Love" (2 Tim. iv:8).

*   *   *   *

Hope goes up the stairs which Love has made, and looks out of the window which Faith has opened.

Wakefulness of Jehovah

"Behold He that keepeth Israel shall neither slumber nor sleep"
(*Ps. cxxi*:3-4)

A little four-year-old inquired of her widowed mother one moonlight night:
"Mamma, is the moon God's light?"
The lamp had just been put out, and the timid little

girl was afraid of the dark; but presently she saw the bright moon out of her window, and it suggested the question, "Is the moon God's light?"

"Yes, Ethel," replied the mother. "His lights are always burning."

Then came the next question from the little girl:

"Will God blow out His light and go to sleep, too?"

"No, my child," replied the mother; "His lights are always burning."

Then the timid little girl gave utterance to a sentiment which thrilled the mother's heart with trust in her God:

"Well, mamma, while God's awake I am not afraid."

One of the most assuring and comforting statements of God's Word is where it is stated, "He that keepeth thee will not slumber;" and then, as if to make His word of cheer the more cheering, it goes on to say, "Behold, He that keepeth Israel shall neither slumber nor sleep" (Ps. cxxi:3, 4).

(1) The Lord is awake to *assist in distress,* as He did the disciples in the storm (Matt. xiv:27).

(2) He is awake to *assure us in perplexity,* as He did the disciples when filled with fear (Luke viii:22-25).

(3) He is awake to *assuage our grief in sorrow,* as He did the widow of Nain (Luke vii:13).

(4) He is awake to *attend us as we journey through life,* as He did the two disicples as they went to Emmaus (Luke xxiv:15).

(5) He is awake to *admonish us when we are growing cold,* as He did the Church in Ephesus (Rev. ii:4, 5).

(6) He is awake to *adjust us in the inner life,* as He did the Apostle Peter, when He appeared to him (Luke xxiv:34).

(7) And He is *awake to accept us, should we fall asleep before He comes,* as He did His faithful servant Stephen (Acts vii:56).

* * * *

God has a hand to help us, a heart to love us, and a hearth to warm us.

Want of Knowledge

"Israel doth not know" (Isa. i:3)

When the Prince of Wales was only the Duke of York, he was speaking on one occasion in the interests of the Royal Caledonian Asylum for the benefit of Scotch children. He related the following anecdote, which he said illustrated the pleasing fact that some Highlanders recognized London as an asylum for their countrymen:

A Highlander, on paying his maiden visit, met a fellow-townsman in the street, who had been resident only a short time, and inquired of him, "Mon, can you tell me where I shall find the Caledonian Asylum?" The other immediately replied, "Why, mon, y're in it."

The reply was not correct in one sense, and yet it may be taken to illustrate that many believers are ignorant of the fact that they are in the realm of all spiritual blessing, and therefore are shut out of blessing by their want of knowledge. For instance, how many times the Holy Spirit has to use the expression, "Know ye not."

In the following Scriptures we may gather the baneful effects of not knowing.

To be ignorant of our oneness with Christ is to miss its power and blessing (Rom. vi:3).

To be ignorant of the consequence of yielding to sin is to lay ourselves open to its power (Rom. vi:16).

To be ignorant of the fact that our bodies are the temples of the Holy Spirit is to miss the safeguard that comes from recognizing His presence (1 Cor. iii:16; vi:19).

To be ignorant of the evil of leaven's working is to permit its contaminating presence to remain unjudged (1 Cor. v:6);

To be ignorant of our future destiny and dignity is to make us act in an unbecoming manner to those who are the Lord's erring children (1 Cor. vi:2, 3).

And to be ignorant of our union with Christ is to miss the inspiration of His grace, and the separation to Himself, which is the practical outcome of it (1 Cor. vi:15).

*   *   *   *

Not to know is not to trust, for they who know the name of the Lord, trust in the Lord of the name.

DEVOTIONAL BIBLE STUDIES

Watchfulness of the Lord

"The Eyes of the Lord" (2 *Chron.* *xvi*:9)

We have seldom seen the idea of perfect trust better illustrated than in the following touching incident of a little daughter's trust in her father. They were travelling together, and in order to reach their home it was necessary for them to travel all night. When it became too dark for them to look out of the windows, and the lamps were lighted inside, the father laid aside the little girl's hat, and spreading out cloaks and shawls, said, "Now we will rest." But a little troubled face peered out upon the strange scene, a mist was gathering in those blue eyes, and the cheery tone of voice changed to a very plaintive one as she asked, "Father, how can we go to bed here?"

"This is your bed, darling," he said, drawing her to his heart, "and a warm one you will always find it." And then he tucked her in so carefully, that in place of what had been a little girl, there seemed only a great bundle of shawls.

But every now and then there was a movement inside the bundle, and a voice would say, "Oh, father, I am afraid to go to sleep here!" Then the father reminded her that he was taking care of her, and would do so all night. So at last, soothed by this assurance and worn out by unwonted fatigue she fell asleep. When she opened her eyes again, after what seemed to her only a few minutes, the sun was shining brightly. The train stopped, and there just in sight was her own dear home. She could even see her dear mother standing in the open door, with arms outstretched to welcome back her loved ones. After the kisses were over, the mother asked, "And so my little girl has been travelling all night? Did she find it a long and weary time?"

"Oh, no, mother, not at all. I had such a good sleep, and father watched over me all night. Only think of it! All night, mother, he watched over me. At first I was afraid to go to sleep in that strange place, but he told me to lean against him, and shut my eyes, and rest easily, for he would stay awake and take care of me. So I crept close to him, and, before I knew it, I was really and truly sound asleep; and dear father stayed awake and took care of me all night. How I do love him for it!" Then the mother with the love-light beaming from her eyes, told her child of that heavenly Father Who watches over each of His children, not only one but every night of their lives.

The Lord is continually watching His people and looking after their interests. He has

(1) *Appreciative eyes* to care (Deut. xi:12).
(2) *Quick eyes* to help (2 Chron. xvi:9).
(3) *Testing eyes* to search (Ps. xi:4).
(4) *Responsive eyes* to answer (Ps. xxxiv:15).
(5) *Omniscient eyes* to discern (Prov. xv:3).
(6) *Preserving eyes* to keep (Prov. xxii:12).
And (7) *Guiding eyes* to direct (Ps. xxxii:8).

* * * *

The eyes of the Lord's regard are watching us, that we may regard Him to our comfort. When the look of our faith meets the look of His love, there is communion.

Wind, an Emblem of the Spirit

"The wind bloweth where it listeth" (John iii:8)

Rotherham's translation is to be preferred to the above. It is, "The Spirit, where it pleaseth, doth breathe."

"Dey jeeted me on der vindmill," complained Big George, the German.

"What's the mattter now, George?" inquired a companion.

"Oh, no-ding," smiled George.

"But you were saying when I came in that some one cheated you on a windmill."

DEVOTIONAL BIBLE STUDIES

"Vell, dey did. I go up to my ranch by Sonoma County to see der new machine if it vork, and dree days I go up dere alreaty and it don't vork, and I von't bay for it; it ain't goot."

"But how do you know it isn't a good one?"

"Vell, didn't I sday dere two hours dree days in der hot sun and fan myself all der time and vatch it and it nefer moved?"

"Maybe there was no breeze, George."

"Of course der was no breeze. Vould I fan myself if dere vas a vind?"

With many of the saints, their experience is like the windmill; there is no move. A saint without the Spirit is as helpless as a windmill without the wind. The saint may have the "mill" of a past experience, and the "wind" of a name-association with the Spirit, but what is the use of the name "windmill" if there is only the "mill" without the "wind"? A windmill is a mill for the wind to move, and sorry a mill it is without the wind to move it. And a sorrier saint is he, who is not moved by the Spirit.

There are three things suggested by the Saviour's words about the Spirit: (1) His personality, for He is "The Spirit;" (2) His Sovereignty, for He goes "where it pleaseth;" and (3) His Vitality, for He "doth breathe."

(1) His Personality—"The Spirit."

What constitutes personality? Intelligence, independence, power, and character. The Spirit is holy in nature, for He is called "the Holy Spirit" (Acts i:5), and what He produces is holy (Luke i:35), and the evidence of His presence is likeness to Himself (1 John iii:9), even as the die pressed on the soft wax, leaves its impression (Eph. i:13; iv:30). The Spirit is powerful in action. Christ's resurrection from the dead is proof of this (Rom. viii:11), and so is the sinner's quickening from the death of sin (Eph. i:19; ii:1). The Spirit is independent of help, for He is the Spirit of God (1 Pet. iv:14); and as God, the Spirit is omnipotent in power; and He is intelligent in mind, for He is the Author of inspiration (1 Cor. ii:11), and the Enlightener of the believer's intelligence (Eph. i:17, 18).

(2) His Sovereignty—"Where it pleaseth." The word "Thelo," rendered "listeth" in the A. V., signifies to will, and is rendered "will" in Mark i:41; "disposed" in 1 Cor. x:27, "pleased" in 1 Cor. xii:18, "desire" in Gal. iv:20, and "intending" in Luke xiv:28. Twice in 1 Cor. xii the sovereignty of the Spirit is emphasized, in speaking of the place which He gives the members in the mystical body of Christ, for they are there as it "hath pleased Him," and He gives the gifts of His ministry to each member "severally as He will." We have no right to His grace. Those who have received spiritual life have got it because of "His own will begat He us with the Word of truth" (Jas. i:18), and the secret of an effectual salvation is to allow Him "to will and to do of His good pleasure" (Phil. ii:13). The sovereignty of God is not an arbitrary fiat which rides roughshod over us, but is an exclusive power which alone can bless us. It is not of him that willeth or runneth, but God that sheweth mercy, who is the cause of our blessing (Rom. ix:16). He none the less is willing to bless those who will be blessed, although their will to bless is not the cause, but God who is willing to bless.

(3)) His Vitality—"Doth breathe." On the day of Pentecost the Spirit in His power came as a "rushing, mighty wind" (Acts ii:2). The word "wind" is rendered "breath" in Acts xvii:25. As the Lord gives "to all life and breath" in a natural sense, so He gives spiritual life and impetus (John xx:22).

*   *   *   *

The virtue of a holy life, the vim of active service, the virility of an ardent love, the voice of earnest prayer, the vivacity of a conforming faith, the victory of a continuous triumph, the vigilance of a watchful outlook, the vigor of spiritual growth, the volition of a better part, and the vivaciousness of a satisfying joy, are all from the vitalization of the vitalizing Spirit.

Witness Bearing

"Ye are my witness" (Isaiah *xliii*:10)

A little girl, who had decided for Christ, and was happy in His love in consequence, was singing in her home, when her father severely rebuked her, and said she was not "to make that row again." The child promised obedience, but, quite unconsciously, was singing again a short time after the father's injunction, whereupon her father said to her, "I thought I told you not to make that row again?"

The child replied, "Feyther, it sings itsel'. I canna' help it."

This is always true in relation to the child of God. The life and joy of Christ, when they are in the life, cannot be hid. They will express themselves some way. They do not express themselves in the same way in all, any more than the life in the floral kingdom does, but where the Christ is within, He will be manifest without.

(1) As the lame man at the Beautiful Gate expressed his wholeness by his walking and leaping (Acts iii:8), so the believer evidences his salvation by walking in newness of life (Rom. vi:4).

(2) As the woman of Samaria bore testimony to Christ's convicting grace when she said, "Come, see a man who told me all things that ever I did, is not this the Christ?" (John iv:29), so those who have come in contact with Christ know the evil of sin, and say, "I know that in me dwelleth no good thing" (Rom. vii:18).

(3) As Bartimæus showed he had received sight from Christ by following Him in the way (Mark x:52), so those whose spiritual eyes have been opened obey the Lord's command, "Follow Me" (John i:43).

(4) As the eunuch testified to his being justified by Christ by his joy in Him (Acts viii:39), so those who are justified by grace "joy in God" (Rom. v:11).

(5) As the two spies who came back from the land of Canaan, laden with fruit, demonstrated where they had been (Num. xiii:23), so those whose lives are full of the fruit of the Spirit tell beyond all dispute that the Spirit has His home in them (Gal. v:22-25).

(6) As the Thessalonians, by their turning to God, were able to turn from their idols and serve Him (1 Thess. i:9), so those who have come to Christ receive power from Him to do the will of God (Acts i:8).

WORD OF GOD, A LIGHT

(7)   As David said of Goliath's sword, "There is none like it" (I Sam. xxi:9), so the soldier of Christ can bear his testimony to the effectiveness of the Spirit's sword— "the Word of God" (Eph. vi:17).

*   *   *   *

True witnessing means the correspondence of the talk of the lips with the walk of the life.

Word of God, a Light

"Thy Word * * * is a Light" (*Ps. cxix*:105)

"I remember," says one, "being shown a beautiful collection of moths some time ago, and I said to the boy who owned the collection, 'However did you catch them?' He said, 'Why, with a light, of course.' He went out at night with a butterfly net, put a light just behind it, and the moths flew straight into the net.   That is the way to catch people—with the light of God's truth."

The Acts of the Apostles illustrates in a striking manner the attractiveness of God's Word.

The "five thousand" after Pentecost (iv:4).

The cause of the revival in Samaria (viii:14).

The means of the Ethiopian eunuch's conversion (viii:35).

The medium of instruction to the Philippian jailer (xvi:32).

The subject matter of every true ministry, as Paul illustrates (xviii:11).

The expeller of evil, as is seen in the power of the Gospel at Ephesus (xix:19, 20);

And the builder up of the Christian life (xx:32) are examples.

*   *   *   *

To have the Word of Life in our minds is good; to have the life of the Word in our hearts is better; but to have the life of the Word in living characters in the life is best.

263

DEVOTIONAL BIBLE STUDIES

Word of God: Ground of Assurance

"The Lord said unto him, surely, etc." (*Judges vi*:16)

The son of a chieftain of the Macgregors, was killed in a scuffle at an inn on the Moors of Glenorchy, by a young gentleman, named Lamont. The manslayer mounted his horse and fled, and though sharply pursued, in the darkness of the night he succeeded in reaching a house. It happened to be the house of Macgregor himself. "Save my life!" cried Lamont to the chieftain; "men are after me to take it away." "Whoever you are," replied Macgregor, "while you are under my roof you are safe." Very soon the pursuers arrived, and thundered at the gate. "Has a stranger just entered your house?" "He has; and what may be your business with him?" "The man has killed your son! Give him up to our vengeance." The terrible news filled the house with lamentation; but the chief, with streaming tears, said: "No; you cannot have the youth, for he has Macgregor's word for his safety, and, as God lives, while he is in my house he shall stay secure." This story has been told for centuries to illustrate Highland honor. What shall we say of the older story, that illustrates Divine love? To Jew and Gentile, high and low, rich and poor, friend and enemy, the grace of Christ is free, and His Word is sure.

The following "I have's" are some of God's assurances, and His Word cannot be broken.

(1) PARDONED—"*I have* blotted out" (Isa. xliv:22).
(2) REDEEMED—"*I have* redeemed" (Isa. xliii:1; xliv:22).
(3) PROTECTED—"*I have* covered" (Isa. li:16).
(4) CHOSEN—"*I have* chosen" (Isa. xliv:1).
(5) ENDOWED—"*I have* put My Spirit upon" (Isa. xlii:1).
(6) REGARDED—"*I have* seen * * * *I have* heard" (Isa. xxxviii:5).
(7) LOVED—"*I have* loved" (Isa. xliii:4).

* * * *

If we meditate in God's Word *continually*, we shall have a prompter to prayer *incessantly*, and trust Him explicitly.

WORD OF GOD VERSUS THE LAWS OF MEN

Word of God: Its Power and Penetration

"Speak unto us smooth things" (Is. xxx:10). "The Lord shall
cause His glorious voice to be heard" (Is. xxx:30)

A certain sermon was described under three heads. In
the first place, it was said to be very moving. In the
second place, it was very soothing. And in the third
place, it was very satisfying. It was moving, inasmuch
as one half the congregation left the church during its
delivery. It was soothing, because the remaining half
fell asleep. And it was satisfying, since they declared
without a dissentient voice that they never wanted to hear
that preacher again.

It is a sorry thing when a Christian worker speaks
"smooth things" (Isaiah xxx:10), for he is in bad company (Psalm lv:21; Proverbs v:3).

> The Word of God, while it is a comforter to the sorrowing
> (Ps. cxix:50), never glosses things over.
>
> It is a sword to kill (Heb. iv:12).
> A rapier to pierce (Heb. iv:12).
> A knife to cut (Acts v:33).
> A fire to burn (Jer. xxiii:29).
> A hammer to break (Jer. xxiii:29),
> A light to search (Ps. cxix:105).
> And a sieve to sift (Ps. cv:19).

*　　*　　*　　*

The Word of God is a two-edged sword. It wounds
to heal, and kills to make alive.

Word of God versus the laws of Men

"Thy testimonies are very sure" (*Ps. xciii:5*)

"A friend of mine who is in a large way of business,"
says the *City Press,* "uses a large quantity of crude
petroleum, and his carts are continually conveying it

from the wharf where it is stored, to the factory where it is used. By the Petroleum Act, he is subjected to a heavy penalty, if he places a light within 20 ft. of the oil; and under the new bye-laws of the London County Council, he is also liable to a fine, if a lamp is not on his wagons. What is he to do?"

Man-made laws are always contradictory, but the law of the Lord, namely, His Word.

Is *perfect* in its revelation, (Ps. xix:7).
Pure in its character (Ps. cxix:140),
Powerful in its operation (Acts xix:20).
Permanent in its endurance (1 Pet. i:23).
Potent in its influence (Luke v:1).
Pointed in its application (Heb. iv:12).
And *protective* in its indwelling (1 John ii:14).

* * * *

The sure Word of promise is a light to gladden and to guide. The harmony of the Word, harmonizes with all man's need.

Worldliness

"'Be Ye Separate" (2 Cor. vi:17)

A story is told of a gentleman who had a splendid singing canary. A friend wanted to see if he could teach his sparrows to sing by keeping the canary with them. He borrowed it, and placed it in the cage with the sparrows. Instead, however, of teaching them to sing, the poor bird got so timid among the strange birds that it stopped singing altogether, and did nothing but chirp like the sparrows. The owner then took it back, but still it would not sing. It then occurred to him to put it beside another canary which sang well. This had the desired effect, and, regaining the old note, it sang as well

WORKS, OR THE WORK?

as ever. Many Christians go, like the canary, into the strange company of worldlings, and consequently they not only do not teach the world to sing their happy glorious note of praise, but they cannot sing the old songs of praise in a strange land themselves, and soon they learn the sorrowful note of the world. The best thing for such is to go back again into the more genial society of happy, rejoicing Christians, among whom they will soon learn to sing the glorious notes of praise again, making melody in their hearts.

We see what contact with the world does in the following examples.

Worldliness robbed Abram of communion and joy when he went down to Egypt (Gen. xii:10-20).

Worldiness vexed Lot and caused him to escape only with his life from Sodom (Gen. xix:17; 2 Pet. ii:7).

Worldiness emptied Naomi of her store and satisfaction (Ruth i:12).

Worldiness nearly cost Jehosaphat his life when he joined affinity with Ahab (1 Chron. xviii:1, 31).

Worldliness blighted and blasted the life of Demas (2 Tim. iv:10; Col. iv:14).

Worldliness tripped Peter up to his hurt and sorrow (Luke xxii:54-62).

Worldliness cursed and damned Balaam (Jude 11; Num. xvi:1, etc.).

*   *   *   *

If we resist the devil he will *flee from us,* but if we resist the world it will *flee at us,* therefore, ignore it.

Works, or The Work?

"To him that worketh not, but believeth on Him that justifieth the ungodly" (Rom. iv:5)

"I have been trying to save myself for fifteen years." So said a young lady in telling how the Lord had met with her and saved her. How many there are who think they have to do something.

Man's religion is—

"Something in my hands I bring."

But God's religion is—

"Nothing in my hands I bring,
Simply to Thy cross I cling."

The first is like Cain, who brought to God the fruits of the earth—the fruit of his own toil—forgetting that the curse of God was resting upon it (Gen. iii:17; iv:3).

The second is like Abel, who brought to God the God-appointed sacrifice, and thus was accepted of Him (Heb. xi:4), for it told out the perfection of Christ's Person, and the completeness of His work (John xix:30).

The devil's gospel is—

DO.

But God's Gospel is, "It is

DONE."

The answer to the question, "What must I do to be saved?" was, "Believe on the Lord Jesus Christ, and thou shalt be saved" (Acts xvi:31). And Christ confirms this, for He says, "This is the work of God, that ye believe on Him whom He hath sent" (John vi:29).

*   *   *   *

Gethsemane, Gabbatha, and Golgotha are a trinity of places where Christ suffered. Their agony, stripes, and gore, are the believer's joy, healing, and glory.

Worries

"Be not anxious" (Matt. vi:25, R. V.)

A shocking tragedy occurred in the public park at Ipswich recently, Mr. W. H. Bond, manager for a well-known tent manufacturing firm, being found unconscious in a fir plantation, with a fatal bullet wound in

WORRIES

his head and a revolver by his side. The deceased was a prominent Nonconformist, being a deacon at a Congregational church. Stocktaking is said to have preyed upon his mind. He was accustomed to carry a revolver when looking round the firm's premises at night, and when cycling. Three children are left orphans by the sad occurrence.

Another case of fatal worry is seen in the following:—A fatal leap of 50 ft. was taken by Mrs. Sarah Aylwin (aged sixty-seven) from the roof of her house, 48, Great Russell Street, London. At the inquest, her brother-in-law said, she "worried herself about trifles in household matters, and made mountains out of mole-hills."

God's people often worry themselves from one cause or another.

> The *fog of doubt* will make us worry as to our safety, as Peter did (Matt. xiv:30).
>
> The *burden of anxiety* (Matt. vi:31) will make us worry about the affairs of home, as Martha did (Luke x:41).
>
> The *spectre of fear* will make us worry as to the future, and fill the heart with the dread of death (Heb. ii: 14, 15).
>
> The *chafing of fret* will make us worry as to the prosperity of the wicked (Ps. xxxvii:7).
>
> The *storm of trouble* will make us worry about the persecution of the wicked, unless the Lord is keeping the heart within (1 Pet. iii:14).
>
> The *weeds of care* will hinder the fruitfulness of the soul, as to its spiritual prosperity (Mark iv:19).
>
> And *the blight of discouragement* will cover the soul with black despair and murmuring, as it did to the children of Israel (Num. xxi:4, 5).

*   *   *   *

When matters of *care trouble* you, make them matters of *prayer* to *take* to the Lord.

Textual Index

The texts with an asterisk against them are the title texts, and the rest of the texts are found in the devotional part which follows the incident.